Kierkegaard's Presence in Contemporary American Life:

Essays from Various Disciplines

Edited, with an introduction and bibliography
by
Lewis A. Lawson

The Scarecrow Press, Inc.
Metuchen, N. J.   1970

Table of Contents

iii

Acknowledgements

I wish to thank the Department of English and the General Research Board of the University of Maryland for valuable support for this project and Barbara, Rachel, and John for invaluable support for all my projects.

Lewis A. Lawson

Introduction

In The Descent of the Dove, Charles Williams wrote
that Kierkegaard had to wait seventy years for his world-
wide acknowledgement. [1] This statement was certainly true
for Great Britain and the United States even in 1940, eighty-
five years after Kierkegaard's death. Perhaps the only
place in the English-speaking world where Kierkegaard's
works were seriously discussed before 1900 was the Garrett
Biblical Institute, Evanston, Illinois. There, as early as
1887, Professor N. E. Simonsen, who had received his
graduate training at the University of Oslo, had his students
read Kierkegaard both for content and style. [2] But apparently no published recognition resulted from this study.

The earliest mention in English was in Andrew
Hamilton's Sixteen Months in the Danish Isles, published in
London in 1852; despite the sketchiness of his treatment of
Kierkegaard, Mr. Hamilton seems to have caught a very
perceptive glimpse of him: "There is no Danish writer more
in earnest than he, yet there is no one in whose way stand
more things to prevent his becoming popular. "[3] After that,
it was forty years before even an English summary of a
French article appeared, in the Review of Reviews.

Mrs. Mabel Annie Stobart was the first English
critic to reveal a genuine interest in Kierkegaard and his
influence. Very probably she had read Georg Brandes'
Søren Kierkegaard in Danish, for she was competent enough
in that language to publish translations. But she attached
a significance to Kierkegaard's religious and philosophical
attitudes that she could not have derived from Brandes' somewhat negative approach to his fellow Dane. Her first article,
in 1899, approached Kierkegaard indirectly; in "New Light
on Ibsen's 'Brand'," she pointed out:

> . . . in his poem Brand [sic] Ibsen has . . .
> clothed in dramatic drapery some of the tenets
> propounded in the neglected works of Kirke-
> gaard [sic] . . . For the religious philosophy of
> this Danish thinker contains none of the usual

vii

narcotics of philosophy or the opiates of religion.
Truth, for Kirkegaard, lies in Subjectivity alone.
"Subjectiviteten, Inderilgheden er Sandheden. "[4]

In her second article, in 1902, "The 'Either/Or' of
Søren Kirkegaard, " [sic] Mrs. Stobart concentrated directly
upon his significance for the twentieth century:

> . . . now the Zeit-Geist of the Age demands a
> bridge over the gulf which has hitherto divided
> the few abstract and purely scientific philosophic
> thinkers on the one side, from mankind with its
> ritualistic and dogmatic religion upon the other,
> and the time has come when, disappointed with
> the illusionary nature of thinkers who, like
> Nietzsche, put away realities to find consolation
> in pretty coloured clouds, the large and increasing
> number of spiritually ambitious who have cast off
> the swaddling clothes of superstition can appreci-
> ate the helpful works of an earnest and vigorous
> thinker such as Sören Kierkegaard [sic].

No doubt Mrs. Stobart would be more widely recognized as an early admirer of Kierkegaard, if she had continued to publish such studies. But her interests soon
turned her to a much more active life. She was Founder of
the Women's Sick and Wounded Convoy Corps, a detachment
of which she took to Thrace in the Balkan War of 1912-1913.
Early in World War I she organized hospitals in Belgium and
France until she was captured by the Germans and sentenced
to be executed as a spy. After her release, she served in
Allied hospitals in Serbia. Her writing after the war most
often dealt with spiritualism, and she served as Chairman
and Leader of the Spiritualist Community from 1924 to 1941.
Before her death in 1954, at the age of ninety-two, she
must often have reflected upon the wide popularity in
England of the thinker whom she had introduced over fifty
years before.

Very little attention was paid to Kierkegaard for the
next ten years, and what little there was occurred in Scot-
land. In Edinburgh, Hugh Ross Mackintosh, Professor of
Systematic Theology at New College, offered a short piece,
"A Great Danish Thinker, " in the Expository Times. Professor Mackintosh was to retain his interest in Kierkegaard,
for in 1929 he offered one of the best of the early specialized
studies, "The Theology of Kierkegaard, " which served as
groundwork for his treatment of Kierkegaard in Types of

Modern Theology, published in 1937, but still a useful volume. Also in the Expository Times, Alexander Grieve provided "Soren Kierkegaard." And in the Danish publication Hovedstaden, James Maitland Anderson, Librarian of the University of St. Andrews, published "Søren Kierkegaard and the English-Speaking World."

The first consideration of Kierkegaard in a professional quarterly occurred in 1914, when John George Robertson contributed "Soren Kierkegaard" to the Modern Language Review, of which he was then the Editor. A student of Scandinavian literature and later Director of the Department of Scandinavian Studies at the University of London, Professor Robertson concentrated, as might be expected, upon Kierkegaard as man of letters, not as theologian or philosopher. He, too, recognized the influence of Kierkegaard upon Ibsen; he pointed out, for example, that ". . . the sinister, gloomy faith of Ibsen's Brand is an embodiment, carried to its logical extreme, of the third great stage in Kierkegaard's life journey, the religious stage." But he saw Kierkegaard as much more than just an influence on Ibsen; indeed, he felt Kierkegaard to be ". . . the writer who holds the indispensable key to the intellectual life of Scandinavia, to whom Denmark in particular looks up as her most original man of genius in the nineteenth century. . ."

The first serious American article, "The Anti-Intellectualism of Soren Kierkegaard," appeared in 1916, written by David F. Swenson, who was to become one of the most admired of the early Kierkegaard scholars in this country. Professor Swenson had first come across Kierkegaard at the turn of the century, when he had picked up a copy in Danish of the Concluding Unscientific Postscript in a local library in Minneapolis, where he was a young teacher of philosophy at the University of Minnesota. He sat up through the night to finish the book and thus began a study of Kierkegaard that lasted all his life. By 1914 he was lecturing on Kierkegaard at the University in a course entitled "Great Thinkers of the Nineteenth Century." These were the first public lectures devoted to the Dane in English ever given in this country. [5] In the article on Kierkegaard's anti-intellectualism, Swenson makes a point about Kierkegaard's attitude which he obviously liked, that the man who is really engaged with existence prefers the thinker, not the professor of philosophy. His own career reveals a man thinking and acting, not a man playing the role of professor of philosophy. Perhaps in part for that reason, his list of publications is not extensive; he seems not to have written for the sake of writing, but rather for the filling of some immediate, usually rather practical, need. His second article on Kierkegaard, a long introductory biographical essay, appeared in Scandinavian Studies and Notes in 1920-1921; his third, "A Danish Thinker's Estimate of Journalism," appeared in 1927. In this article he synthesized "fourteen points" about journalism that Kierkegaard had written in his diary in 1849-1850, then used his evaluation of the points to arrive at a judgment of some contemporary members of the press, Walter Lippmann, H. L. Mencken, and Upton Sinclair.

The first extended English translation from Kierkegaard, Lee M. Hollander's Selections from the Writings of Kierkegaard, appeared in 1923. Dr. Hollander had received his Ph. D. in Germanic Philology from Johns Hopkins University in 1905. With an interest professionally directed toward Scandinavia, he had been aware of the controversy between Norway and Sweden which was then raging. When the countries agreed to settle their differences by arbitration rather than war, Dr. Hollander was pleasantly surprised to discover some rational thinking left in the world. Since he had decided to specialize in Scandinavian literature and language, he felt that further study in such a remarkably humane area of the world was desirable. He went to Oslo to attend the University as a post-doctoral student, spending a quarter of each year either in Copenhagen or Stockholm.

Like Swenson, indeed like so many other scholars, Dr. Hollander was an inveterate browser in libraries and book stores. In the public library, either in Oslo or in Copenhagen, where the library stacks were just, in the American fashion, being opened to the public, he came across Stadier i Livets Vei, which impressed him as being one of the "profoundest as well as wittiest and most delightful" books he had ever come across. After returning to this country to begin his teaching career, he translated Stadier, "Stages," and selections from other volumes by Kierkegaard. Although the manuscript was sent to a number of publishers, none would publish it, and it lay in Dr. Hollander's desk for years. 6

Then, by chance, a friend, Howard Mumford Jones, who was then the Editor of the University of Texas Bulletin, asked Dr. Hollander if he had any material to submit to that publication. When he received the "Selections," he immediately asked for permission to publish them. Their appearance in print, however, did not evoke any response from scholars or students. By law the Bulletin was sent to the newspapers of the state, "where it no doubt helped, " Dr. Hollander speculates, "fill many waste paper baskets. " Nor was his work any more successful in gaining attention outside of Texas. And it did deserve attention, for Professor Hollander was a good translator and, as his Introduction reveals, a good student of Kierkegaard's thought, though he never professed to be a scholar of Kierkegaard's work. He was content to be a distinguished man in his own area. Very probably publication of the "Selections" in a more prominent place would have made very little difference in the amount of attention received--not with the country as materialistic as it was in the late Twenties.

There was some awareness in the seminaries of the new "Theology of Crisis, " which Karl Barth and Emil Brunner had based in part upon Kierkegaard. Such an article as K. E. J. Jörgensen's "Karl Barth in the Light of Danish Theology" reflects such awareness. And a few people, like John Mackay, who was long a leader in American theological thought, were learning of Kierkegaard through his presence in Miguel de Unamuno's "The Tragic Sense of Life. 7 But the few articles to appear between 1925 and 1935 mainly record Kierkegaard's unchanged status: "Kierkegaard: A Neglected Thinker" or "A Neglected Prophet. "

The early Thirties marked a time of individual labor for the men who were to be jointly responsible for the great popularity of Kierkegaard in England and America in the Forties. Swenson continued teaching Kierkegaard, of course, as he began to translate some of his favorite passages, apparently only for his own satisfaction. The publication in the Dublin Review of Georges Cattaui's "Bergson, Kierkegaard, and Mysticism" in an English translation by Alexander Dru was the first public announcement of the English Catholic Dru's advocacy of Kierkegaard. He was to continue to translate Kierkegaard and speak and write in his behalf for the next twenty-five years; thus he was more responsible than anyone else for introducing Kierkegaard to England.

The early Thirties also marked the arrival of Walter Lowrie upon the scene of Kierkegaardian scholarship and translation. Dr. Lowrie had served as rector of St. Paul's American Church in Rome from 1907 to 1927. During his last years in Rome he had begun to read the works in German of Karl Barth that were revolutionizing conventional Protestant theology. Barth frequently referred to Kierkegaard (although he was later to dissociate himself from Kierkegaard somewhat), and soon Lowrie was reading Kierkegaard in German. When he returned to Princeton in 1930, Lowrie was so involved with Kierkegaard that he had begun to teach himself Danish in order to read him in the original. And as he read more of Kierkegaard, he became convinced that other Americans should be informed of Kierkegaard's views.

In December, 1934, Alexander Dru suggested to Lowrie that the two of them support the translation of Kierkegaard into English. [8] Even though he was past sixty-five years of age, Lowrie agreed, and so Dru proposed to Charles Williams, Editor of the Oxford University Press, that Oxford be the house to publish Kierkegaard in an English translation. After carefully weighing the proposal Williams recommended to Sir Humphrey Milford, the Publisher, that Oxford undertake the project. Sir Humphry agreed to lend the prestige of Oxford to the project, provided that some other source be located for financial support. Since Dr. Lowrie could find no other source, he agreed to provide the necessary support from his personal funds, an amount which reached at one point over fifteen thousand dollars. In return for his support, though, Oxford had agreed to very attractive royalty rate, so that Lowrie was handsomely rewarded for his decision when the great interest in Kierkegaard began to develop in the late Forties. Williams, it should be added, had more than just an editorial interest in Kierkegaard; religiously inclined himself, he found the ideas of Kierkegaard challenging and applicable to his own day. He was soon lecturing on him at the City Literary Institute, giving the first public lectures on Kierkegaard in England. [9]

Swenson and Lowrie had also begun to correspond, and at Lowrie's urging, Swenson decided to translate Philosophical Fragments, choosing this particular work because his interest was in Kierkegaard as thinker, not necessarily as religious polemicist. Incidentally, his choice of the word "fragments" as a translation for that concept in the Danish title was to provoke a friendly controversy between Lowrie and himself that lasted throughout their friendship. Philosophical Fragments was published in 1936; it marks the beginning of the decade during which almost all of Kierkegaard was translated. As if to signal the beginning of this fruitful period, Lowrie and Swenson sponsored the visit of the noted Danish Kierkegaardian

Eduard Geismar for an American lecture tour. Geismar had earlier written an introductory article for the American audience, so his name was not completely unknown when he gave the Stone Lectures at Princeton and then repeated his views elsewhere.

Lowrie, Swenson, and Dru had agreed about their individual responsibilities in the joint project of translation and about the order in which the various translations were to be made. Swenson was to undertake the Concluding Unscientific Postscript after he had completed Philosophical Fragments, and he must have looked forward to the task with great anticipation, since it had been the Postscript which had so captivated him forty years before. Dru was to complete his translation of Haecker's Danish biography and then to excerpt and translate those parts of the whole that were to be published as The Journals of Kierkegaard; after that he planned to undertake The Concept of Dread. Lowrie completed his massive biography, Kierkegaard, in 1938, dedicating it to Swenson and paying tribute to Charles Williams in the Preface. Then he planned to begin work on The Sickness Unto Death.

By 1940, because of the impetus provided by the appearance of the various translations and by the arrival of refugee Continental scholars at American seminaries and universities, articles about Kierkegaard were appearing with accelerating frequency in journals devoted to scholarship in half a dozen different disciplines. Whether or not he would have liked it, Kierkegaard was being taken over by the professors, who were, though, usually not nearly so Germanic as the "Professor" of his conception. The phenomenologist could view him in discussing "The Concept and the "Thing" in the Journal of Philosophy, while the theologian could focus upon his religious role in "Søren Kierkegaard: Hamlet or Jeremiah?" in the Evangelical Quarterly. The patient and scholarly David Swenson provided "The Existential Dialectic of Sören Kierkegaard" for Ethics. Others began to place Kierkegaard in his historical context, in such articles as "The Cleavage of Minds: Kierkegaard and Hegel" or "Kierkegaard and His Century." A few, such as Julius S. Bixler in "The Contribution of Existenz-Philosophie" and Dorothy Emmet in "Kierkegaard and the 'Existential' Philosophy," recognized Kierkegaard as one of the origins of the new philosophic school being faintly heard from across the Atlantic--existentialism.

It should have been that Lowrie, Dru, and Swenson

would have continued their labors of translation free of outside cares. But the now Major Dru was wounded in the early part of the war and then was retained on active duty after his recovery. He had not completed his translation of The Concept of Dread and had to ask Lowrie to undertake it in his stead. And, although he was younger than Lowrie, Swenson died in 1940, leaving unfinished his translation of the Concluding Unscientific Postscript. Thus, in addition to those works that he had originally planned to translate, Lowrie accepted three more texts. Despite the fact that he was then over seventy years old, Lowrie was able to translate fifteen or so of Kierkegaard's works by 1945.

The time had come for knowledge of Kierkegaard to break out of the seminaries and colloquia. The many translations were of course reviewed, not only in philosophical and theological journals but also in general periodicals, so that a large audience thus learned of the existence of Kierkegaard, even if it did not read his works. Even President Roosevelt, with concerns so apparently foreign to those of Kierkegaard's, learned of him through Howard Johnson, then a young clergyman in Washington. Apparently he read the just translated Concept of Dread, for he told Frances Perkins, "Kierkegaard explains the Nazis to me as nothing else ever has. I have never been able to make out why people who are obviously human beings could behave like that. They are human, yet they behave like demons. Kierkegaard gives you an understanding of what it is in man that makes it possible for these Germans to be so evil."[10]

The periodicals of general interest followed up their reviews of the translations of Kierkegaard's work with brief introductions to his life and thought. Representative of this trend are Norbert Guterman's "Kierkegaard and His Faith," which appeared in Partisan Review in 1943, and W. H. Auden's "A Preface to Kierkegaard," which was published in New Republic, May 15, 1944.

Nor was this the end of Auden's association with Kierkegaard. Nearly twenty-five years later he wrote of "A Knight of Doleful Countenance" in the New Yorker, and his poetry of the period between the two articles reveals his deep interest in Kierkegaard. Auden had first learned of Kierkegaard through Charles Williams. In 1938, when Auden had conferred with Williams about the publication of The Oxford Book of Light Verse, he had undergone a religious experience of deep intensity. In his contribution to Modern Canterbury Pilgrims, Auden himself describes Williams' effect upon him: "Shortly afterwards, in a publisher's office I met an Anglican layman, and for the first time in my life felt myself in the presence of personal sanctity." As a result Auden ". . . started to read some theological works, Kierkegaard in particular, and began going, in a tentative and experimental sort of way, to church."[11]

Kierkegaard had a dramatic impact upon Auden's creative imagination. His first long poem published after his meeting with Williams, The Double Man, in 1941, several times quotes from The Journals of Kierkegaard, which Dru had translated. Since then his poetry has been colored by his continuing interest in Kierkegaard, as Edward Callan has pointed out in "Auden and Kierkegaard: The Artistic Framework of For the Time Being" and "Auden's New Year Letter: A New Style of Architecture," as Justin Replogle has pointed out in "Auden's Religious Leap," and as Lee Whitehead has pointed out in "Art as Communion: Auden's The Sea and the Mirror."[12]

Although Auden was perhaps the first English-speaking author to reveal a significant reliance upon Kierkegaard, there had been a tradition of such reliance on the Continent since Ibsen, a tradition that includes Kafka, Rilke, Dürrenmatt, and Unamuno. In recent years there have been studies in English-language periodicals of the indebtedness of these writers to Kierkegaard; such studies are cited in the bibliography of the present work. What should be said here is that these studies are frequently in complete disagreement about the extent of dependence upon Kierkegaard that a given author exhibits, as for example in the two opposed positions revealed in the two articles cited in the bibliography on Unamuno and Kierkegaard, "Observations on Unamuno and Kierkegaard" and "Kierkegaard and the Elaboration of Unamuno's Niebla." Such disagreements seem to arise from the narrowness or broadness of the critic's approach; it seems beyond doubt that Kafka, Rilke, Dürrenmatt and Unamuno were affected by the image of Kierkegaard as the isolated, suffering artist, but whether or not they reveal any conceptual dependence upon Kierkegaard has become a matter of critical controversy.

Certainly Kierkegaard's influence has been evident in post-war literature. In England both William Golding and Graham Greene have revealed a utilization of Kierkegaardian concepts; in America the reliance on Kierkegaard has been especially strong since 1952. In that year Ralph Ellison, in Invisible Man, alluded to The Sickness Unto

Death and it may well be that the fundamental truth of that novel is based upon the Kierkegaardian insistence that only faith is the alternative to the sickness, to despair. In the next year Richard Wright revealed in his novel, The Outsider, a strong attraction to The Concept of Dread. J. D. Salinger has also been influenced by Kierkegaard's thought, as was Carson McCullers in Clock Without Hands (1961). The most recent novels to display a use of Kierkegaard have been William Styron's Set This House on Fire (1960), John Updike's Rabbit, Run (1961), and Walker Percy's The Moviegoer (1961), and The Last Gentleman (1966).

The attraction that Kierkegaard holds for these writers lies in two entirely different areas of experience. The unparalleled horrors of World War II served to remind the world, as in the case of President Roosevelt, that man could be evil, that he could will to destroy his fellow human beings by the millions, that he could desire to be as God Himself. Kierkegaard had said as much, and the contemporary reader who begins to study Kierkegaard must often be struck by his prophetic vision. For one thing, then, Kierkegaard has become a spokesman for those who cannot accept the extreme liberal, humanistic view that man is innately good and will be incapable of evil if all of his material needs are met.

But aside from the philosophical insights that they might derive from Kierkegaard, recent writers have also gotten some very practical help from his works. The novelist must always be concerned with two technical elements: the depth of characterization and the movement of the narrative. Kierkegaard has offered new strategies in both these areas. Before World War II Western culture had almost completely succumbed to the idea that man was rather completely a determined creature, that either economic or psychological forces propelled him forward to do what he was destined to do. Since the war, however, there has been a renewal of interest in man as the isolated individual, perhaps buffeted by economic and psychological forces, but still capable of willing his own most significant behavior. With that dreadful kind of freedom, he has felt his estrangement from the Supernatural and consequently dwells in dread and despair. Since these states of existence are chief topics in Kierkegaard's work, novelists have turned to him for explication of the psychology of the characters that they wish to depict. Thus Styron's Cass Kinsolving or Wright's Cross Damon or Updike's Rabbit Angstrom, for example, are better understood in terms of Kierkegaardian, rather than

Marxian or Freudian psychology.

Kierkegaard has also helped the novelist achieve a convincing narrative sequence. It is no longer sufficient for a novelist to begin at the beginning and tell his story until it ends. Ever since Bergson men have acknowledged the falsity of compartmentalizing time into three separate and distinct spheres, past, present, and future. Rather, human experience is always a state of becoming; thus the present is always a blur. And since, as an objective entity Time has become so unreliable, the novelist has turned to other conceptions of narrative progression. Mythic cycles have long offered levels or steps of progression that could be utilized by the artist. Now, too, the novelist has available the scheme of individual progression developed by Kierkegaard, that of the spheres of existence. In his view, man lives in one or another of three states of attitude: the aesthetic, the ethical, or the religious. Most men remain buried in the uncontemplative aesthetic stage, but the thoughtful man, hence the man worth writing a novel about in the first place, at least attempts to reach the other stages, in order to become aware of himself in the presence of his fellows and ultimately in the presence of the Supernatural. Such men, looking forward and at the same time dreading and despairing about the future, lend themselves to depiction through Kierkegaard's stages, and men like Percy's Binx Bolling and Will Barrett can better be experienced when it is realized that they are struggling to attain another level of existence.

At the same time that English and American authors were beginning to embody Kierkegaardian concepts in their fiction, a new generation of American preachers was offering the same concepts in its sermons. Trained by such theologians as Paul Tillich and the Niebuhrs, Reinhold and Richard, these young pastors insisted that the existential insight need not be abandoned to the atheistic views of such philosophers as Jean Paul Sartre. They were able to keep American religious culture alive and questing at a time when it was beset on the one hand by the sentimental middle-class complacency of Norman Vincent Peale (so superbly satirized as "Irving Franklin Bell" in Styron's Set This House on Fire) and Billy Graham, and on the other hand by the proponents of one or another kind of "humanistic" religion. Thus there developed in American theological thinking a quality that a recent critic has defined in the following manner:

> Lacking a better term, I call it "Kierkegaardian, "
> for no other adjective so effectively implies the

xvii

major features of the movement in question: its
critique of group, class, and personal complacency;
its demand for personal appropriation of Christian
truth; its insistence that man's moral obligation
under the Gospel cannot be stated in terms of
legalistic precepts; its warning against the dangers
of rationalizing the great Biblical paradoxes; its
emphasis upon a radically personalistic understanding of the self, of other selves, and of God; above
all, the reality, the objectivity, and the sovereignty
of God and His judgments. [13]

With an awareness of Kierkegaard fostered by introductory periodical articles and books, sermons, and literary
references, almost every facet of American life seemed
ready to celebrate the centenary of his death in 1955. There
was a Kierkegaard Festival at the University of Chicago and
a Kierkegaard Colloquium at the Cathedral Church of St.
John the Divine in New York. Nor does this mean that
there were no celebrations in other countries; there was a
very significant Congress for Kierkegaardian Research, for
example, held appropriately enough in Copenhagen.

There was also an outpouring of periodical articles.
In the years just after World War II there was an average
of fifteen articles on Kierkegaard in English per year. But
there were in 1955 almost forty articles, a number reached
in part because several journals puplished all-Kierkegaard
issues. Although, as would be expected, there was a decrease in the number of articles after 1955, the average,
especially since 1960, has been around twenty. Moreover
the nature of the articles has changed; no longer are the
articles introductory in their content; rather, Kierkegaard
has become so much a part of the expected general
knowledge of the literate American that most articles now
deal with one specialized aspect or another of his thought.

But although Kierkegaard may be a familiar enough
subject in current American thought, there is no indication
that the amount of attention paid to him in American periodicals will begin to decrease. On the contrary, Kierkegaardian scholarship has only reached what Harold Durfee
calls the "second stage." As Durfee, speaking from the
camp of the philosophers, views the matter, American
theologians seem content to remain at the level of introductory, unevaluative description in their treatment of Kierkegaard. But Durfee detects a movement by American
philosophers toward a level of serious weighing and testing

xviii

of that part of Kierkegaard's thought which lends itself to philosophic analysis. This, says Durfee, is the true beginning of the second stage. And it will be very important, he continues, for only by such analysis can the professional philosopher ever be convinced of the validity of any philosophy grounded as heavily upon the subjective as is that of Kierkegaard and his heirs. So it appears that the old animosity continues between "Denmark's Dead Man" and the professors, and until one or the other is victorious (and hopefully that will never occur), there will be many additions to the bibliography attached to this study.

Notes

1. Charles Williams, The Descent of the Dove (London, 1939), p. 212.

2. Howard A. Slaatte, "Kierkegaard's Introduction to American Methodists, " The Drew Gateway, XXX (Spring 1960), 161-167.

3. Quoted in John Heywood Thomas, Subjectivity and Paradox (Oxford, 1957), p. 1.

4. Quoted in Thomas, pp. 1-2.

5. Lillian Marvin Swenson, Kierkegaardian Philosophy in the Faith of a Scholar (Philadelphia, 1949), p. 8.

6. The information regarding Lee M. Hollander was generously supplied by him in a letter to the author dated July 20, 1969.

7. Nelson R. Burr, A Critical Bibliography of Religion in America (Princeton, 1961), Volume IV, p. 1082.

8. See Walter R. Lowrie's "Translator's Preface" to The Concept of Dread (Princeton, 1957), p. vii, for corroboration of this statement; see the various other prefaces and introductions to translations of Kierkegaard by Lowrie for additional information about his role in the introduction of Kierkegaard to that part of Christendom called America.

9. Alice Mary Hadfield, An Introduction to Charles Williams (London, 1959), p. 126.

10. Frances Perkins, The Roosevelt I Knew (New York, 1946), p. 148.

11. James Pike (ed.), Modern Canterbury Pilgrims (New York, 1956), p. 41.

12. The most extended discussion of Auden's indebtedness to Kierkegaard occurs in Justin Replogle's Auden's Poetry (Seattle, 1969), especially pp. 50-82.

13. Sidney E. Ahlstrom, "Theology in America: A Historical Survey, " in The Shaping of American Religion, ed. by James Ward Smith and A. Leland Jamison (Princeton, 1961), pp. 315-316.

Essays from Various Disciplines

A Word about the Essays

My intent in selecting essays for inclusion in this anthology was to demonstrate the far-reaching impact of Kierkegaard upon contemporary American life. For that reason I have chosen articles which originally appeared, for the most part, in the journals of one or another of the professional disciplines. The articles vary greatly in their understanding of Kierkegaard's thoughts and in their application of those thoughts to research in a specific discipline. What they all share is the realization that his observations about human existence remain as rich and provocative as on the day they were written, over a hundred years ago.

Lewis A. Lawson

The Anti-Intellectualism of Kierkegaard[1]

David F. Swenson

First published in the Philosophical Review, XXV (July 1916), 567-586, the article is here reprinted with the kind permission of its editors and of David Swenson's literary executor, Paul L. Holmer.

The aim of the present paper is two-fold: to give an introductory characterization of Kierkegaard's individuality as a thinker, and to elucidate in some detail the epistemological position from which the paper takes its title. This position I have characterized as anti-intellectualism, in order to establish a point of contact with present-day currents of thought; but I warn the reader that Kierkegaard resists a facile classification, and that one cannot, without danger of misunderstanding, transfer impressions derived from a study of James or Bergson, unmodified, to the interpretation of this most profound and original thinker. The introductory section of the paper deals briefly with Kierkegaard's style and method of writing, in its relation to his philosophical ideas; with his doctrine of 'indirect communication,' as the consistent form of a reflectively conscious protest against intellectualism; and with the method and program of his constructive philosophy of values.

I

Although the author of a literature rich in philosophical content, Kierkegaard wrote no systematic treatise on pure logic or metaphysics. It most often happens that philosophical writers who thus wear the less professional air, have their treasures of truth so submerged in feeling, or so suffused with imagination, that their position is not abstractly clear, and consequently not readily susceptible of a sharp definition. But in Kierkegaard we have a rare combination of dialectical power with an imaginative and dramatic intuition, so that picturesque characterization in the concrete is to be found in his writing, side by side with exact and

23

algebraic definition. His native dialectical powers were
disciplined by a serious study of Hegel; and though emanci-
pating himself from the tyranny of Hegel's dominant influence, he acquired through his aid the mastery of a precise
and finished terminology. The absence, therefore, of any
systematic treatise covering the logical and metaphysical
disciplines is due, not so much to a limitation or a
peculiarity in his genius, as to the nature of his philosophical position; indeed, it is the deliberate expression
of a well-considered choice, the carefully planned application of a corrective against a onesided and abstract intellectualism. [2] This feature of his thought makes his ideas
extremely difficult to convey at second hand, since the task
resembles the translation of poetry, where the form is inseparable from the content. One is constantly exposed to
the danger of utterly failing to interpret the spirit of his
philosophy, in spite of having correctly transcribed its
chief salient propositions, --a danger which the reader will
note is somewhat ironical in its nature.

        Kierkegaard calls himself a subjective thinker. His
meaning may perhaps be conveyed, in one of its aspects,
by calling him also an artist-thinker. For he strove constantly to reduplicate his reflection in an artistic form,
attempting to assimilate and transmute its objective content
so as to make it serve the purposes of a communication
in which due regard should be had both to the giver and to
the receiver. This care for the subjective elements in
communication demands that thought should be doubly reflective; by the first reflection it then attains to its ordinary
and direct expression in the word or phrase, and by the
second reflection it receives an indirect expression in style
and form, as the concrete medium of human intercourse. [3]
Such an indirect expression, inasmuch as it is the result of
reflection, is artistic; and such a thinker is therefore an
artist in another and higher sense than that which is implied by the possession of mere literary skill. Kierkegaard
maintains the validity and necessity of this two-fold reflection, whenever the subject matter to be communicated
concerns Reality in its most concrete aspect, as rooted in
the very nature of Reality itself, and as grounded in the
fundamental relation between objective thought and real
existence. Reality is such that a form of communication
may be chosen which contradicts the very thought that it
assumes to convey, thus "transforming the supposed communication into a non-communication."

        I cannot undertake to convey, within the limits of

this paper, an idea of the literary resourcefulness, the reflective ingenuity, the keenness of irony and profundity of humor, the variety and multiplicity of forms and devices, that give to Kierkegaard's writings their peculiar individuality of stamp and coloring, as a consequence of the method described as 'double reflection.' One expression of the method is the absence of a volume of pure logic or metaphysics from the list of his published works; the principle by which this choice was guided I wish briefly to explain.

The problem of Reality is of course, in one sense or another, the problem of all philosophy, and it was also Kierkegaard's central problem. As a student of the philosophy of his day, he soon began to feel, like many other students in his day and our own, the inadequacy of what philosophers are accustomed to say on this all-absorbing topic. "What philosophers say under the head of Reality," he complains in one of his aphorisms, "is sometimes as illusory as a sign displayed in a window, 'Clothes pressed here.' If you enter the shop to have your clothes pressed, you are disappointed to learn that the sign is held for sale, and that clothes are not pressed on the premises."[4] Philosophers tend to forget that the categories which are usually the first to attract their attention, and to which objective thinking is apt exclusively to devote itself, namely the logical and the metaphysical, are not as such the categories of Reality. The entities of metaphysics and the forms of logic do not exist <u>as such</u>; when they exist, they exist as imbedded in the flesh and blood of the esthetic, the ethical, and the religious. Their reality or being is not identical with the reality of factual existence, but they constitute an abbreviation of, or a <u>prius</u> for, the above three fundamental spheres of existence. Hence it is that no man lives in categories that are purely logical or metaphysical, but exists on the contrary in categories that are esthetic, ethical or religious in their nature.[5] A philosopher thoroughly conscious of this fact should be impelled to give his intercourse and his writings the stamp of a broad and sympathetic humanism; he will certainly wish to bear in mind that a philosopher is not only <u>sometimes</u> a man, as a Greek sceptic once frankly confessed, but always and essentially a man. In the attempt to express this consciousness, Kierkegaard made his work approximate, as nearly as possible, the essential features of the living reality. Now, in the concrete, the logical both is and is not, being imbedded in life's moral substance; hence the skeleton of Kierkegaard's own logical position was likewise imbedded and hidden in a certain 'thickness,' to use a sig-

25

nificant expression of James. It was wrapped up in a covering of humor, wit, pathos, and imagination, and interwoven with mimic and lyric expressions of doubt, despair, and faith; so that we have presented before us, instead of a mere logical web of paragraphs, a thinking personality who exists in his thought. The subjective is shown appropriating and using the objective; on this account the style has a certain breadth, an unsystematic lingering ease of conversational tone; and there is displayed a pregnant and decisive energy of acceptance or repudiation which is unusual in philosophical composition, but which brings us incomparably nearer to the breath of life.

Pascal has noted that there are few who show themselves able to speak of doubt doubtingly, or faith believingly, or modesty, modestly. It is no slight tribute to the noble simplicity of William James as a thinker, that he put in practice so large a measure of what he had learned to understand, and actually taught pragmatism in a pragmatic spirit. A student of Kierkegaard is in like manner impressed by the fact that his doctrine and method and spirit are consonant, and may be called genuinely pragmatic in a high and noble sense. In Kierkegaard, abstract logical thought is not merely dogmatically described as having an instrumental function, but it is actually made to perform its duty as instrumental; it is every moment held in subjection to a realistic aim. Moreover, so concrete is the conception of this realistic aim, so reflectively apprehended are the difficulties in the way of its actualization, that the problem which it sets gives rise to a philosophic theory of the art of communication respecting it. This theory seeks to define the nature and limits of the mutual dependence of individuals upon one another, in such a way as to exhibit and respect their real and ultimate independence. The theory is expressed and summarized in the category of 'indirect communication,' which is the logical outcome of the method of double reflection, and the consistent consequence of the thorough-going anti-intellectualism which Kierkegaard represents. [6]

That communication on the subject of the highest and most concrete phase of Reality must necessarily be indirect, has its ground, according to Kierkegaard, in the fact that the actualization of the real is always in process, and also in that independence of the individuals which makes any essential discipleship a false relation; it is an expression for the ethical isolation which makes it impossible to judge of an individual justly, or with unconditional certainty,

26

by means of any code of general rules or laws; finally, it
is a consequence of the metaphysical incommensurability
between the particular and the universal, language being
the vehicle of the abstract and the universal, Reality being
essentially concrete and particular. When communication
deals with the abstract, or with such aspects of the concrete as can be apprehended through essentially valid analogies, i. e. , the whole realm of purely objective thinking,
there is no good reason why it should not be direct and
positive; but when it attempts to deal with the absolutely
individual and concrete, i. e. , the realm of the ethico-
religious inwardness, its apparent positive and direct character is illusory; such communication becomes real only on
condition that its negative aspect is brought to consciousness, and embodied in the form. A lover, for example,
may feel the need of telling others of his love, though he
also feels that he neither desires to convey, nor is able to
express, its deepest and most intimate secret. And that
which is only relatively true in the case of the lover, since
the lover's experience has analogies, is absolutely true for
the ethico-religious individual. A concrete subjective thinker,
like Socrates, has no positive result that can be truly or
adequately conveyed by a formula or a sum of propositions;
he has only a way, he is never finished, and he cannot
therefore positively communicate himself.

A protest against intellectualism needs a category of
this kind in order to free itself from the last vestige of
subservience to the dominance of the principle of identity.
In my opinion, Kierkegaard was the first critic of intellectualism who burned his philosophical bridges behind him,
and thereby liberated himself from the trammels of the
intellectualist application or misuse of logic in the world of
life and reality. Certainly not the first to discover the
category in question, or the first to use it, he was nevertheless the first, as far as I am aware, to give it a clear
and dialectical formulation. What I have said about it here
is simply for the purpose of calling attention to the concept,
and does not pretend to play the part of an exposition. [7]

James characterizes intellectualism as the claim that
conceptual logic is the final authority in the world of being
or fact, and as the assertion that the logic of identity is
the most intimate and exhaustive definer of the nature of
reality. [8] Kierkegaard meets this claim and assertion by
the proposition that logic does not and cannot define reality;
that it merely predisposes reality for our knowledge without
itself coming into contact with its actuality. [9] With this

27

proposition his anti-intellectualism begins, but it by no means ends there; and although this attitude toward logic is the primary concern of the present paper, I wish also to indicate, very summarily and only by way of introduction, the philosophical advance which he has made in the application of this initial proposition to more concrete problems.

The chief forms of positive objective knowledge--mathematics, the historical disciplines, sense perception and the natural sciences which rest upon perception, and metaphysics--are subjected to a critical estimate, in the endeavor to establish the fundamental fact that these disciplines, despite their real and obvious value (Kierkegaard is no obscurantist), when viewed as revelations of Reality, suffer from two fundamental defects of abstraction. First, they are either entirely hypothetical in their application to reality, as in the case of logic and mathematics, or they are endless approximations to the truth, as in the case of history and the natural sciences. Secondly, they are, and indeed wish to be, purely objective disciplines; as such they realize a knowledge which from the standpoint of the real knower is non-essential, since it does not express his actual and concrete position in existence. Hence they do not essentially concern him, but concern merely a fictitious objective subject-in-general, not identical with any concrete human being; in the last analysis, the degree and scope of such knowledge is a matter of indifference, and only knowledge whose relation to existence is essential, is essential knowledge. No form of positive objective knowledge, no logical system, no metaphysical result (a metaphysical system embracing reality is an illusion), can attain to a Truth in which Reality is adequately and definitively revealed. [10]

If the problem of Truth and Reality is not to be given up in despair, one must seek for a solution elsewhere, and seek for it in another spirit. There is but one sphere in which such a solution can be sought, and this is the sphere of the subjective attitude of the knower, the realm of the subjective 'how' as distinct from the objective 'what.' Such is the fruitful turn which Kierkegaard gives to an analysis of the adequacy of knowledge that is nearly as old as thought, and which, according to the temperament of the philosopher, has served variously as a starting point for scepticism, for positivism, for relativism, for mysticism, or for an abstract idealism. Kierkegaard makes it the point of departure for an elaborate and profound critique of the personality in its chief subjective modes, in order to discover a 'how' which shall adequately express and grasp the real in its human accessibility and concreteness. He offers us a delineation of the whole range of typical subjective life-attitudes, describing them in their ideal self-consistency and sharpness of distinction.[11] In this way he presents a variety of esthetic points of view, from hardened understanding to sympathetic-egoistic melancholy; esthetic and ethical despair in many forms; prudent eudemonism and worldly wisdom; executive irony, or irony as a fundamental attitude toward life; ethical self-assertion in terms of moral courage and pathos; marriage as the most concrete ethical realization of life; the struggles of conscience and remorse under exceptional and irregular conditions, for the purpose of throwing light upon the normal; humor and resignation; religion. The forms of the religious attitude are reduced ultimately to two, which Kierkegaard regards as fundamental: immanent religion and transcendent religion, the latter being distinguished from the former by the decisiveness in which it grasps, and the passionate concreteness with which it expresses, the deepest paradox of life.[12] This critique of the personality is evidently equivalent to a philosophy of values. But the uniqueness of Kierkegaard's contribution to such a philosophy lies in the fact that the evaluations of life which form its subject matter are by his method made to reveal themselves, and therefore in a sense to criticize themselves, through representative personalities; they are embodied in the self-expression of a variety of authors or pseudonyms, whose ideas constitute typical and rival views of life.

The results of this dramatic and imaginative exploration of the personality are abstractly summarized, and culminate in a definition of Truth, as Subjectivity raised to the highest intensity of which it is capable; or, in order to make explicit its negative relation to the objective, as the objectively uncertain, held fast in subjective inwardness with the highest possible degree of passionate appropriation.[13] This formula also defines Faith, which is the subject's mode of apprehending the Truth, sensu eminenti. A more concrete and epigrammatic characterization of the Truth is embodied in the maxim: "Only the Truth which edifies, is Truth for you."[14] This is evidently a concrete way of acknowledging the individual himself as the test and standard of Truth, not indeed in the sense of Protagoras, but in the opposite sense of Socrates. 'Know thyself' becomes the ultimate categorical imperative.

This self is not, however, a transcendental ego serving as a starting-point for metaphysical speculation, as in Fichte; it is, very simply, the concrete personality that constitutes for each one his appropriate ethical task. Realistically, the above definition of Truth involves the consequence that the only reality accessible to any existing individual is his own ethical reality. To every reality outside the individual, even his own external reality, his highest valid relation is cognitive; but knowledge is a grasp of the possible, and not a realization of the actual; the knowledge of actualities transmutes them into possibilities, and the highest intellectual validity of knowledge is attained in an even balancing of alternate possibilities with an absolutely open mind.[15]

Each of the brief characterizing phrases used in the above schematic outline stands for an entire section or volume in Kierkegaard's comprehensive literature of the personality; and he has himself given the content of these treatises an abstract categorical formulation, conceived with almost algebraic exactness. This is indeed a brilliant double achievement, by the recognition of which Kierkegaard's permanent fame as a thinker will be historically assured.

II

We now pass to a more detailed consideration of Kierkegaard's estimate of logic, formally taking up the reasons which constitute his critique of intellectualism. These reasons may be summarized under four principal heads. 1. Logic cannot, from its own resources, provide for transitions from one quality to another; in the world of fact, such transitions take place by a leap. 2. Logic cannot acknowledge, within its own sphere, the contingent; but the contingent is an essential constituent of the actual. 3. Logic deals only with universals; the particular, however, is absolutely inseparable from the actual. 4. Logic deals only with essences, whose being consists in their conceivability; factual existence is not an essence, and it involves a kind of a being which cannot be logically conceived. Let us consider each of these points in turn.

A. A logical transition from one quality to another is impossible. The static character of the concept has often been contrasted with the dynamic character of temporal experience, sometimes with the intent of proving the concept, and sometimes temporal experience, unfit for knowledge. Of course, we may define knowledge in different ways; but in the generally accepted meaning, it would seem to be this static characteristic of the concept

30

which makes knowledge of a changing experience possible. [16]
Kierkegaard succeeds, perhaps, in obviating much superficial misunderstanding of the doctrine of the static concept,
by formulating the distinction between a logical and an
actual transition, and in calling attention to the fact that
the change from one concept to another, whether in the
revision of judgment or in the course of history, is not
logical, but actual. A concept does not change itself,
either into its opposite or into a mere other, but reality
makes the transition from one concept to another by means
of a leap. In logic, everything is and nothing comes into
being--a truth which the Eleatic philosophy transferred to
the realm of factual existence in consequence of a misunderstanding. [17] In a logical system of concepts, every
movement is immanent, since the relations by which the
system is constituted are, by the existence of the system,
rendered internal relations; the whole is therefore presupposed in every part, and that which emerges from the
logical development of such a system is exactly the same
as that which was there at the beginning. [18] Movement,
transition, mediation, are all transcendent concepts, and
have no legitimate place in logic. To ignore this is to
confuse both logic and the historical sciences, where these
concepts belong, and makes ethics impossible; for it leads
to the misunderstanding that the actual, whether past or
future, may be viewed as necessary. By this interpretation
all real movement is taken away from history and from the
individual life, and the illusory introduction of movement
into logic is a very poor substitute for such an irreparable
loss.

In the realm of the actual, transitions come to pass.
This is the essential nature of existence; its salient characteristic is change and striving, which is the source of all
its pathos. All actual transition involves a breach of continuity, a leap. The leap is present in manifold forms,
and it is one of the most important of philosophical problems to distinguish between transitions of different orders. [19]
The most significant and decisive are those which take place
in the ethico-religious life of the individual; this is the
sphere of the essentially qualitative distinctions. But every
leap possesses the logically negative character that it cannot be construed, except out of an immanence which has
first included it, and the gap between two qualities can
never be bridged by a demonstration; it must either be
given or be achieved.

The historical actuality is thus marked by a transition to the new as a leap, whence is derived the sense of wonder. Wonder is the philosopher's receptivity for the historically new. Under a logical construction of history, wonder would be abolished; "for who could possibly wonder at a necessary construction?"[20] But such a construction of history is illusory, as everyone would easily understand if he attempted to construe the life of a single individual, say his own. Kierkegaard pithily remarks that the Hegelian interpretation of history helps us to understand the past by apprehending it as if it had never been present or future; it interprets the heroes of the past as if they had never been alive; and it seeks to aid us to an understanding of ourselves by treating us as if we were dead. [21] The futility of this kind of explanation of life, and the need of replacing it by an interpretation more human, is expressed in the following epigram from one of his journals: "The motto of all philosophy hitherto has been, There is nothing new under the sun; the motto of the new Danish philosophy will be, There are more things in heaven and earth than are dreamt of in your philosophy. "

B.   Logic cannot assimilate or acknowledge the contingent aspect of the actual, within its own realm of truth. This is an immediate consequence of the fact that change transcends the sphere of logic, since change is a contingency.   In a logical system all relations are necessary, precisely because in such a system no changes actually take place.   Hence the logical as the necessary cannot exist, for everything that exists has come into being, i. e., has suffered the change involved in passing from potentiality to actuality ($\kappa\acute{\iota}\nu\eta\sigma s$).   This change the necessary cannot undergo; the necessary is, and never comes to be; its being is sub specie aeternitatis, in the realm which is the essential medium of thought.   In logic, every movement is in consequence of a logical ground, and is hence both necessary and immanent; in reality, nothing happens in consequence of a ground, but everything takes place by virtue of a cause.   The apparent necessity of a natural law, binding cause to effect, is no real or unconditional necessity; the appearance of necessity arises through an abstraction from the fact that the causes (the secondary causes) have themselves come into being, and by a forgetfulness of the fact that their becoming is not explained, but only presupposed, by the law; "should such forgetfulness perhaps also be necessary?"   The past is indeed unchangeable but it does not share the unchangeableness of the necessary, for when the past came to be, it did not exclude the change by which it came to be; but the necessary excludes every change.   The possibility of a systematic apprehension of

32

the past, ex post facto, cannot alter the fact that the past is
not more necessary than the future. Just as the optical illusion
of seeing the square tower round is one which is induced by
distance in space, so the intellectual illusion of apprehending
the past as necessary is induced by distance in time. [22]

C. The incommensurability between the universal
and the particular reveals the impotence of logic in its
attempt to define the actual. The logical concept is always
a universal, and even the so-called concrete universal is
not concrete in the same sense that the actual is concrete,
for the particular quâ particular is essential to the actual,
and repels every attempt to conceive it logically. [23] When
abstract thought tries to conceive the particular, it transforms it into a universal. To ask what reality is in general, is one thing; to ask what it means to call this particular thing or situation a reality, by bringing the ideality
of thought to bear upon its concrete particularity, is an
absolutely different thing. The former question is perhaps
not even legitimate; in any case the question and answer
remain within the sphere of the abstract, and do not reach
reality as actual. The latter question is a concrete question,
and cannot be put in a logical or metaphysical system, or
in any science; it can only be answered by the individual as
an individual, who finds in the definiteness of time and
space the particularization of his experience and his thought.
Abstract thought solves all the difficulties of life by ab-
stracting from them, whence arises its complacent disinterestedness; the concrete thinker, who faces the concrete
problem of reality as above specified, discovers that this
problem brings his subjective interest to a climax, since
it reveals a future presenting a critical and decisive alternative. For abstract thought there is no 'either-or,' no
absolute disjunction; "why in the world should there be,
since abstract thought abstracts from existence, where the
absolute disjunction belongs?" But for the thinker who
faces the future with the subjective passion inherent in
voluntary action sensu eminenti, there exists an absolute
disjunction, a valid contradictory opposition; "whoever
attempts to take this away, takes existence away, and does
not therefore take it away in existence. "[24]

On the universality of the universal rests the possibility of communication, and on its validity rests the acknowledgment of the existence of other selves. The universal is that which is common to different thinkers, or to the
same thinker at different times. [25] But the incommensurability between the universal and the particular makes doubt

33

and belief, truth and error, possible. When I interpret a
particular sense impression as a star, I give it a place in
a conceptual order; and when I interpret it as the same
star which I saw yesterday or a year ago, or as a star
which my neighbor means or sees, or as a star which
once came into existence, whether an instant or ages ago
makes no essential difference--I am in these interpretations
or judgments identifying a present immediacy of sense with
some conceptuality of the memory or the imagination.
Scepticism is a protest of the will against every such
identification, on the ground that it involves an inference
transcending the immediately given, and because it is
impossible to prove that such inferences may not turn out
to be erroneous. Belief is a contrary movement of the
will, an affirmation which recognizes that another interpretation is possible, but nevertheless risks the assertion
of this interpretation as real. That alternative interpretations are always possible, is most frequently a latent
consciousness; stupid and passionate people ignore it; and
the immediate suggestions of sense, together with the
familiarity of the habitual, not to speak of the partiality of
the will, tend to lull this consciousness to sleep. On the
other hand, the experience of error tends to rouse the
mind from its dogmatic slumbers, thus positing the choice
between belief and belief, or between belief and doubt. [26]

In the inner life of the self, the contrast between
the universal and the particular finds its highest significance.
The self is a synthesis of the universal and the particular.
The ethical individual has the task of realizing the universal
man in a concrete particular embodiment, and the individual
is both himself and the race. The ethical solution of this
contradiction constitutes the history of the individual, by
which he also participates in the history of the race, and
is essentially interested in the history of every other individual. Here lie all the ethical and religious problems
of the individual life. [27]

D. The heterogeneity of the logical and the actual
is revealed, finally, in the fact that logic deals only with
essences or qualities. Factual existence, which is the mark
of actuality, is not an essence or a quality; and the difference between the possible and the actual is logically
non-determinable, because the change from the one to the
other is not a change of essence, but a change of being. [28]
From this follow two important consequences: it becomes
evident that demonstration or proof with reference to existence is a misunderstanding, and that to speak of degrees

of reality without clearly distinguishing between ideal
reality and factual existence, involves a similar misunderstanding.

It is impossible to reach existence by means of a
demonstration. All demonstration operates by essences or
quales, and their existence is either assumed or irrelevant.
(The objective existence of the essences postulated by logic
is simply their reality for thought, but is not their factual
existence.) Hence I can never demonstrate the existence
of a stone or a star, but only that some existing thing is a
stone or a star. The testimony offered in a court of
justice is not for the purpose of proving that a criminal
exists, but in order to show that the accused, whose existence is given, is a criminal. It cannot be proved that
God exists; every such attempt inevitably reduces itself to
a development of the consequences which flow from having
assumed his existence, i.e., to a making explicit the
logical content of the conception of God. If God does not
exist, of course it is impossible to prove his existence;
but if he does exist, it would be the height of folly to
attempt it. The procedure has esthetically the form of an
insult, as if one were to assume to demonstrate, in the
presence of someone, that he exists; for existence is higher
than demonstration, and requires a more adequate form of
acknowledgment. The only adequate expression for the
existence of God is worship, and the attempt to demonstrate
it, is consciously or unconsciously to ignore his existence,
i.e., his presence. All reasoning is _from_ existence, and
no reasoning is _toward_ existence.

Factual existence not being a quality, is not subject
to distinctions of degree. A fly, if it exists, has precisely
as much existence as a God. The dialectic of existence
is the dialectic of Hamlet, 'to be or not to be.' Ideally,
it is not improper to speak of degrees of reality, but when
we deal with reality from the ideal point of view, we do not
deal with factual existence, but with ideal essence. Spinoza's
proof for the existence of God is thus a profound tautology,
resting on the identification of reality with perfection. It
avoids the real difficulty, which is, to bring God's ideal
essence into relation with factual existence.

The category which relates the ideal to the actual
is the possible, and knowledge is always a system of
possibilities; intellectually and esthetically, though not
ethically, the possible is higher than the actual, just as
Aristotle says that poetry is more philosophical than

history. [29] Belief is the application of knowledge to the determination of the actual, and constitutes our point of contact with the historical as such. The historical comes into being by setting aside the antecedent alternative possibilities; in precisely analogous fashion, belief comes into existence by setting aside as invalid the alternative possibilities of knowledge. And just as the former transition is a leap which cannot be logically construed, so the latter transition, the transition from the many possibilities of knowledge to the one reality of belief, is not necessitated by knowledge, but is an act of the will. [30] The choice of the will in believing is the means whereby the personality constitutes, expresses, and reveals itself, on the different levels of its subjectivity. Every deeper ethico-religious conviction, as an interpretation of the universe and of life, is an expression of the inner depths of the personality, rather than a necessary consequence of knowledge. Faith is never grounded in the objective necessities of logic or of metaphysics, and its firm conviction in incommensurable with the approximations and probabilities of history or of natural science; it is forever transcendent of every positive external objectivity, and its object exists only for the infinite subjective interest in which and through which it lives and works. [31]

* * * * * *

Such is, in brief outline, and largely in free paraphrase, Kierkegaard's anti-intellectualism, viewed from the standpoint of logic. The reader may wish to compare these views with current attacks upon formal logic, and with the radical evolutionism of Bergson. The attacks upon logic charge that this discipline or no-discipline, as the impetuosity of its critics leads them to stamp it, does not describe actual thinking, does not reveal the actual motives of thought, and does not explain the actual progress of knowledge. This is evidently the same contrast between the formal and the actual which Kierkegaard has attempted to illuminate and to interpret. When compared with Bergson, Kierkegaard's position shows both essential resemblances and essential differences; but the comparison raises so many problems that the present paper cannot undertake even to mention them. Current controversy is almost wholly preoccupied with the problem of knowledge, leaving the problem of action far in the background. It is here, however, that the distinction between intellectualism and its antithesis is most sharply defined, for the mere knower is not as such the concretely real subject; as knower he makes an effort, the better to realize the function of science,

36

to abstract from his real existence. It is by such an abstraction that he seeks to become disinterested and objective, and to identify himself, as far as may be, with the objectivity that he knows. It is true that this undertaking is but an approximation, and is never completely successful; but it is folly to ignore the reality of the effort, and futile to deny that it may and does meet with a relatively adequate degree of success. On the other hand, it is surely necessary for every thinker to understand what relation his abstract thought and objective knowledge bear to life; if he seeks to forget life in a complete absorption in the tasks of objective thought, or assumes that the latter is the highest and noblest human pursuit, then he becomes, as Kierkegaard has shown in a style and manner worthy to be ranked as classic, personally insignificant and fundamentally a comic figure, a type of the absent-minded professor whose real life is lived in distraction, "and who even marries--in distraction." This species of abstract thinker Kierkegaard has immortalized in the figure of the 'privatdocent.' With greater objectivity than Schopenhauer, but with a point of view akin to his, he has drawn the picture of the "professor of philosophy, in the German sense, who is bound, a tout prix, to explain everything"; over against this picture he has set the ideal of the "thinker, in the Greek sense, whose life is an attempt artistically to realize his thought," and who does not, therefore, need "many thoughts, all valid to a certain extent," but is satisfied with "one thought, which is absolute."

Notes

1. Sören Aabye Kierkegaard, a Danish thinker (1813-1855), author of an extensive esthetic, ethical, and religious literature. The latest edition of his collected works was published in Copenhagen in 1904, under the editorship of A. B. Drachmann et al. References in the article apply to the separate volumes of this edition. A German translation in twelve volumes has recently been published by Eugen Diederichs in Jena. Georg Brandes, S. K., Leipzig, 1879, offers a critical analysis of the Kierkegaardian literature in its esthetic aspects; Hoffding, S. K. als Philosoph, Stuttgart, 1902, deals with his philosophical position.

2. Afsluttende Uvidenskabelig Efterskrift, pp. 210, 303.

3. Ibid., pp. 55-62.

4. Enten-Eller, I, p. 16.

5. Stadier paa Livets Vei, p. 443.

6. A study of Professor Royce's Problem of Christianity reveals an interesting parallel between the category of 'interpretation' as developed by him, and Kierkegaard's doctrine of 'indirect communication.' These two categories play analogous and central rôles in two antithetical views of life and reality. Kierkegaard's conception of Christianity is therefore the precise opposite, at every essential point, of that offered by Professor Royce. Interpretation is direct and positive, is an expression for objective certainty, and is related, despite strenuous efforts to avoid the implication, to an essentially static view of life. Indirect communication is a negative expression for an underlying positive principle, involves the denial of objective certainty, and is related to an essentially dynamic view of life. To take one illustration of many: Royce has a doctrine of the Spirit in the Community, but does not make paramount the question of how the Community comes to be, since for him it simply is; he does not ask how the Spirit comes to constitute the Community, or to dwell in it. When this question is raised and answered, as Kierkegaard would answer it, by an insistence upon the primacy of the individual, and a recognition of the fact that the Spirit must first come to dwell in the individual in order to dwell in and constitute the Community, instead of vice versa; then the life of the individual is turned inward rather than outward, and is made inwardly, and therefore radically, dynamic; the relation to God becomes prior to, and fundamental to, the relation to humanity, instead of an ambiguous variant expression for the latter, or a powerless shadow of it; and the distinction between pantheism and theism receives its true significance.

7. Cf. Indøvelse i Christendom, pp. 115-134.

8. A Pluralistic Universe, pp. 213-220.

9. Begrebet Angest, p. 10.

10. Cf. Afsluttende Uvidenskabelig Efterskrift, passim.

11. Op. cit., pp. 212-257; and the entire literature.

12. Ibid., pp. 484-587.

13. Op. cit., p. 170.

14. Enten-Eller, II, p. 318.

15. Afsluttende Uvidenskabelig Efterskrift, p. 271.

16. It is one of the many merits of Hüsserl's Logische Untersuchungen to have abundantly set forth and illustrated this point.

17. Begrebet Angest, p. 13.

18. Hence when logic rejoices in the orderly beauty of its ballet of the categories, it is pledged not to forget that this ballet is devoid of all actual motion; reason enough for its 'unearthly' character!

19. For the sake of greater clearness, I append a few examples, culled mostly from material in Kierkegaard's journal. H_2 plus O becomes water, and water becomes ice, by a leap. The change from motion to rest, or vice versa, is a transition which cannot be logically construed; this is the basic principle of Zeno's dialectic, and is also expressed in Newton's laws of motion, since the external force by which such change is effected is not a consequence of the law, but is premised as external to the system with which we start. It is therefore transcendent and non-rational, and its coming into existence can only be apprehended as a leap. In the same manner, every causal system presupposes an external environment as the condition of change. Every transition from the detail of an empirical induction to the ideality and universality of law, is a leap. In the actual process of thinking, we have the leap by which we arrive at the understanding of an idea or an author. Kierkegaard finds a pardonable pleasure in noting the inconsistency of certain followers of Hegel, who have tried to invest with romantic glamour the experience by which they awoke to an understanding of his philosophy; as if a man were to boast of the miracle by which he became an adherent of the philosophy which denies all miracles. The change from scepticism to belief is a leap of

fundamental importance; a radical doubt cannot work itself out into belief by an immanent development of its presuppositions, in spite of the fact, exploited by a too fᵃᵈile idealism, that scepticism always posits an abstract certainty in the background   Doubt consists in falsely interpreting this certainty; hence it cannot be overcome except by the assumption of a new point of departure, reached in a decision of the will. In the inner life, the radical transitions are not merely given, but must be achieved as an expression of freedom. They are therefore both non-logical and pathetic; the breach of continuity which they involve necessitates an experience surcharged with pathos. Thus the transition from esthetic Eudemonism to ethics, or from the contemplation of nature to the idea of God, or from an intellectual knowledge of the good to its ethical realization, is in each case a pathetic transition. Cf. Sören Kierkegaard's Papirer, V, pp. 371-375.

20. Philosophiske Smuler, p. 74. Cf. Aristotle's remark that science tends to abolish wonder, by exhibiting as necessary that which at first appears to be contingent; citing the example of the geometrician who has demonstrated the incommensurability subsisting between the circumference of the circle and its diameter.

21. "Misled by the constant reference to a continued process in which opposites come together in a higher unity, and so again in a higher unity, etc. , a parallel has been drawn between Hegel's doctrine and that of Heraclitus, that everything is in a state of flux.   But this is a misunderstanding, since everything that Hegel says about process and becoming is illusory.   Hence the System lacks an ethic, and hence the System knows nothing when it is asked, in real earnest, by the living generation and the living individual, to explain becoming, in order, namely, that the individual may learn how to act and live.   In spite of all that is said about process, Hegel does not understand the world-process from the point of view of becoming, but understands it, by help of the illusion incident to pastness, from the point of view of finality, where all becoming is excluded.   Hence it is impossible for a Hegelian to understand himself by means of his philosophy, for he can only understand that which is past and fin-

ished; but a living person is surely not yet deceased. Possibly he finds consolation in the thought that when one can understand China and Persia and six thousand years of the world's history, the understanding of a particular individual matters very little, even if that individual happens to be one's self. To me it does not seem so, and I understand it better conversely: that he who is unable to understand himself must have a somewhat peculiar understanding of China and Persia, etc. " Afsluttende Uvidenskabelig Efterskrift, p. 263. Cf. also James: A Pluralistic Universe, pp. 243- 244, where Kierkegaard is quoted.

22. Cf. Philosophiske Smuler, pp. 65-79.

23. Begrebet Angest, p. 75.

24. Afsluttende Uvidenskabelig Efterskrift, p. 261.

25. The 'ego-centric predicament' is an imperfect expression for the more fundamental 'present-moment'
predicament; it is just as impossible to know one's
own past, or conceive one's own future, or realize
the full significance of one's own present, without
assuming the validity of universals, as it is to conceive the possibility or acknowledge the reality of
another person without making the same assumption.
To characterize the universal as indeterminateness
of meaning is confusing, since it needlessly breaks
with traditional terminology, and necessitates distinguishing between two kinds of indeterminateness,
one of which is sui generis. To call universals
dead dictionary definitions, verbal forms without
content, is likewise confusing, and is excusable only
as a sort of vehement argumentum ad hominem
relevant to a particular misuse of the universal, but
not tending to clarify logical terminology.

26. The philosophers who confidently appeal to Experience,
spelled, like the Absolute, with a capital, as the
adequate immanent guarantee for the security of
judgment, seem not to have learned from experience
that the consequences always come last, and cannot
therefore be appealed to in the moment of judgment;
their utility for the shaping of future judgments
never reaches the point where it abolishes the risk
of error, or the incommensurability between the
given and the inferred. On the other hand, the

41

idealists seek to heal the open wound of this situation by reference to an Absolute Knower, failing to realize the power of the actual uncertainty and risk of error involved to depress the ideal certainty which the Absolute Knower possesses, to the status of an abstract possibility; other motives than those derivable from the realm of epistemology are necessary, in order to transmute this abstract conception into a concrete faith in a real actuality. But by this transference of the problem from the logical to the ethico-esthetic sphere, the content of the conception is radically altered, and we pass from the Absolute of metaphysics to the God of religion.

27. Begrebet Angest, p. 28

28. Philosophiske Smuler, Chap. 3, and "Mellemspil."
    It is this transition which, as Bergson teaches, offers a problem that no intellectual knowledge succeeds in solving; Kierkegaard insists that the problem is irrelevant to knowledge as such, and that the attempt to find a new form of knowledge that solves the problem (intuition) is illusory.

29. Afsluttende Uvidenskabelig Efterskrift, pp. 273-312.

30. The reader will note the identity of what is here called belief, with what modern logic calls judgment, as something distinct from the ideal content of propositions.

31. For Kierkegaard, faith is by no means objectless; but its object is not given positively, outside the individual, but only negatively, within the individual; there is an absolute correspondence between the nature of this object and the individual's subjective mode of apprehending it. Kierkegaard's achievement is, so to have defined this subjective mode as uniquely to determine the object to which it corresponds.

42

Kierkegaard's Theory of Knowledge
and New Directions in
Psychology and Psychoanalysis

Bruce W. Wilshire

First published in the Review of Existential Psychology and Psychiatry, III (1963), 249-261, the article is here re- printed with the kind permission of its editor and of the author, who is at present Chairman of the Department of Philosophy, University College, Rutgers University.

Introduction

There is a self-critical reassessment currently being carried out in psychoanalytical quarters. It is a turbulent discussion, heated, and frequently confusing. Questions are being forced into the discussion that bear on the very nature of psychology itself: Is psychology Geisteswissenschaft, a science in the sense of the social sciences and humanities, or Naturwissenschaft, a natural science? Old questions are being asked in new garbs. Can all experiments be quantified, rigorously controlled and replicated? Is evidence of other minds publicly accessible to all qualified observers? What is a qualified observer? What is the nature of the psyche, the mind? How is it known?

It becomes obvious that the nature of these questions about psychology is philosophical and that answers to them can derive only from philosophical assumptions concerning the nature of the self, the nature of knowledge and the nature of science itself. Discussion between psychologists and philosophers is called for.

Existential psychologists attempt to do this. In dialogue with philosophers they wish to re-think depth-psychology at its philosophical foundations. Unfortunately, though, the issue "What kind of science is psychology?," raised within the properly broad context it deserves, has not been vigorously pursued by the great body of philoso- phers of science. Especially is this true in the Anglo-

43

American world where a settled and tacit bias to conceive of every science, even psychology and the social sciences, after the model of the natural sciences seems to prevail. This being so, the issue is usually pre-judged, and with perfect equanimity. [1]

With the recent interest in existential philosophy among psychologists, an abrupt redirection of inquiry and concern has unsettled the atmosphere. In fact some of the very psychologists instrumental in introducing existentialism have admitted that the dust it raises is terrific. Rollo May warns of the possibility of obscurity, confusion and a Tower of Babel. [2]

That such a warning should be given is understandable. Existential philosophizing ranges broadly and boldly through ontology, ethics and theory of knowledge, and existential psychologists have dipped into it at many points. If it were merely a matter of fitting existential insights into a pre-existing framework of psychoanalytical theory, confusion could be minimized; but many of these same psychologists question the framework itself. And too, if the introduction of existentialism could be placed within the confines of a well-established discussion of the philosophical foundations and scientific status of psychology, then confusion could be minimized a second way; but such a discussion is not to be found. * The purpose of this paper is to isolate and clarify a centrally important insight of existential philosophy concerning the nature of knowledge and to discuss the reasons psychologists give for finding it relevant to their work.

Ever since Freud psychoanalysts have noted cases in which the self-knowledge a patient gains is merely intellectual. Though the patient can formulate a multitude of true judgments about himself, he cannot experience and feel the very things within himself about which he judges truly. He can judge truly, say, his own desire to be destructive, but never fully feel this desire. And ironically enough, his intellectual knowledge can be a psychic defense against ever fully feeling it, because the knowledge convinces him that he already knows about himself and therefore has no further need of feeling desires and volitions which could pain and disgust him in the extreme. As Franz Alexander puts it, "The substitution of understanding for feeling is one of the principal defenses of the compulsive

_____
*Note that this article was written in 1961--B. W. (Author's note, 1970.)

44

personality. "[3] Merely intellectual knowledge, then, is a form of self-alienation and it stands in the way of an integrated self.

All this has implications for the communication that goes on between analyst and patient. According to Edith Weigert it is often not wise to tell the patient the truth about himself, because precisely when he intellectually accepts and affirms it, he blocks his deeper experiencing.[4] The patient is convinced that he has already arrived and that there is no need of going further. Dr. Weigert writes, "I am convinced that the truth of psychoanalysis has to be experienced; it cannot be indoctrinated."[5]

What intrigues psychoanalysts is that Kierkegaard appears to have advanced a theory of knowledge which takes this further experiencing and feeling into account. There is a peculiarly relevant theory of knowledge in Kierkegaard that challenges the intellectualist tradition of western philosophy (as he construed it). The theory, however, is notoriously unsystematic, unacademic and, some would say, strange. In the first place he wished to be known as a religious writer and poet, so his theory must be winnowed patiently from a mountainous mass of religious and poetic writings. At least a rapid and pointed survey of this mass is necessary.

Kierkegaard indicted the Christians of his day. He charged that their affirmation of their dogmas was a purely intellectual affair: that they tacitly denied with their total behavior what they judged to be true with their intellect. But having actually affirmed they were blind to their denial, and he called them the most hopeless of people--unwitting hypocrites. They had not fully experienced the very things they claimed to know: their sinful condition, their willingness to repent, their desire for an immortal life. They were emotionally and volitionally disconnected, lacking inner, subjective involvement, having failed to know with their whole selves. Kierkegaard taunts them for existing as ghosts, with their intellects floating detached somehow from the rest of the self.

Here we see the first point of affinity between psychoanalysts' patients and Kierkegaard's Christians. Though the Christians claimed knowledge of things not typically claimed by psychoanalysts' patients, and not necessarily on the same kind of evidential grounds, yet both groups share the common problem of intellectualization:

they never fully experience the very things about themselves that they claim to know.

Subjective Knowledge

Kierkegaard's study of Socrates put the problem in sharp focus. Kierkegaard observed that Christians claimed to have progressed beyond the pagan Greek, and yet they had never squarely faced his ancient challenge to "know thyself. " Socrates is conceived by Kierkegaard as a master of intimacy: concerned with how men really think. And by this is meant not so much what a man thinks and knows as the subjective involvement with which he thinks and knows; in other words, how he thinks, how fully he feels the things he knows to be true.

Kierkegaard recalls these facts about Socrates: To test how men really think as moral beings he asked them to imagine themselves owning a ring which makes them invisible and puts them beyond reach of punishment for criminal acts. Do their previous moral judgments change? These new conditions imaginatively entertained clearly reveal the subjective involvement of their previous judgments and the extent to which they felt the goodness of what they judged good. Then to test how men really think as mortal beings Socrates concerned himself with how they die. For if a man judges immortality to be true, affirms his own immortality but proceeds to die like a coward, then the subjective involvement of his judgment, the extent to which he felt its truth, is certainly open to question. One should say that he really did not believe at all.

Thus Kierkegaard conceives of Socrates as a master of irony as well as of intimacy, for the Greek shows that men know and affirm but that they carry around with them deep seated denials--denials which are, in effect, deep seated fractures of the self. It is not so much what men know (the store of true judgments may be no more than excess baggage), but how they know; it is the subjective involvement of the judgment and what is judged about.

Now Kierkegaard calls this subjective involvement a kind of knowledge which is different from intellectual or objective knowledge; it is subjective knowledge. By so doing he sounds an unusual note in the history of philosophy. For the central tendency since Aristotle has been to limit the word "knowledge" to true propositions or judgments, ones which conform exactly with what they are about--their

46

objects. Traditionally conceived, then, knowledge is so many whats known about, and it is objective. Thus the judgment "I have only one hand" is true if I actually have but one hand, and no matter what kind of subjective involvement characterizes the judgment, no matter how impassionedly I feel my one-handedness or how little I feel my one-handedness, still the judgment is true and constitutes knowledge if and only if I actually have but one hand, and the subjective involvement with which it is judged is irrelevant.

This is the traditional view, and it applies to judgments about all things: A thing is as it is, and the subjective involvement of the judging which judges it changes it not a whit. The subjective involvement is itself a thing to be judged about! The world is a world of objects.

Kierkegaard, however, wants to say that when we make judgments about ourselves the subjective involvement with which we make the judgment is itself an inexpugnable and requisite part of self-knowledge, and not merely another object to be judged about. Though it is necessary to know objectively facts about oneself, it is not sufficient. Kierkegaard is saying that there is a difference between scientific knowledge (using here natural science as the locus of science) and self-knowledge. Perhaps an example will underline his meaning. A geologist would be said to have knowledge of a stone if he can identify it, make accurate judgments concerning the chemical structures of its component minerals, state the atomic structures of its atoms, etc. He needn't feel or fully experience what he judges about; his tactual, psychological or aesthetic feelings vis-à-vis the stone are irrelevant. He needn't in any way appreciate or possess the stone; he is the detached observer. In Santayana's vivid sentence, he needn't digest the stone to know the stone. What Kierkegaard is saying is that adequate knowledge of oneself makes additional demands: it does require that in addition to having objective knowledge we must experience what we judge about--that in some sense we do digest it.

Kierkegaard's reasons for his theory of subjective knowledge spring from his analysis of his own experience. This he carried out in the isolation of his own subjectivity; thus it is introspective in some sense. Yet he constantly moves to point out the limitations of introspection. He finds that he cannot achieve a view of his whole self at any given moment and render a judgment of it; because that

47

portion of the self which is then doing the viewing and judging will always be excluded from the judgment. The "I" that views and judges cannot simultaneously view and judge itself. To turn attention to the mirroring, judging "I" is to pass out of the given moment, to miss the "I," and to get only a mirrored and objectified "me." The "I" and the new moment will lie behind one, impossible of examination because doing the examining, as a lone mirror can reflect everything in turn except itself.

Here is Kierkegaard's major point: to turn upon a moment in a succeeding moment is to miss its immediate reality and to miss the how of subjective involvement (the involvement of judging and judged, of "I" and "me") which characterized it. Consequently it is to miss the reality of subjective knowledge. And since all judgments miss or nullify it, subjective knowledge must be inexpressible. Kierkegaard characterizes subjective knowledge and the immediacy of subjectivity as elusive, inexpressible and yet eminently real, the very core of the conscious self.

In a work of our own time, The Concept of Mind, Gilbert Ryle also deals with "the systematic elusiveness of 'I.'" He writes,

> So my commentary on my performances must always be silent about one performance, namely itself, and this can be the target only of another commentary. 6

But Ryle cleaves to the tradition of western philosophy by regarding reality as expressible by judgments (or commentary), and by regarding objective knowledge as sufficient knowledge. Notice carefully:

> Yet nothing that is left out of any particular commentary . . . is privileged thereby to escape comment . . . forever. On the contrary it may be the target of the very next comment . . . 7
> (italics mine)

The elusive emotivity, the degrees of which Kierkegaard makes so much, Ryle is content to mention and then drop because he believes that the accuracy with which it can be referred to or hit in the next moment's judgment is sufficient to express its reality, and because, too, he evidently believes that the elusive emotivity itself is not an essential part of self-knowledge.

> 'I' is like my own shadow; I can never get away
> from it, as I can get away from your shadow.
> There is no mystery about this constancy, but I
> mention it because it seems to endow 'I' with a
> mystifying uniqueness and adhesiveness. 'Now'
> has something of the same besetting feeling. [8]

This is Ryle's last mention of the subject and in concludes
his chapter on self-knowledge. What Ryle dismisses because it is an elusive feeling, Kierkegaard accentuates
because it is an elusive feeling! When the same fact is
given a wholly different interpretation and evaluation, as in
the case here, we can suspect that we are in the presence
of two antithetical world-views.

Because of the elusiveness and inexpressibility of
subjective involvement at the core of the conscious self,
Kierkegaard contends that a person must cease to turn on
the involvement in a succeeding instant in the expectation
of pinning it down completely. For not only will the succeeding instant's judgment of the involvement miss the
momentary quality of that involvement, but it will throw
the self into a posture vis-a-vis itself which impedes any
further involvement; it will be a posture of past oriented
detachment. Such a posture is the precise antithesis of a
future oriented posture of acceptance; that is, acceptance
of the inexpressible quality of the involvement and, implicitly,
a trust in the consequences of allowing such an involvement
to occur (a trust in one's future). It is this posture of
acceptance, trust, total commitment to the truth of one's
judgment and, really, submission which is the heart of
Kierkegaard's theory of knowledge. Submission because in
such a posture the self so orients itself that what is judged
in the self, one's urges, purposes and fears, is allowed to
emotively inform the judging. This is the full subjective
involvement which can complete the requirements for self-
knowledge.

Kierkegaard breaks from three related traditions in
western philosophy. The first is that knowledge consists
only in true judgments which conform to their objects. The
second is the subordinate tradition of introspection which
dates in explicit form from Descartes and Locke. He insists that the self cannot turn within itself and mirror and
objectify itself successfully, because the judging cannot be
detached from the thing judged as it can from other objects.

49

The judging and the judged are inevitably involved and connected in some kind of way--whether it be that of full subjective involvement or not; after all, he reasons, they occur within oneself and not between oneself and another. Then the important point: the kind of involvement and connection resists expression and reference by the next instant's judging. Though the involvement can be the target of such a judging, and can be hit with all the accuracy that objectivity affords, the succeeding judging cannot have the brute quality of experience it judges about. And at this point we can see that Kierkegaard is breaking from still another related tradition in western philosophy, one which stretches from Aristotle to Dewey. This is that brute qualities of experience are the raw materials for judgments and knowledge but are knowledge not yet.

When Kierkegaard's radical theory of subjective knowledge is grasped as a judgmentally inexpressible and future directed subjective involvement which overcomes the alienation of the selfconscious self, then much of his other thinking, such as his concern with the future in The Concept of Dread, is illuminated. The future--"that which isn't yet," "the possible," "the nothing"--[9] is all the more dreadful to him because he throws himself naked into it; because he is sufficiently trusting to take the consequences of a full subjective involvement in a subjectivity, a self, of obscure and frightening dimensions. Illuminated also become his provocative and cryptic early Journal references. For instance,

> I believe . . . that it is a good thing . . . to let my thoughts appear with the umbilical cord of their first mood . . .[10]

> But just as a heavenly body, if we imagine it in the process of constituting itself, would not first of all determine how great its surface was to be and about which other body it was to move, but would first of all allow the centripetal and centrifugal forces to harmonize its existence, and then let the rest take its course--similarly, it is useless for a man to determine first of all the outside and afterwards fundamentals.[11]

This idea of the "outside," while it refers to the externals of life--fame, position, prestige--is seen to refer also to the misguided attempt to treat one's own subjectivity as an "outside"--something to be objectified, contemplated and manipulated. J. V. L. Casserly grasps beautifully the in-

50

wardness of Kierkegaard's subjectivity.

> (Subjectivity) does not mean mere self-centered-
> ness . . . the self is known not as an object,
> regarded from outside itself, but as the active
> subject which performs the knowing. Indeed, the
> use of the customary grammatical form, 'I know
> me,' falsifies the self-conscious situation . . .
> 'I know I,' though deplorably bad syntax, would
> express the truth about self-consciousness more
> accurately. [12]

We can summarize the paper to this point. Kierkegaard criticizes the traditional tendency in western philosophy to regard only true judgments as knowledge. He
does not criticize tradition where natural science or many
forms of common sense are concerned. He does question
the ability of the traditional position to fully encompass the
requirements of self-knowledge. Here he maintains that
full subjective involvement, inexpressible by judgments in
its immediate and brute experiential quality, is essential to
self-knowledge and should be classed as subjective knowledge.
To put his deviation from tradition in a different way, he is
claiming that the judgment itself as a brute quality of experience is knowledge of a kind quite distinct from the objective accuracy with which it conforms to what it is about,
its object. The brute quality of experience is the quality
of the judged which pervades the judgment. For example,
if a man adequately, i. e. subjectively as well as objectively,
knows his own desire for a certain goal, then he will at
the same time experience that desire and the full emotional
and volitional matrix of the self in which it moves.

From Philosophical Foundations to Therapeutic Technique

When psychoanalysts point out the affinity of Kierkegaard's theory of knowledge to the needs for knowledge
which they find in their patients, they give impetus and
direction for tying-back current scientific problems into the
history of philosophy, a history out of which many of the
problems grew in the first place. By so doing they make
possible a more comprehensive and basic evaluation of
working assumptions in their own science, assumptions
which might otherwise remain tacit and unacknowledged.
The benefits from their insight spread in all directions,
from philosophical foundations to therapeutic technique. For
example, if subjective knowledge is construed as inexpressible, if no judgment (either the patient's or the analyst's)

can adequately express the reality of one's subjectivity and the integration of oneself, then the analyst, at a certain point, will cease pushing for objective knowledge and will cease pushing the patient to get it; for if Kierkegaard's theory is correct then the scope of objective knowledge is limited; to try to push all the patient's experience and knowledge within the scope of objective knowledge would mutilate and distort it. Such readjustment in therapeutic technique is not the only significant thing, however. Some of the most significant developments in the history of philosophy as a whole have stemmed not from a robust claiming of knowledge but a disclaiming and a tempering (e. g. , Aristotle's warning that we should seek no greater accuracy in knowledge than the subject matter allows, and Kant's critique of metaphysical knowledge). After waiting a century for perceptive readers, Kierkegaard's theory of knowledge may now prove to be such a development.

But always a leading obstacle impeding fertile inter-action between psychological science and historically oriented philosophy, particularly existential philosophy like Kierkegaard's, is the difficulty in isolating-out relevant issues from a tangled philosophical mass of poetic, ethico-religious and metaphysical considerations. The difficulty is compounded by the fact that our scientific age and place is markedly averse to poetic, ethico-religious and metaphysical considerations, and is thus tempted to dismiss out of hand the whole matter of existential philosophy, before issues relevant to science have been isolated-out. The purpose of this paper is to combat confusion and aversion by isolating the issue of knowledge in its most elementary form. Other issues which need isolation fall beyond the scope of the paper.

However, there is another matter making for confusion which is so closely tied-in with what we have discussed that it must be disentangled here and now. Rollo May writes,

> A second important contribution of Kierkegaard to dynamic psychology lies in his emphasis upon the necessity of commitment . . . Truth becomes reality only as the individual produces it in action, which includes producing it in his own consciousness. Kierkegaard's point has the radical implication that we cannot even see a particular truth unless we already have some commitment to it. [13]

Now it is not clear to me what May means by "see." It seems to function as a synonym for "know," but does he mean subjective knowing or objective knowing? If subjective knowing is meant then the passage boils down to tautology: we cannot subjectively know subjective involvement, and the commitment it involves, unless we are committed. But if he means objective knowing--if he means the commitment of subjective involvement brings to consciousness facts of the personality not otherwise accessible to awareness, facts which would be the objects of judgments and which would thus constitute objective knowledge--then he is saying that subjective knowledge is not merely a complement to already existing objective knowledge, but that it produces new objective knowledge. If he means this then he is claiming that there is a strand of Kierkegaard's theory of knowledge which we have not yet disentangled and isolated--a dimension which could be most confusing if not isolated.

Let us assume that objective knowing is meant. There are other passages which suggest this is what May means. [14] Besides, if we assume this we shall be investigating an interpretation (or extrapolation) of Kierkegaard's theory which is tempting to make and which falls in line marvelously with certain techniques now used in psychoanalysis. The extrapolation is this: the inward orientation of the self which characterizes subjective knowledge is necessary for the attainment of further objective knowledge of the self; that is, it is necessary to make the sub-conscious conscious and thus to attain knowledge of elements of the self not knowable otherwise. This is objective knowledge, even though it be known also subjectively; for it is knowledge of facts about the self--hopes, urges, perceptions, purposes and fears, previously unknown--which are now the objects of judgments.

What is the basis in Kierkegaard for such an extrapolation? We have seen that subjective knowledge requires a peculiar attitude and orientation towards oneself. In the crucial but elusive moment of judging, that which is judged must be allowed to inform and move the judging. Kierkegaard repudiates the idea that adequate objective knowledge of this is ever possible, for an objective judgment in the next moment entails a detachment which misses the very involvement characterizing the crucial moment in question. What we have, then, is a rudimentary act of faith in, and commitment to, the factuality and legitimacy of the emotions and volitions which move and involve the judging of them, and a trust in the consequences of allowing this involvement to occur.

For Kierkegaard consequences there must be. The knower cannot be detached from that which he knows when that which he knows is himself. Differences in knowing will produce differences in the known. If one objectifies involvement one alters or precludes the consequences of involvement as well as misses it in its immediate subjective quality. If one chooses involvement there will be consequences which change the self. This basic involvement is the first step away from the aesthetic life in Kierkegaard's schema of the stages of existence.

> The ethical individual knows himself, but this knowledge is not mere contemplation . . . it is a reflection upon himself which itself is an action, and therefore I have deliberately preferred to use the expression "choose oneself." So when the individual knows himself he is not through; on the contrary, this knowledge is in the highest degree fruitful, and from it proceeds the true individual. If I desired to be clever I might say at this point that the individual knew himself in such a way as Adam "knew" Eve in the Old Testament sense of the word. By the individual's intercourse with himself he impregnates himself and brings himself to birth. [15]

But how is the self brought to birth? Is its behaviorial organization so changed that the subconscious mind is made conscious, or are new habits formed and goals adopted, or what? Or is it merely a matter of broadening the self in the sense that any new experience enlarges us and gives us more to know about ourselves? In this last sense any new experience would enlarge us, such as joining the Peace Corps, jumping from the roof or changing a dull occupation for a bizarre one. One thing is sure: Kierkegaard denies that it is any mere matter of quantitatively broadening the experience of the self. Rather, the self must achieve new levels or qualities of experience, and this depends on the kind of commitment in subjective involvement.

Kierkegaard's famous stages of existence are the aesthetic, the ethical and the culminating conversion experience of Christianity. He intends these stages to be different levels of behavioral organization, not merely more and more experiences. From the primordial commitment of brute subjective involvement the developing person is to

54

make commitments of progressively greater scope and difficulty. Finally, to fully accept and feel the truth of what he judges true he makes a leap of faith: he commits himself totally to the object of his greatest desire--communion with God--and in overcoming the tension of doubt the "passion of the infinite" is generated. The person's life is changed and he utilizes the energy of his passions.

We may, however, be tempted to put our own interpretation upon Kierkegaard's idea of the self changing and developing through subjective involvement and commitment. Especially would existential psychoanalysts be tempted, I think. True, most of them are concerned with the ethical and religious stages of their patient's existence, but also they are concerned with bringing their patients to a particular new level of psychic behavior and self-awareness; awareness of subconscious and semi-conscious emotions, volitions, ideas and perceptions. They make the point that only when the patient first commits himself in subjective involvement to his own emotions and volitions, and allows them to work out their own consequences, can he bring subconscious material adequately to consciousness. More particularly, they make the point that only when the patient becomes fully involved subjectively with a desire to believe, and a willingness to believe the truth of the analysis which his psychoanalyst offers him, can he bring to consciousness those volitions, ideas and perceptions to which the analysis refers, and which verify the analysis. Thus existential psychoanalysts set up their own leap of faith, their own style of commitment.

> The significance of commitment is not that it is simply a vaguely good thing or ethically to be advised. It is a necessary prerequisite, rather, for seeing truth. This involves a crucial point which has never to my knowledge been fully taken into account in writings on psychotherapy, namely, that decision precedes knowledge. We have worked normally on the assumption that, as the patient gets more and more insight about himself, he will make the appropriate decisions. This is half truth. The second half of the truth is generally overlooked, namely that the patient cannot permit himself to get insight or knowledge until he is ready to decide, takes a decisive orientation to life, and has made the preliminary decisions along the way. [16]

The theory operating here seems to be this: elements of the self are not accessible to awareness because of emotionalized resistance to awareness; therefore only an initial commitment and emotional involvement in the self, a decisive willingness to believe, which is not the result of objective knowledge (for the person lacks this because he lacks awareness) can move the emotionalized resistance and allow the elements to come from subconsciousness to consciousness and awareness. It is the opposite of intellectualism: a radical voluntarism. Commitment and involvement precede knowledge rather than follow it.

But there is nothing explicit in Kierkegaard like this. Several times he mentions the subconscious mind, and once speaks of the value of dreams for disclosing it,[17] but these are rather isolated references, unconnected with his exposition of both subjective knowledge and the stages of existence. New kinds of behavior and awareness are to be reached through subjective involvement, to be sure, but as to the subconscious becoming conscious Kierkegaard leaves us pretty much in the dark.

Still, it must be admitted, Kierkegaard's theory of knowledge offers almost an irresistible stimulus to extrapolate. And if we distinguish what is quite definite in Kierkegaard, that is, his view of subjective knowledge, from what is extrapolated from it, that is, the view that subjective involvement renders the subconscious concious, then confusion need not result. A prime example of confusion would be to use the words "see" and "know" in the sense of objective discovery (of previously unconcious processes) where Kierkegaard's analysis and evidence would justify only the sense of subjective discovery or subjective realization of what is already known objectively.

Conclusions

After stressing the importance of making and adhering to the distinction, and stressing the confusion which awaits us if we do not, we can evaluate such an extrapolation quite apart from its source. What is its value in the current psychoanalytic reassessment of psyche and mind, the problem of knowing the mind and the status of psychology itself as a science? Existential psychoanalysts are suggesting that scientific method in psychology be re-thought. As in May's telling words, they are suggesting that the usual emotional detachment and objectivity in the natural sciences is not always appropriate in psychology. They are working with the hypothesis that just as one must perform the operation of placing his eye behind a telescope of such and such quality if he would observe the polar caps on Mars, so he must perform the operation of attaining a certain quality of subjective involvement in his thinking if he would observe a fact about himself. And just as a geologist must detach himself from his emotions when he tests for a rare metal, so, in reverse, a person must at some point involve himself in his emotions if he would judge accurately about himself.

The importance of the question of readjustment in scientific method is further heightened when one considers the procedures of inquiry adopted by existential psycho-analysts. For most of these analysts admit that even they themselves cannot read-off the concealed subconscious facts of the patient's personality in the way an astronomer, say, would detachedly read-off absorption spectra and calculate the chemical constitution of a star, but rather, the analyst must emotionally involve himself with the patient so that together they can, in the uniqueness of their relationship, open-up and discover the sheer factuality of the patient's personality--his perceptions, hopes, motivations and fears. The theory operating here is that if the analyst coolly and detachedly (scientifically?) objectifies the patient, the patient will tend to coolly and detachedly objectify himself; and this premature objectification will interfere with the patient's uncovering of himself, an uncovering upon which the analyst depends for his own information on the patient.

Kierkegaard's insights, then, in whatever way they prompt such a basic re-thinking, must be considered valuable. Many of the bogging places in the progress of psychology suggest that an ill-fitting philosophical framework has been thrown over them. Surely any wholesale equation of knowledge and objectivity should be questioned. Questioned too should be that tendency to relegate all which is difficult or impossible of objectification and expression through judgments, such as the emotional and volitional matrix of subjectivity, to the limbo of the non-cognitive, as many philosophers of science under the influence of positivism have done. We needn't be Zen Buddhists to suspect that the predominantly intellectualist tradition of western science and philosophy slights some important emotional and volitional aspects of our experience--aspects which are essential to an awareness and grasp of ourselves, thus aspects which are cognitive in the fullest sense.

Notes

1. There are some encouraging signs, however. See
   Psychoanalysis, Scientific Method and Philosophy,
   ed. by Sidney Hook. This attempts to achieve some
   meeting of minds and unanimity of endeavor among
   psychoanalysts and philosophers. Another fledgling
   attempt is The Foundations of Science and the Concepts
   of Psychology and Psychoanalysis, ed. by Fiegle and
   Scriven. Particularly promising is Scriven's short
   article at the end of the book. See also the monographs edited by R. F. Holland, published by Routledge & Kegan Paul.

2. Psychoanalysis and Existential Philosophy, ed. by
   Ruitenbeek, p. 179. For the major statement of
   existential psychoanalysis in English see Existence:
   A New Dimension in Psychiatry and Psychology, ed.
   by May, Angel and Ellenberger.

3. An Outline of Psychoanalysis, ed. by Thompson et. al.,
   p. 449.

4. Contribution to the problem of terminating psychoanalysis,
   Psychoanalytic Quarterly, 21:465 (1952), p. 467.

5. Ibid.

6. Ryle, The Concept of Mind, p. 195.

7. Ibid.

8. Ibid., p. 198.

9. In addition see Kierkegaard's Philosophical Fragments,
   p. 60.

10. The Journals of Kierkegaard, ed. and transl. by Alex-
    ander Dru, Fontana Books, p. 56.

11. Ibid., p. 46.

12. Casserly, The Christian in Philosophy, p. 155.

13. Existence: a New Dimension in Psychiatry and Psy-
    chology, Rollo May's introduction, p. 28.

14. May, op. cit., p. 87.

15. Kierkegaard, <u>Either/Or</u>, Vol. 2, Anchor Books, p. 263.

16. May, <u>op. cit.</u>, p. 87.

17. "Moreover the poor opinion in which dreams are held nowadays is also connected with the intellectualism which really only values the conscious, while in simpler ages people piously believed that the unconscious life in man was the more important as well as the profounder." <u>Journal</u>, ed. by Dru, p. 175. Kierkegaard's theory of knowledge is set forth primarily in his <u>magnum opus</u>, <u>The Concluding Unscientific Postscript</u>, but important insights are scattered throughout all his writings.

Kierkegaard and Logic

Paul L. Holmer

First published in Kierkegaardiana, II (1957), 25-42, the
article is here reprinted with the kind permission of its
editor and of the author, who is at present Professor of
Theology, The Divinity School, Yale University.

Kierkegaard is certainly one of the most prolific
thinkers of the nineteenth century. And he bids fair to
becoming also one of the most influential. Though there
are numerous testimonies to his persuasive powers, especially among religiously sympathetic readers but also
among many of his intimate critics, there are to date
relatively few studies of his dialectical powers and the
implementation of these in his writings. This statement is
not made simply to draw attention to the lack of critical
philosophical studies--there is such a lack despite the
plentitude of secondary works--but also to highlight those
factors in Kierkegaard's authorship which gave validity and
intellectual form, this independently of one's persuasion or
proclivity, religious or otherwise. Kierkegaard was also a
philosopher and, furthermore, was so acute intellectually
and more particularly logically, that he articulated his
writings with their enormous persuasive content with an
apparatus, simple and chaste, for which any contemporary
analytical and anti-metaphysical philosopher would be justly
proud. This is not to say that he was an analtyical thinker
in the contemporary Anglo-Saxon and Scandinavian senses of
the term--he was too many-sided to be a member of any
school--but by the canons of even today's rigorous philosophical movements he was certainly a philosopher. He
may have had too many strings in his bow for modern
readers but it hardly seems plausible to accuse him for a
richness of personality that most of the rest of us are but
the poorer without.

Without the support of the environment and by efforts
that intellectually considered must have been prodigious,

60

Kierkegaard defined his position against the most formidable philosophical positions of the day. Not only did this demand courage, but in his case there was more involved. He had to forge the weapons for his attack in virtue of his own understanding. That he did this in two different directions is sometimes forgotten. On the one side, he opposed the Church of Denmark, though his polemic is aimed, of course, at features of organized Christianity everywhere, with an extremely well articulated view concerning the meaning of Christian belief and practice; on the other side, he opposed the metaphysical philosophies, and especially Hegel's, with humor and wit, precision and exactness, all of these held together by severe views concerning the limits and validity of human speech. The neglect by his readers of this latter feature is perhaps to be explained by the fact that the religious interest is both so obvious and so attractive that little else is expected. But Kierkegaard's writings are here deceptive. What is apparent on the surface, the give and take of the literary creation, is analogous to the parts of the iceberg above the water level. Seven-eighths are below the surface and make possible the portion which is apparent. So too with Kierkegaard's literature. The logical and epistemological views which make his writings so effective as argument, which make his issues conceivable, are usually hidden but are not, for this reason, either irrelevant or unimportant.

An attack upon another's philosophy is not in itself unusual. But it is the mode of Kierkegaard's attack which marks him as a philosopher and thinker of first rank. He does not quarrel with particular factual claims within a philosopher's writings nor does he do as rival metaphysicians frequently have done, namely, show that all of the facts can be accounted for by another metaphysical hypothesis. He chooses instead to level his attack at the possibility, the logicality, of the metaphysical factual claims. The possible is his philosophical domain. He leaves the factually real to the scientists and scholars. The sallies addressed to the metaphysicians are directed to the logic of their discourse as well as the ethical and religious inadequacies inherent in taking such extravagant claims seriously. Detailed considerations of the limits of validity, of coherence, of non-contradiction, of system and sundry other logical values, are replete in his papers and incidental remarks. That all of this impinges upon religious and ethical considerations which admittedly were of paramount concern to Kierkegaard goes without saying; but, it is likewise true that if any of his remarks on the most abstract issues have validity, they

61

have validity independently of Kierkegaard's literature too.

In what follows I am intentionally trying to sketch the features of that seven-eighths which is hidden to view. I am admittedly dependent here upon the casual remarks, the jottings and notes of the Papirer, the footnotes within the literature proper. But still I admit to constructing logical views, systematic structures, where they do not obviously obtain. The references given in the notes at the end are intended to give only an approximate clue to the important materials, enough, however to indicate why I believe the views herein articulated are congruent with the Kierkegaard literature.

I shall here address myself to three questions whereby Kierkegaard's philosophical and logical positions can be illumined: What is logic? Is Kierkegaard a logician or logical? What are his specific insights?

I

Logic is for Kierkegaard the disciplined inquiry into the meaning structure and principles of knowledge. Unlike modern logicians who might say as much, Kierkegaard does not exercise himself greatly on questions concerning the methods of knowledge, partly, one suspects, because the climate of opinion was not very rich on this topic in his Denmark. Logic is, by him, not conceived to be immediately methodological nor a biological weapon. Throughout his literature he seems to make clear, too, that logic is a spectator's science, it is broadly descriptive. But the question is--of what? It is surely not ontological description; for this is the almost constant criticism made in the Postscript, and every other occasion permitting in the literature, of the Hegelian philosophy.

Kierkegaard is a singular 'via media' thinker. Denying that logic is ontological, or a science about being, does not entail the affirmation that logic is an arbitrary invention, or simply conventional, or only rules like those governing a parlor game. He seems to be insisting that logic is a descriptive science, but descriptive principally of the structures implicit in the meaningful use of language. Logic describes the idealties, rules and norms, principles and criteria, in virtue of which meanings are communicable.

It is interesting to note that Kierkegaard always roots the prescriptive functions of language in the subjectivity of the user and hearer of the language. Unlike many post-Hegelian philosophers who disparaged both human subjectivity as the locus of anything important and the tendency to make all language descriptive, Kierkegaard did not posit two realms, one of fact and another of value. He did not suggest that logic, esthetics and ethics were prescriptive because their objective correlates were values; instead he explored the character of subjectivity and came to the conclusion that it was not completely arbitrary, nor was it formless and to be discounted. His authorship therefore vindicates, subjectivity by the contention that ethically it ought to be each man's concern and, intellectually, by insisting that it had formal and regular features and was subject to categorization.

Thus, on logical matters he can admit that there is a facticity to the meaning structure of language which acquires its prescriptive power, its oughtness, in the general interest (a subjective factor to be sure) that we all have in making language meaningful. Without the wish on the part of would-be knowers, logic is only a descriptive science. Just so, too, can Kierkegaard's views on ethics be described. From one standpoint, everything he says about ethics can be couched also in a disinterested form appropriate to ethical theory. But, admitting a personal responsibility for stirring the reader to new ethical enthusiasms, Kierkegaard used every literary device available to keep the reader from reading him dispassionately. However, he was under no illusion, for he continually asserts that the ethical exists as an ought only in virtue of a movement within the man. So too, we might say on matters of logic. It is a tool to everyone with the wish and interest to be meaningful and therewith logic has immediately--as immediately as the wish is present--a prescriptive character.

For Kierkegaard, then, it is meaning which is the vehicle of knowledge. Obviously enough, meaning is a possible vehicle of other functions too. That structures of various kinds are involved in meanings seems to be a major burden of the long history of logic. Thus, concepts, judgments, propositions, inference, categories, etc., are all names for parts of the structure of meaning. But how these structures could possibly refer to a real world and things outside of discourse has been a tempting question that has continually strained philosophers' intellectual modesty. That the relation between meanings and the world was also a meaning structure, that it was itself logical, has been a kind of secular piety overarching vast difficulties

not otherwise amenable to intelligent discourse. It is
relatively recently that criticisms of such brave pieties
have become fashionable. Kierkegaard's criticisms of
Hegel are directed to this very issue. He denies that the
relation between discourse and the world discoursed about is
itself a logical relation. Meanings are logically inter-re-
lated, but not meanings and the world. Likewise, and here
he may seem to be out of step with modernity, the position
which says that there are no meanings in knowledge, is in-
admissible, not least because it denies the genuinely descriptive character of logic.

Logicians formulate principles which become in
virtue of their usage, laws. This is what is meant by
saying that certain ideal values are implied in different
kinds of meaning. Order, truth, consistency, system,
simplicity, definibility, etc. , are seemingly the conditions
of meaningfulness. To describe these is a major responsibility of anyone who studies the meaning structure of knowledge. Such 'values' are different than methods, either
special or general, relevant to the sciences. Knowledge,
Kierkegaard insists, is a synthesis of logical and a-logical
factors. Human experiencing is individuated and cannot
be communicated in its original forms. But, knowledge
which is a synthesis of experience and logical factors is
communicable. The meaning structure of a language is the
vehicle of the communicable. Thus, logic is the science of
that in a language which makes it communicable and cognitive. To say that logic makes knowledge meaningful or
even language meaningful is again to invert the order of
discovery and to play Zeus all over again to the order of
reflection. Logic is the description of what is involved in
knowledge. Logic does not then invent nor impose. It
becomes normative only if the meaningfulness thus described
is desired.

This, in brief, is what Kierkegaard's views on logic
add up to. That persons are logical without knowing the
subject matter of the logicians is a fact. But this is only
to report 'via' persons what one would expect if a meaning
structure is implicit in knowledge. Persons do know about
the world and themselves without first recognizing logical
forms. They have knowledge without possessing knowledge
about that knowledge. But, the reason for stating this
position here is principally to draw the reader's attention
to a facet of Kierkegaard's thought and writings which is
almost completely neglected. For, the position here described is the position from which Kierkegaard attacks the

pretensions of idealistic logic. Some of the reasons for saying this will be noted in the ensuing sections. If the above account is correctly to be attributed to Kierkegaard, then we can say that he is one with contemporaries in denying that logic is a description of ontological structures, but, that against both the ontological logicians and the contemporaries, he asserts that logic is descriptive of knowledge and hence is neither metaphysical nor purely formal (except when considered in abstraction from knowledge).

II

There is certainly a difference between a logician and being logical. The logician, I take it, is one who makes his subject of inquiry what for the other man are the tools of reflection. The logical man may also be a logician, but properly, we mean by a logical man one who uses the tools of reflection correctly, so that the meaning of his language is apparent. He may or may not reflect upon logic but certainly he uses it. The question is therefore appropriate: Was Kierkegaard a logician or was he logical?

In respect to the first question it seems clear enough that Kierkegaard was not a logician in any of the usual senses. He did not, for example, write a treatise on logic nor did he suggest at length any new logical theory. The appearances seem to be against him in this respect. But, on the other hand, if we ask whether he was logical, the answer is certainly in the affirmative. He is not irrational nor illogical in any wide sense of either term. With almost maddening regularity Kierkegaard too escapes all neat summary remarks. His logicality is not simply inadvertent nor is it as fortuitous as one might assume from the literature by and about him. For, despite the lack of what one might call strictly technical and detached works such as might qualify for the label, 'works on logic,' Kierkegaard did provide a whole series of judgments about his own writings. He did what in the modern idiom is called, provide a language about his own language. More strictly, he provided a literature about his pseudonymous literature.

In an older philosophical language, probably a little more appropriately expressive for Kierkegaard's accomplishments, Kierkegaard wrote with a high degree of self-consciousness. Hence his logicality is not accidental or haphazard. When you read him at any length you acquire the strange feeling that this man has just about exhausted in his own person the possible vantage points from which his works could be viewed and judged. And a logical and detached standpoint from which the norm and validity of specific works as well as the entire authorship can be understood is never very far from the reader's grasp as he reads Kierkegaard's books, principally because this standpoint is so frequently invoked, though not expounded, by the author himself in his running commentary which his footnotes, his accounts of his books, his journals and papers, yes, and even his letters, give in such abundance.

Kierkegaard's books are many in number and are ostensibly possessed of two kinds of meaning; one kind of meaning is intrinsic to each work, the other extrinsic to each work and provided by the role of each book in the entire authorship. Kierkegaard's sweep was a very broad one and his literature taxed his own ingenuity as well as his readers. Just what all of the pseudonymous works were aiming to do and how they hung together with all of the religious works was not immediately clear. Whether one must assume that Kierkegaard's literature was too complex to let his plan stand clearly forth is a moot point for the literary critics, but, what Kierkegaard did do is obvious enough, he supplied a written explanation. Whether his Point of View for My Work as an Author is correct in its factual judgments about the earlier works is again an issue for the critics but that this book provides another standpoint outside of the kind given in the earlier works is the interesting point to note for any philosophical reader. For, here one does have in fact discourse about his earlier writing. True, it is a language that provides a kind of 'telos' for other books; but even this admission does not negate the significance of there being also a standpoint from which the author could comment upon esthetic, ethical, and religious standpoints. The latter triparite division is said to be an exhaustive classification of ways of living one's life (i. e., if one admits the Christian to be a variant on the religious). If there is another point of view from which all of them can be described and written about, what is this point of view? Certainly it is not another way of living one's life. But, it would seem that such a disinterested standpoint is exactly what Kierkegaard would have called a logical standpoint.

This standpoint is compatible also with the standpoint which permits Kierkegaard's critiques of other logicians in the Fragments and Postscript. Also, it seems to be identical with that which permits the incidental remarks, sometimes in footnote form (notably in The Concept of

66

Dread), which are frequently and specifically on questions
of logic and even logical theory. And, if one adds to these
still somewhat casual appearing sources, all of the remarks
on logic and epistemology to be found in the Papirer, then
one has an imposing array of testimony for the existence of
another standpoint, a logical and disinterested standpoint,
from which Kierkegaard could write and could construe
(albeit only logically!) the life views within his literature
as well as all else which were his as a most richly talented
poet-dialectician.

It behooves Kierkegaard's reader to distinguish carefully therefore between his anti-intellectualism and what
might seem to be an anti-logicality. Because the metaphysicians of the idealistic variety invariably use logic to
define the real and because they claim that the categories
of the real are the categories of logic, Kierkegaard's
criticisms of this position are easily construed as criticisms
of all logical reasoning. They in fact are not this at all.
He is protesting against those philosophical rationalisms
which purport to find that intellectual categories, or more
particularly, logical categories are descriptive of something
more than the meaning structure of knowledge. For Kierkegaard the objectivity, and in a limited sense, the real,
to which logic stands related, is knowledge. His cross-
fire is directed to those who wish to make categories descriptive of the world, of history, of God, or of anything
else metaphysical or empirical. That there may be knowledge about any or all of these, he grants. But, logic and
rationality in Kierkegaard's sense (somewhat analogous to
Kant's), has as its subject for analysis, meaningful discourse and not the world. An intellectualism which seeks
to mitigate the differences between categorization and
facticity, between the non-logical and the logical, is a
confusion for Kierkegaard. Kierkegaard finds no logical
or epistemological ground for identifying logical categories
and those of reality. He does admit however plenty of
extra-logical grounds. The admission of the latter, however, is fatal for the intellectualist's claim, for this is to
admit that non-intellectualistic interests or non-logical
motives are essential for intellectualistic systems.

None of this is to say however that Kierkegaard is
anti-logical. He is not 'anti' system, order, or precision.
For, if the categories of logic are not the intimate definers
of reality, they may still be the intimate definers of knowledge. And knowledge may in turn be about almost anything
you please, even fictional entities and/or God, and still be

logical. The extramental reference of knowledge is another issue altogether which logic cannot construe nor explain. Readers of Kierkegaard's literature well know the importance of 'the leap' in this regard. While remembering that Kierkegaard did not write in 'extenso' about logical matters it is not difficult to construct something of his logical theory from his many criticisms of the kind of intellectualism represented by Hegel and the Hegelians of his own day. For purposes of brevity I enumerate a few of his criticisms:

A) He protests first and always against giving logical categories immediate empirical and factual content. He denies that they are historical, theological, metaphysical, etc. But, he does not deny that there is historical knowledge, knowledge of nature, and with serious reservations which demand special attention, a kind of religious knowledge called theology.

B) He rejects any understanding of an implicative relation or a logical conclusion which imputes ethical or religious significance to the logical consequent. The neutrality of logic is as relevant to the premises and the conclusion as it is to the inferential transition and nowhere within logical discourse is it possible to slip from the neutral and the logical to the non-neutral and the ethical or the religious.

C) He deprecates also the identification of validity and truth. Though he distinguishes sharply between the truth of sentences and religious and ethical truth, he distinguishes equally sharply between both of these and the kind of claim usually described by the word 'validity' which a logical conclusion possesses.

D) He strikes out too against the extension of other logical values, most clearly perhaps 'system,' to non-cognitive issues. What he has to say about the passions in respect to esthetics and religion bear immediately upon this problem. Here he wishes to free the passions from the artificial and restricting formality which an inappropriate logical categorization imposes. That there may be knowledge about esthetics and about religion again may be the case but then logic would describe properly the meaning structure of

68

esthetic and religious discourse. It would not,
should not, predispose esthetic creativity or
appreciation nor a religious decision.

E) He protests too against the extension of the
truth which is the logicians to analyze, viz. ,
truth as a quality of a sentence or 'propositional
truth, ' to all other enterprises and especially
ethics and religion. Kierkegaard denies cate-
gorically that any kind of propositional truth is
of direct and immediate religious and ethical
importance. The assent to cognitive truth is not
a religious act. This is the point made indirectly
by the insistence that religious and ethical truth
is a matter of subjectivity.

F) All of this can perhaps be summarized under
Kierkegaard's general repudiation of an identity
between the logical and the real. But to say the
latter within the appropriate context is Kierkegaard's merit. For he does not deny the possibility of knowledge of the real--he is not like
Bergson, supposing that conceptualizing is 'ipso
facto' a deception--but he does again deny only
that logic and reality are co-extensive.

When drawing distinctions between 'logician' and
'logicality, ' between 'anti-intellectualism' and 'anti-logicality' and especially in reference to Kierkegaard, it is
well to remember that he was throughout his career of
author a polemicist. He was delightfully argumentative.
One of the ways to most clearly describe his ideas is to
determine what he was against. In contemporary theological language he was a 'dialectical' thinker. Again in
contradistinction to the idealistic tradition, Kierkegaard
decried the panlogical efforts to include even ethics and
religion within logical sequences. He proposed that there
was an existential dialectic, a qualitative dialectic, separate
in kind from a logical dialectic. The first was non-logical
and had to do with the life of passion and interest--it was
dialectical only in the sense of being descriptive of the
opposition, the give and take, of the inner life; the logical
dialectic is that which gives anything about which we can
have knowledge its argumentative and structural form. As
dialectician, Kierkegaard is logical about non-logical matters
and this is what makes his polemic so biting and gives
irony to his entire endeavor. But he is not inconsistent.
In order to draw the distinction between an existential and

a logical dialectic and in order to make this distinction
stick against opposition who deny the distinction, he uses
a logical form in which to state his case for the passions.
He uses poetic and passional forms too--he does in truth
have many strings in his bow--but to the extent that he
would have created only interesting poetical works, to that
very extent he would not have been the polemicist and dialectician that he was. He was at once poetically creative
and a logical thinker who used his own creativity for reasons which his intelligence commanded. This is why we
can argue that his logical dialectic includes the expressions
of the existential dialectic and the poetic content within its
own scope. But, if what he has said about the life of
passions is true, then it is also relevant to note that the
existential dialectic, the life of passions and the conflict of
passions, is itself not the logical dialectic. The oppositions
within logic are contrariety and contradictoriness and these
are essential to the understanding of the relations between
anything conceived. That the confrontations within the life
of the passions are something quite different than logical
oppositions, this is, of course, the burden of much of the
Danish Socrates' literature.

As will be subsequently noted Kierkegaard was
acutely aware of the fact that his own literature was both a
poetic achievement and yet an argument. As an argument
it was informed by principles of logical reasoning. This
can also be said about the bitter fight against the Church
and the surprisingly bombastic literature produced during
1854-55. If Kierkegaard is correct on the delineation of
what logic is, then it is appropriate to draw the distinction
already noted between validity and truth and I believe it
becomes possible to draw a distinction between the validity
and the truth of Kierkegaard's attack upon the Church. His
argument is valid if his premises are correct. His premises
are discussed and discussed again in the earlier literature.
To say this is not to say that they are true. However,
this is to draw attention to the fact that it is invidious and
logically fallacious to accuse him of logical faults when one
ought to criticize the truth of his premises. But the latter
is not easy. It is altogether too simple for most readers
to read the earlier writings, even to praise them, and then
to explain away the later attack upon the Church as if it
were not integral to the earlier. This from the logical
standpoint is a major fault. Kierkegaard's systematic acuity
was not wasted--his literature whatever else one might say
and feel about it is an expression of a masterful polemicist
who kept his argument always to the point. If he has faults

they are not logical in kind.

III

But with all of this it behooves us to turn to the
consideration of Kierkegaard's specific logical achievements.
One must note always that his literature is logically unified.
It is internally consistent; it focuses diverse materials upon
the same issues; it provides a description of the life of
subjectivity but does it also in the spirit of objectivity and
detachment. The literature is about the problems of existing but is ordered and articulated by a logicality which
remains almost hidden but which helps to press all of the
books to purposes which are Christian in intention and
'edifying' in Kierkegaard's special use of this term. Because it is meaningful and because the literature is discourse
containing an argument, logic is a necessary instrumentality
for both writing and understanding its structure and pur-
posiveness. The complete account of Kierkegaard's intellectual prowess could not be written without a very detailed
examination of the internal consistency and logicality of the
literature adjudged as a unit.

But again an indirection must be noted. The literature includes discussions about many topics, many of them
of great interest to philosophers. Logic is not treated at
the same length as some of the rest of these. For example,
music, language, the Bible, duty, passion, system, truth,
sin, faith, speculation, etc. , are all discussed and in surprising detail. Supposing for the moment that Kierkegaard
occupied a kind of vantage point while writing about all of
these other topics, then it should be possible to discern
this vantage point or at least to approximate to its description in virtue of (a) identical (and self-identical) characteristics in all of his judgments about different things which
characteristics are formal properties not identical with any
described by the literature, and, (b) the fact that his descriptions of other topics give us the outlines when pieced
together of logic itself. One of Kierkegaard's pseudonymous authors gives us precedence for this latter use of
the literature when he tells us that by going to the 'utmost
boundaries' of the 'kingdom' best known to him, namely
language, he can then discover also the boundaries of the
neighboring kingdom, music. By describing with precision
so many other spheres of intellectual interest, it is almost
as if Kierkegaard has circumscribed the sphere of logic
without ever quite entering it.

And, we are not without his direct comment on these issues either. Repeatedly, Kierkegaard defines his logical ground (albeit briefly most of the time in 'extenso' only once and then in a polemical situation where other issues are of paramount concern). Nonetheless, putting all of these sources together, we can state a number of theses which seem in fact to state Kierkegaard's logical position. These are sufficient in number and rich enough in quality to occasion a revision in judgment about his status as a thinker. Granted that he is not a logician in the ordinary senses, still he shows the diagnostic and analytical powers of the greatest of them. He seem actually to have anticipated privately what are some of today's public logical modernities. Therefore, despite what has been said, he begins to loom as a logician and a very good one.

In what follows I shall list some of the theses which seem to me to give a clue to Kierkegaard's logical theory. These are not in any order of importance. These are, in most instances, constructed and constituted in their present form, from contexts in which other issues are discussed. But I point each thesis toward a logical consideration, and this intentionally. I shall in each instance state first a thesis and then add only sufficient comment to relate each thesis to others.

1. The logical standpoint is one of disinterestedness. Disinterestedness and logicality cannot perhaps be completely identified. The Stoics talked about 'apathy' and gave this psychological state of personality ethical and even religious significance. Kierkegaard's esthetic pseudonyms do the same. Kierkegaard believes that the state of disinterestedness is the 'sine qua non' of logicality, but to make such disinterestedness a life-view, was to impute more significance that it could ever contain.

2. Ethical and religious standpoints are instances of interestedness. There are qualities and kinds of interest and therefore there are kinds of ethical and religious positions and ways of life. These are described in Kierkegaard's own literature. There is, however, only one logical standpoint, if pure disinterestedness is attained. Logic is centripetal.

3. Logicality is the necessary condition for all knowing, including the knowing about ethics and religion. Logic does not describe the necessary

conditions for being ethical or being religious. Logic therefore describes the conditions permitting intelligible discourse even about passional matters. Disinterestedness is the necessary condition for 'discussing' and 'knowing' about interestedness.

4. Interestedness is the necessary condition for being human. To substitute a state of logical disinterestedness for a form of interestedness is to confuse a noetic condition with a moral condition. The logical standpoint is neutral and properly a-moral; to impute moral qualities to it is to negate its neutrality.

5. Identity describes the condition under which knowledge can be remembered (i. e., known by the same person in different moments of time and in different psychological complexes or states of mind) and communicated (i. e., known by different persons). Logical connections and the acts of inference are between identities in different complexes of things, of thoughts, of meanings. The law of identity in logic, therefore, describes a minimal condition for knowledge and communication.

6. Tautology is the highest logical principle. The identity between premise and conclusion is the guarantee of validity. That there is nothing new in the conclusion describes the paucity of logical discourse but from the point of view of disinterestedness this paucity is the token of certainty and validity.

7. There is no proof for logical laws or principles. Insofar as logic describes the meaning structure of knowledge it is 'descriptively' either true or false. But insofar as logical laws are true and therefore 'ought' to be obeyed, it becomes ridiculous to assert their truth. They describe only the conditions for valid inference; they do not provide logical grounds for being logical. Logic is not its own proof.

8. There is a necessity described by logic which is implicative necessity. There is a necessity which is 'for' logic which is not described by logic. The first is logical necessity; the second is a pragmatic and psychological necessity. There is no logic

mediating between persons and logic or being logical.
The only proof for logic--or better the ground for
being logical--is the demonstration of the pragmatic
need or the absurdity of being illogical.

9. Logic and non-logical (existence, e. g.) are
not logically related. But, reflection secures a
homogeneity between all things by first converting
them into possibles. Logic provides a homogeneity
in possibility, in knowledge, only by disregarding
through abstraction the actuality. Existing things
as conceived are logically amenable. That the world
is an 'existing (not as conceived) logical homogeneity, '
Kierkegaard finds to be a gratuitous and unwarranted
assumption. To assert that this is true 'sub specie
aeternitatis' is to pretend to a standpoint that is not
the logical standpoint.

10. The heterogeneousness of 'existence' is an
expression for the differences between passions and
thought and also for the difference between the thought
of a thing and the existence of the thing. Reflection
translates actuals into possibles and thus secures
homogeneity within possibility, which homogeneity
logic then describes. A contrary and non-logical
effort is to convert possibles into actuals, out of
homogeneity and out of possibility into the heterogeneity of existence.

11. All necessity is implicative, not causal. It
is a metaphysical leap to impute to natural events
and history the necessity characteristic of natural
and historical knowledge. The necessity describing
logical relations and any and all possibles does not
describe nonlogical relations. Logic describes the
necessity within the meaning structures of knowledge,
not truths of knowledge, not the world.

12. Logical movement, from premises to conclusions, is a necessary movement. It is sharply
differentiated from 'kinesis' or change in nature and
from qualitative changes within human subjects.
Logical movement is between possibles; 'kinesis' or
motion is (from the logical standpoint) the transition
from a possibility to actuality; ethical and religious
change, conversion, repentance, a new life, etc. , is
to deny one kind of actuality in favor of another,
which is at present only a possible. It is to 'become'

a possible.

13.   Knowledge is a synthesis of the real and the
ideal.   Logic describes the duality but does not
explain it.   Metaphysical logic purports to describe
and/or explain nature and history as a duality.   A
non-metaphysical and non-ontological logic describes
only knowledge.   It does not nor can it explain or
construe the duality that the world and knowledge is.

14.   That ethical-religious truth is 'subjectivity'
is from a logical point of view a sentence purporting
to be true about an objective state of affairs.   Kierkegaard's logical theory permits the objective and
logical and disinterested understanding of this assertion without mitigation of the religious and ethical
standpoint on the one hand or the logical on the
other.

15.   That 'ethical-religious truth is subjectivity'
is itself of logical and empirical significance:
  a)   As a sentence it stands within a systematically
       related group of sentences which detail the
       limits and validity of cognitive meaning struc-
       tures.   This sentence has therefore validity
       within Kierkegaard's delineations of the logic
       of meaningful sentences.
  b)   The sentence purports to be true about mat-
       ters of ethical and religious fact.   Whether
       it is or not, is another question.   In prin-
       ciple, the assertion can be treated as an
       empirical hypothesis.

16.   Logic permits of a high degree of certainty.
The certainty about knowledge which is what logic
provides is of a different order than the certainties
within or of knowledge.   The certainties of knowledge about knowledge are greatest where only the
ideal meaning structure is described; knowledge
about knowledge becomes hypothetical also to the
extent that the duality that knowledge is must be
described.   Logic is most certain because it seeks
to describe that which is self-identical (not as some
contemporaries say because it is all a matter of
staying consistent with one's original definitions).

From all these, and there could be listed many
more,   it becomes clear that Kierkegaard's logical reflec-

75

tions describe a 'via media' position in logical theory. He
was a formalist in logic but with significant differences from
most contemporaries. He did not believe that logic or reflection stood logically or reflectively related to any content.
He believed the meaning structures commanded by reflection
were in truth empty of content and by themselves without
existential and metaphysical significance. His case against
the ontological logicians makes this quite clear. But, on
the other hand, he does not make the logical forms simply
inventions either. He believes them to be discovered within the knowledge enterprise which again did not wait for
logicians or the logical forms before beginning. Once discovered and isolated it is clear enough that a reference to
a non-logical content is not itself a logical matter. The
content of the logical forms (which is what knowledge is) is
gained only by extra-logical and intentional acts. But again
to speak of logical forms as if they were pre-existent is a
mistake. They are abstracted from knowledge and have
separate existence only to the thought which abstracts them.

Kierkegaard refuses all of the extreme resolutions
of the problem that can be raised respecting the relation of
the logical and the real. He refuses to translate the homogeneity of essences to the realm of existence as do all the
intellectualists of human history. This is his case against
Hegel finally and, most particularly, against the Eleatic
philosophers of the ancient world. But, against the other
extreme he is equally opposed. He refuses to translate
the heterogeneity of existence and the inner life to logic
and the realm of essences. This is his point in denying
so candidly the Hegelian effort to introduce movement
('inesis') into logic. His position keeps him a kind of
dualist. All of the unities are logical; the differences and
the clefts between people, between people and thoughts,
between thoughts and things, he accepts to be what they
are. Philosophy, and certainly not logic, is no legerdemain
by which to discover their underlying unity. No metaphysics heals the breaches, no ontology gives any understanding of the duality. Kierkegaard has no philosophical
instrument to make the world different than it appears.

Kierkegaard's understanding of logic secures his
intellectual modesty. To re-trace his thought on metaphysics is a refreshing and novel mode of seeing how his
understanding of the province of validity tempered his
hopes and his conjectures about what may or may not be
the truth about nature and history.

A Note Concerning Sources

I should like to suggest that the principle sources for the remarks here offered are Kierkegaard's Concept of Dread, Fragments, Postscripts, and volume II of Either/Or; Samlede Vaerker, II (2. Del, Enten-Eller), IV (Philosophiske Smuler og Begrebet Angest), VII (Afsluttende Uvidenskabelig Efterskrift). Numerous places in the Papirer are important too, of which I list only a few: Vol. I A, 317; II A (entire section), C 20; III B, 177; IV A, 68; IV B, 118; IV C, 62, 63, 66, 79; V B, 5-8, 49; VI A, 335; VI B, 88; X 2 A, 195, 328, 439. Also, the incomplete "De Omnibus Dubitandum est," Vol. IV, is appropriate as are the lengthy ruminations about logical problems, indirect communication, etc., which were parts of projected books included in the Papirer.

V. Kuhr's Modsigelsens Grundsaetning (Kierkegaard Studier, Vol. II, København, 1915) is an able work on these matters and D. F. Swenson's essay, "The Anti-Intellectualism of Søren Kierkegaard" (included in Something About Kierkegaard Minneapolis, 1945, and in the present text, pp. 23-42) is a penetrating endeavor by a student of modern logic to show what Kierkegaard's criticisms of intellectualism actually meant. To both of these, and a host of others, I am, of course, greatly indebted.

Some Insights for Ethical Theory
From Kierkegaard

E. D. Klemke

First published in the Philosophical Quarterly, X (October 1960), 322-330, the article is here reprinted with the kind permission of its editor and of the author, who is at present Chairman of the Department of Philosophy, Roosevelt University.

I would like to discuss two issues in this paper. The first has to do with what I take to be Kierkegaard's views about ethical theory--the question, roughly, as to whether a science of ethics is possible. The second deals with a more specific issue within ethics--the question as whether intersubjectively valid ethical judgments are possible. The two are closely related. Indeed, the second is perhaps a more specific formulation of the first. The method of approaching each will differ, however.

The interpreter of Kierkegaard faces a problem in connection with the first of these issues--Kierkegaard's views on ethical theory. The problem arises from the fact that Kierkegaard nowhere fully states his theory about ethical theory. He, rather, for the most part, demonstrates it and allows the reader to develop the exposition of it. Thus, in my discussion of the first issue, I am not always able to cite specific passages by which to support my statements. I can only recommend that the reader study Kierkegaard's "aesthetic" writings plus some of the religious works. I believe that if he has done so, he will find my exposition to make explicit what is implicit in Kierkegaard's works. On certain points there is ambiguity in the Kierkegaardian literature. I might say, however, that my discussion is, in large measure, compatible with the views of two capable Kierkegaard scholars--David Swenson and Paul L. Holmer. [1]

The second issue which I shall discuss--whether or

not intersubjectively valid ethical judgments are possible--
does not involve the problem of the lack of explicit textual
statements. On the contrary, Kierkegaard deals with the
issue at great length. [2] However, another problem arises
here. Kierkegaard's discussion of the issue is an extremely
difficult one. Perhaps this is why most commentators have
avoided the subject. After considerable effort, I hope to
be able to explicate Kierkegaard's views on the problem.

In a third section, I shall, briefly, comment upon
Kierkegaard's views on the two problems, indicating the
measure of my agreement with the Danish author.

I

Kierkegaard's theory about ethical theory is expressed
through his doctrine of the Stages. As I mentioned, the
theory is not merely stated or expounded in his literature.
It is portrayed. The portrayal was accomplished by means
of the device of using pseudonyms--invented authors who
structuralize various modes of existence. Each of the invented authors expresses his likes and dislikes, concerns,
interests, and theories. Each is construed "ideally," that
is, in the form of a normative type, rather than after the
fashion of most existing men, who are often complex and
multiple personalities. Each invented author, then, develops in a literary and reflective form the ideal propor-
tions and characteristics of one mode of existence. These
are so delineated that several distinctively different modes
result. Four of these stand out: the aesthetic, the ethical,
Religion A, and Religion B (Christianity).

What is the philosophical purpose underlying this
literary kind of presentation? It is to show that to a disinterested and cognizing subject there are always genuine
ethical alternatives. Reflection does not reduce the multiplicity to a unity. Rather, it increases the plausibility of
each of the various multiples. A scientific or philosophical
ethics--in the sense of a discipline which can resolve ultimate differences concerning the good, etc.--is, hence, a
chimera. All of the various modes of existence, that is,
all of the alternative answers to the questions 'What is the
good?', 'What ought I to do?', etc., can be given equal
rational plausibility to the genuinely reflective man. Intelligence can give no "higher" plausibility to any one of
the various modes.

Thus, since a neutral, disinterested intelligence can

never solve the problem of the multiplicity of alternatives, since it can never decide objectively that this mode of existence is the right one whereas others are wrong, no science of ethics is possible. To a disinterested knowing subject, there is no single good. There are, similarly, no rational or logical grounds for any ethical choice. Rather, the more one's intelligence is maximized, the more one finds that there are only numerous possible modes of existence, each of which remains as a genuine and valid alternative. For such maximization of intelligence gives better reasons for all of the alternative possibles.

Kierkegaard, thus, writes in opposition to such thinkers as Hegel, e.g., who thought that the multiplicity of alternatives could be reduced to a unity by means of a more enlightened reflection. Kierkegaard suggests that all such theories are inadequate as they do violence to the facts which confront one who reflects on this matter. As I have said, intelligence does not merely discover alternatives; it gives greater credence to each of them. Hence, one is always left in objective uncertainty in the area of ethical decision.

How, then, does one "resolve" the uncertainty? One obtains a non-intellectual resolution through passion, interest, inwardness, and concern. Whether pleasure is the good, or duty is the good, or following Christ is the good, etc., is not intellectually ascertainable. Yet if one passionately gives himself to the task of actualizing one of these alternatives in his existence, he may find that X (whichever it may be) is right (or good, etc.) for him. But the important point here is that the condition for such certitude (as distinct from rational and objective certainty) is passionate inwardness, not reflection. The problem is, therefore, "resolved" by an existential choice, a leap. [3] Reflection increases the multiplicity and brings objective uncertainty. Passionate choice reduces the multiplicity which always remains at the intellectual level to a unity at the existential level, and brings a subjective certitude, but always in a temporary and insecure way. Thus, reason has its limits, beyond which one must make a passional leap. Whether or not the leap was the "right" one or "true" one, no man could ever know.

Kierkegaard's view is also in opposition to all who argue that further reflection, consideration of all the data, etc., will reveal common, objective values. As far as I can determine, Kierkegaard neither affirms nor denies that

values have phenomenally or ontically objective status. His
position seems to be that, even if values did possess such
status, who could know it, except, perhaps, God? And,
especially, who could know which actions, characteristics,
etc. , were valuable, and which were not? Who could know
which were right and which were wrong? Intelligence is
neutral on such issues. It can make a case for both sides,
and for all the positions in between too. And to simply
decree that a moral intelligence could resolve moral per-
plexity is begging the issue. Such a manoeuvre also confuses two realms: thought and reality. These are not, as
Hegel said, identical; they are, rather, with one exception
to be noted later, absolutely separate. [4] The former deals
with idealities which "exist" only for one's thought, as
possibilities. The latter concerns existence which cannot
be comprehended by objective thought. [5] One cannot, then,
by greater reflection, find one clear theory which may be
shown to be right on matters of existence. All one finds
are various alternatives, each of which is rationally plausible.

Thus, we are, precisely because of the empirical
data (when fully considered), involved in ethical disagreement. This is so because what one believes concerning
ethical matters (and all matters having to do with human
existence) is a function of one's passion, interest, and
subjectivity. As long as there are varying passions, in
unique individuals, there will be varying views. Similarly,
ethical agreement (to the extent to which that is possible)
is a function of passional likeness among subjects. Ethical
judgments, then, are interested judgments. They are, as
Kierkegaard suggested, non-cognitive. This is not to say
that they are nonsense, however. For although they are
not objectively meaningful, they are subjectively meaningful.
They are expressive of a man's passion, interests, and
concerns. [6]

I anticipate an objection: "But was not Kierkegaard
a Christian? Did he not speak as a religious man? Did
he not say that the Christian mode of existence was the
highest? Did he not think of the Stages as being progressive
steps? And did he not urge his readers to make the progression from the aesthetic, through the ethical, and into
the religious?" Yes, Kierkegaard said things of this sort,
and spoke from the religious mode when he said them.
But this is precisely the point. His utterances of this type
were made from the standpoint of a religious man. Therefore, they were interested judgments. This does not contra-

dict the views of Kierkegaard which I expounded earlier. For I insisted throughout that those views (e. g. , that no one mode of existence was the right one, etc.) were made from a disinterested, neutral standpoint. Kierkegaard's brilliance lies in the fact that he saw that there were at least two types of reflection and their appropriate forms of discourse. There is, first, the reflection (and discourse) of the interested man. This does not require much perspicuity or practice. All men can speak interestedly. There is, second, disinterested, neutral reflection (and its form of discourse). This requires training and a maximization of the intellect. Perhaps few achieve it, and perhaps only on occasions. Yet it is a genuine possibility.

Thus, Kierkegaard's point remains intact. From a disinterested, cognitive standpoint, there is always a multiplicity of alternatives, on any issue. From such a standpoint, all possible modes of existence can be given equal rational plausibility. Hence, which is right can never be known.

II

I turn now to the second issue, which flows directly from the first. This, it may be remembered, is the matter of the intersubjective validity of ethical judgments. The following discussion is based upon a long chapter of the Postscript. [7]

Kierkegaard's discussion may be summed up in the following theses: "The ethical requirement is imposed upon each individual, and when it judges, it judges each individual by himself. . . . This implies that there is no immediate relationship, ethically, between subject and subject. "[8]

Kierkegaard attaches a double meaning to the word 'ethical'. The first meaning is that which is commonly associated with ethics or morals. The second meaning refers to that which is existent, rather than merely an object of thought. Perhaps 'behavioural' or 'existential' are better terms in this second sense of 'ethical'. Kierkegaard makes some pertinent remarks about the ethical in the second sense, but these comments also have an important bearing upon the ethical when considered from the standpoint of morality. Let us see what these insights are. We may use some of Kierkegaard's statements as a kind of outline for this purpose.

83

1. "From the poetic and intellectual standpoint, possibility is higher than reality, the aesthetic and the intellectual being disinterested."[9]

By 'possibility' Kierkegaard means the realm of the non-existent, or that which "exists" for thought alone. A possibility is an essence, or ideal, or that which may be conceived and reflected upon. By 'reality', on the other hand, Kierkegaard means the realm of the existential, that which actually exists.

Aesthetic and intellectual enterprises, where disinterestedness and objectivity are involved (in the sense that one's existence is not involved), are carried on in the realm of possibility. To have knowledge is to be able to have that which is known "exist" for one's thought. If one merely experienced something without reflecting upon it, this would not be knowledge. Thus, from the intellectual standpoint, possibility is higher than reality, since the intelligence cannot manipulate actual objects, existents, and experiences, but can manipulate thoughts about objects, existents, and experiences. Furthermore, in the realm of the intelligible, the greater the degree of disinterestedness and objectivity, the more precise is the knowledge. The thinker who best fulfils his task as a thinker is he who minimizes the influence of his own passions, interests, and concerns, with respect to his thinking.

2. "Ethically regarded, reality is higher than possibility."[10]

From the ethical (behavioural and moral) standpoint, that which is real, actual, existent, is of greater significance than that which is merely ideal or possible. E. g. , there is nothing moral about being able to talk about morality as a possibility. But to concretely actualize the possibility and become a moral man (however 'moral' is defined) is a different matter. Thus, the ethical proposes to do away with the disinterestedness of the realm of possibility by making existence the primary realm and "worthy of infinite interest." The ethical has to do with the concerns and interests of the subject's existence. Therefore, the ethical is in opposition to all attempts to merely contemplate man in general, or to contemplate the world in this fashion--an act which keeps man or the world in the realm of ideality, rather than in the realm of existence. To contemplate humanity in a system (whether from a metaphysical or a moral standpoint) is, therefore, impossible, since all attempts to contemplate anyone but one's self are endeavours which are carried on in the realm of ideality, and have nothing to do with existence. "There is only one kind of ethical contemplation, namely, self-contemplation."[11] This contemplation, however, is not to be confused with rational cognition.

Hence, it may be affirmed that ethics, whether considered descriptively or normatively, must always centre about the individual. It is the individual and not mankind who receives the imperative (a self-imposed imperative) to exist ethically.

Not only is the ethical requirement imposed upon each individual, but when the ethical requirement judges, it judges each individual by himself. This is so because the ethical is internal to each individual. It has as its locus the being or selfhood of each individual. Therefore, it cannot be observed or judged by an outsider. The ethical demand can only be actualized by each individual, who alone knows what it is that "moves within him."

Before the ethical life of a person became a reality to him, he was able to know it in a conceived form, as a possibility. When he actualized the possibility, it became a reality to him. But no individual can have knowledge about another person's reality unless, in coming to know it, he conceives it. But as soon as he conceives the reality of another person, he transforms it from a reality in that person's life into a possibility for his own thought. And it is impossible to incorporate another's existence into one's own. Thus, no one knows another person's reality or existence. He only knows ideas or thoughts about the other person's reality. The reality itself is not known, is never conceivable, by another. Only thoughts about the reality may be known.

With respect to the reality of everyone external to one's self, then, one can "get hold of it" only through conceiving it. In order to get hold of it actually, one would have to make himself into the other person and make his reality one's own. But this is impossible. One cannot so acquire the actual existence of another person. In other words, when any reality, say another individual, is external to myself, I can only appropriate it by thinking it. To acquire it actually, I would have to be able to make myself into him and make his reality my own. At the realm of existence such a procedure is impossible. I can appropriate thoughts about another's reality, but not his reality itself.

The upshot of the matter is: There is no immediate ethical relationship between one individual and another. [12] Therefore, any individual can question only himself ethically. None can question another. None can judge another. This is true because, again, no individual can understand another except as a possibility, an ideality, and this understanding may not conform to the actual concrete existence of the other. Another's thoughts may be conceived. His existence may not. For existence itself is not (in any objective sense) conceivable. It just is. Hence, each individual is isolated and exists by himself with respect to his ethical requirement. Thus, none can legislate for another concerning his existence and behaviour. Therefore, the attempt to find intersubjectively valid ethical judgments ('One ought to do . . .') is futile. There are, and can be, no such judgments.

III

I find myself in agreement with Kierkegaard on the two issues which I have discussed. In this section, I would like to show why I am in agreement by reformulating the Kierkegaardian position on the two issues, conjointly (with emphasis upon the second), in my own terms. For this purpose, I shall use, as an outline, two sentences from another context of the Postscript. [13]

(1) "A logical system is possible."

With respect to thinking, as distinguished from existing, or behaving, common norms may be established to which all thinking must conform. Some logicians have conceived the task of logic to be to provide such norms. Logic, in this view, is not a descriptive study of the way in which people do think. It is, rather, a prescriptive study of the way in which people ought to think. [14]

But, of course, even in the effort to provide norms for thinking, the content of thought may not be prescribed, but only the method or form. Being logical has nothing to do with the content of one's statements. Thus, the norms provided by logic refer merely to the structure of thinking. If one follows the rules, his thought is logical. If the rules are violated, one's thought becomes illogical. The difference between being logical or illogical, then, has to do with the presence or lack of such characteristics as contradictoriness, etc.

(2) "An existential system is impossible. "

We may agree, then, that the act of establishing a
normative procedure for thinking is an entirely appropriate
one. However, with respect to methods of behaving, no
norms may be established to which all behaviour must conform. This is so because behaviour has to do with the
realm of existence, rather than the realm of thought. Behaviour refers to that which is existent, not that which is
an ideal entity. And, whereas it is appropriate to prescribe rules for correct thinking, it is not appropriate to
prescribe rules for correct behaviour.

Why is this so? A thought, that which "exists" for
reflection, may possess a kind of commonness. That is,
I am able to think the thoughts of another, provided that
they are clearly expressed and that I have a mental capacity
sufficient to understand them. But no similar commonness
with respect to the existence of individual selves external
to one's own may be found. Hence, whereas I can think
the thoughts of another, and can even think thoughts about
his existence, I cannot think his existence. His existence
is not amenable to thought. Ideas about his existence are
amenable to thought, but one can never know whether the
ideas actually "correspond" to his existence. Thus, the
existence of another resists being translated from the realm
of the existential to the realm of thought or reflection. No
matter how hard I might try to think his existence, I cannot succeed, as such a procedure would involve a transformation from the realm of reality or existence to the
realm of ideality or reflection, which is impossible. The
same applies to impersonal objects. Anything which actually
exists, externally to any given subject, cannot be thought,
even though one might have probable ideas about the existent
object.

Since I cannot think another's existence, I cannot
truly know it either. Knowledge has to do with the realm
of reflection. I can know ideas or the concepts and thoughts
which sentences express. But I cannot strictly know anything which is existent, except my own self.

Consequently, each individual is an isolated self.
His existence is peculiar to him, and is not shared with
any other existent self, not even those who are most closely
associated with him. This is so, again, because no indivi-

dual can appropriate the existence of another individual to himself. The other always remains a separate self and maintains his own being.

Since each individual is an isolated self, and since no individual can know the existence of another, it follows that no individual may prescribe as to how another individual ought to act. Rules of behaving are, thus, inappropriate. Whereas a logical system (prescribed rules for thinking) is possible, a system of ethics (prescribed rules for existing or behaving) is impossible. One can only prescribe rules where there is a common quality shared by all who participate in the endeavour, or, at least, all who can meet the requirements. The realm of thought permits this common quality. The realm of existence does not.

With respect to existing, therefore, each individual must establish his own rules. No one can legislate for another. No one can truly know what is appropriate for any other individual than himself. Since each individual participates only in his own existence, he can only prescribe as to the way in which he (himself) must act. The effort to establish any sort of science of ethics, on the one hand, or a codified morality, on the other, is, therefore, entirely inappropriate. For, since each individual is an isolated self, no one can know what is right or wrong for any other existent self. He can only know this about himself.

I anticipate another question: "How can an individual know what is right or wrong even for himself?" Two questions are implied here: (a) If he can know only thoughts, how can he know anything with respect to any existence, even his own? (b) How can he know for certain which actions (etc.) are right and which are wrong? One might suggest the following answers. (a) Any individual is, of course, more than an intellect. He is a synthesis of knowing, imagining, feeling, etc., in existence. Therefore, he can, with respect to his own synthesis, have an awareness of matters pertaining to his behaviour or existence. This is so because in his own case, and only then, are the subject who knows and the object known identical. (b) He cannot know for certain which actions are right and which are wrong, etc. He can only posit certain modes of behaving as being more "right" than others, upon the basis of his relative and limited awareness. No objective certainty is possible here. Furthermore, many factors may enter into his account of what is right.

I might add that these conclusions are not entirely attractive to me. But I cannot, of course, reject them merely because they are unpleasant. The conclusions at which Kierkegaard arrives are, I believe, true. I cannot, therefore, distort what seems to be the case. I cannot mould the scheme of things to suit my heart's desire. I cannot yield to a sentiment, such as positing the ontic objectivity of values, by which to escape the predicament. I must accept what is, or seems to be, the case, even though it may be, and is, unpleasant.

Thus, we find verification again of an ancient proverb: "Increase of knowledge means increase of sorrow."

Remarks by the Author (1970)

I still believe that the first two sections of the above article constitute an accurate characterization of Kierkegaard's ethical theory--in spite of the fact that it is difficult to claim any definitive interpretation of Kierkegaard's works, due to such factors as the pseudonymous writings, etc. However, I no longer agree with Kierkegaard on the main theses of his ethical theory, and hence I no longer hold the central points developed in the last section of the paper. It would require far more space than the original article to state my reasons for this disagreement, and therefore I shall not attempt to present them at this time.

(E. D. K.)

1. David F. Swenson, Something About Kierkegaard.
   Mpls: Augsburg, 1941, passim. Paul L. Holmer,
   "Kierkegaard and Ethical Theory," Ethics, Vol.
   LXIII, N. 3, April 1953, pp. 157-170. I am
   especially indebted to Professor Holmer in the first
   section of this paper.

2. S. Kierkegaard, Concluding Unscientific Postscript.
   Tr. by Walter Lowrie and David F. Swenson.
   Princeton: Princeton University Press, 1941,
   pp. 267 ff.

3. Postscript, p. 105.

4. Ibid., pp. 112, 283, 296.

5. Ibid., p. 274.

6. Ibid., p. 279.

7. Ibid., pp. 267-322.

8. Ibid., pp. 282, 285. I have elsewhere ("Some Misinterpretations of Kierkegaard," Hibbert Journal,)
   warned against taking the views of the pseudonymous authors to be Kierkegaard's own. Kierkegaard himself stressed this point. Nevertheless, he
   also held the Postscript (and Fragments) to have a
   special status between the purely aesthetic works and
   the religious writings. He says, for example, that
   he has affixed his name as editor, which he did not
   do for any of the strictly pseudonymous works.
   Hence, we may, I believe, hold that, while the
   Fragments and Postscript do not express the reflection and discourse of an interested religious man,
   they do express that of a disinterested man dealing
   with a problem.

9. Ibid., p. 282.

10. Ibid., p. 284.

11. Ibid., p. 284.

12. Ibid., p. 285.

13. <u>Ibid.</u>, p. 99. My use of these statements does not follow Kierkegaard's exposition of them.

14. I am aware that this view of logic, in terms of <u>thinking,</u> etc., is not too well-received by many <u>present-day</u> logicians.

The Existential Reality of God

A Kierkegaardian Study

J. Preston Cole

First published in The Christian Scholar, XLVIII (Fall 1965), 224-235, the article is here reprinted with the kind permission of the Department of Higher Education, National Council of the Churches of Christ, and of the author, who is at present a Professor of Religion, Lycoming College.

I. Methodological Considerations

We are proposing an investigation of the existential reality of God. To do so is to set rather precise limits to the area of our concern. In the first place it restricts our study to only one mode of being. We are not concerned to examine the essence of being itself, but to investigate only one specific kind of being--human being, that mode of being peculiar to man known as selfhood. More particularly this investigation is for the purpose of disclosing the function of God in human existence.

In the second place we are concerned here to examine only the existential reality of God. We do not intend to investigate the ontological reality of God on the one hand or the psychic reality of God on the other. This is neither a study of the being of God nor a study of the psychology of man, though it may have important consequences for both. Its ambition is much more modest. It simply seeks to give a phenomenological description of the God-phenomenon in human existence.

The method employed here is that of existential analysis, which is closely akin to the phenomenological method of Edmund Husserl. The existential analytic seeks to accomplish an epoche, to use Hüsserl's term, a suspension of judgment with respect to both the ontological question and the psychological question. Existential analysis "brackets out" both the objective judgment and the subjective judgment concerning the reality of God and confines itself to a description of the God-function in the dialectic of selfhood. The study, therefore, seeks to disclose only the existential reality of God, to enunciate an "operational" understanding of God, as it were, derived from an analysis of human existence.

The data for this study is not original. It is wholly dependent upon the existential analytic of Søren Kierkegaard. Though his method has been refined and modified by his successors, none, we think, has achieved a more profound or sensitive analysis of the phenomenon of selfhood than that which he sets forth in his perceptive little monograph The Sickness Unto Death. Dependent, then, upon this existential analysis, we shall simply seek to extract from it the existential reality disclosed therein, to which we give the designation "God."

The existential limitation which we have placed upon this study of the reality of God does not intend to negate the possibility and importance of similar analyses of modes of existence other than the human nor does it mean to preclude any ontological conclusions. It simply intends to set aside such considerations as consequent to the analysis of human existence.

II.   The Dialectic of Selfhood

The most striking fact about human existence is its restless questing character. In stark contrast to other modes of existence, the human mode is characterized by a certain indeterminacy with respect to its essence. Other types of existants tend to become what they are. Their "becoming" is actually an unfolding of what they already are. But man, on the contrary, is a being in search of an essence, as it were. Or, to put it another way, it is the essence of man to create his own essence. Of course, this is to use the term "essence" in two different senses. In the first instance it refers to the original essence of man; while in the second instance it refers to the historical essence. The original essence of man is historicity; the historical essence is the consequence of that historicity. The former is given with his existence; the latter comes into being historically. This original essence Kierkegaard calls "spirit." It is the source of both the grandeur and misery of man. It gives to man a kind of grandeur because he of all the creatures participates in his own creation.

But it also constitutes a source of misery, for it posits for man the central problem of his existence, the endless search for his self. Man begins his existence as an "it" or at best a "me," a self "in the dative case," as Kierkegaard puts it. He has to become an "I." And the very fact that becoming a self is a process which does not transpire by necessity is the source of man's misery and despair.

The consequence of this "spiritual" character of man, his essential historicity, is that man is a relationship. That is to say, because man is a being in search of an essence, his selfhood consists in the relationship whereby he relates himself to that essence. Selfhood is not simply self-consciousness, it is self-consciousness relating itself to an essence. But on the other hand, neither is selfhood identical with that essence to which it relates itself. Selfhood consists in the relationship wherein the self relates itself to its essence.

This does not mean that selfhood is an autonomous mode of being. The self does not become a self simply by willing to be one. Rather it is radically contingent upon a power other than itself. Kierkegaard documents this by an appeal to the phenomenon of despair. If the self is self-constituted, there could be only one form of despair: that of not willing to be one's self--the despair of weakness. But phenomenologically there is also a more despairing despair: that of despairingly willing to be one's self--the despair of defiance. That is to say, despair is found not only among those who lack the courage to affirm the historicity of their existence, but it is also found among those who defiantly seek to become the self of their own choosing. And, indeed, Kierkegaard insists, this is the most desperate form of despair. Nothing is more despairing than the despair of the "self-made man" when he discovers he has not become a self. Kierkegaard insists that "the self cannot of itself attain and remain in equilibrium and rest by itself, but only by relating itself to the Power which constituted the whole relation.* And the self-made man despairingly wills to be a self which he is not. "What he really wills," Kierkegaard says, "is to tear his self away from the Power which constituted it. . . . He wills to be rid of himself, to be rid of the self which he is, in order to be the self he himself

*All references are to The Sickness Unto Death, by Søren Kierkegaard, Anchor Book Edition, Doubleday and Company, Inc., Garden City, New York, 1954. P. 147.

has chanced to chose (sic). " (p. 153) Selfhood, therefore, is profoundly contingent upon the power which constitutes it, that is, spirit. Spirit is the power of human being. Selfhood, then is the continual relationship of the self to that power, spirit, which posits the relationship. And despair is the dis-relation in that relationship. Whether that dis-relation is due to weakness or defiance, both are attempts to avoid the terror of history, the dread of freedom.

Both modes of flight are doomed to failure, for spirit is given with human existence. Selfhood is given as a task from which a man can never be free. He is condemned to the continual task of becoming a self. "The relation to himself a man cannot get rid of, any more than he can get rid of himself, which moreover is one and the same thing, since the self is the relationship to oneself, " Kierkegaard says. (p. 150) Selfhood is a task which is never done. By its very nature it requires continuous affirmation. The collapse of that relationship is always imminent. "The thing of not being in despair must mean the annihilation of the possibility of being this; if it is to be true that a man is not in despair, one must annihilate the possibility every instant. " (p. 148)

Thus, the self, as a relationship is a task which is being continually posited by spirit, the power of human being. It is inescapable, relentless, necessary; but it is also precarious. It requires for its actualization man's responsible enactment. The relationship of selfhood is consummated only when the self relates itself to the power which constituted it.

Kierkegaard has here set forth the basis for an existential doctrine of God. "Spirit" certainly performs a god-function in the dialectic of selfhood. It is spirit which posits the self. The self is wholly contingent upon this power of selfhood for its very existence. Spirit is thus the creator and sustainer of selfhood. While the self is contingent upon spirit for its existence, its existence is not consummated except insofar as it relates to this power which constitutes it. Here is preserved the classic insistence upon both the initiative of God and the response of man.

III. The Dialectic of Selfhood: Viewed Under the Categories of Space

Proceeding with a more detailed examination of the

95

dialectic of selfhood, Kierkegaard employs the categories of space, time, and causality in a highly original manner. He says, "Man is a synthesis of the infinite and the finite, of the temporal and the eternal, of freedom and necessity." (p. 146) Under the aspect of the finite and the infinite, he discusses the dialectic of the self with respect to its definition, its "de-finition," its delimitation or demarcation. Under the aspect of necessity and freedom, or necessity and possibility as he more characteristically expresses it, he discusses the dialectic of the self with respect to its becoming. And under the aspect of the temporal and the eternal he discusses the dialectic of the self with respect to the reality· of that to which the self relates itself.

The definitive proposition with respect to the dialectic of selfhood, construed under spatial categories, is this: "The self is the conscious synthesis of infinitude and finitude which relates itself to itself, whose task is to become itself, a task which can be performed only by means of a relationship to God." (p. 162) The significance of the theological reference will become clear only after we have examined more closely the dialectic of the finite and the infinite. The key terms here are, of course, "finite" and "infinite." By "finite" Kierkegaard means "de-finite," circumscribed, final. The connotations of the Latin origins of the word are not unintentional. The overtones of limited, finished, having a definite end, are certainly intended. So, by his emphasis upon finitude in the dialectic of selfhood, Kierkegaard means to make clear that in order to be a self one must become a definite self, a specific self. One cannot become a self in the abstract, but only a self in the concrete. One cannot become "mankind," but only the "individual"; he cannot become a self "in general," but only a definite self.

But finitude does not exhaust our understanding of the self. Indeed, it is only one pole, though an indispensable one, in the dialectic of selfhood. Equally indispensable to becoming a self is infinitude. By "infinite," Kierkegaard means "in-finite," without restriction, limitless. Infinitude, therefore, ascribes to the self an uncircumscribed openness to what it can become, a capacity to transcend continually all definition, all "de-finition," of the self.

Now selfhood, as Kierkegaard understands it, is neither the finite, "de-finite" self one is, nor the infinite, "in-definite," self one is not yet, but a dialectical relation

96

between the two. "The self," he says, "is a synthesis in which the finite is the limiting factor, and the infinite is the expanding factor." (p. 163) And again, selfhood "consists in moving away from oneself infinitely by the process of infinitizing oneself, and in returning to oneself infinitely by the process of finitizing." (pp. 162 ff.) Selfhood consists in continually opening up the vistas of selfhood, while at the same time continually giving concretion to the self.

The "infinitizing process" is a manifestation of spirit, that power in human being which continually impels the self beyond itself in quest of itself. It is accomplished by means of "imagination." Again, we will best understand what Kierkegaard means by taking the term literally: "image-ination." Imagination is the ability of the human being to depict the abstract, to project it in pictures, to give it an image. More specifically, in reference to the dialectic of selfhood, it is the capacity to project an image of the abstract possibilities of the self. There is, of course, nothing absolute about this image. Indeed, it is what Kierkegaard calls a "counterfeit presentment of the self," for it is our own creation, and hence not absolute but relative. Nevertheless, it is essential to the dialectic of selfhood, for it is an image of the infinite to which the self relates its finite self, and therefore makes possible the relationship which constitutes selfhood.

It cannot be stressed too strongly that selfhood consists in the relationship; and this is dissipated if either pole is lost. One can lose his selfhood if he mistakes the infinite transcendent self for his real self, for then the self becomes fantastic and illusory. Kierkegaard illustrates this with respect to feeling, knowing, and willing. If feeling is infinitized without respect for the finite, it becomes an abstract sentimentality without a definite object. Love becomes the illusory love of mankind which cannot love a specific individual. Knowledge which does not sustain a reference to the concrete self becomes a kind of "inhuman knowing," a knowledge of the abstract without a corresponding self-knowledge. And one may also lose himself in the fantastic if his resolve to do great things is not kept in dialectical relation to a resolve to do that finite portion of the project which is immediately at hand. In each case, the individual has become infinitized, in a way; "but not," Kierkegaard notes, "in such a way that he becomes more and more himself, for he loses himself more and more." (p. 164)

One can also lose his selfhood, however, if he mistakes the finite self for his real self. Here the self is lost "not by evaporation in the infinite, but by being entirely finitized, by having become, instead of a self, a number, just one man more, one more repetition of this everlasting Einerlei. " (p. 166) He allows some finite image of the self to become definitive for him. He allows some cultural consensus to become normative for what it means to be a man. He loses his selfhood in the loss of the capacity to transcend this finite image. Of course, by his culture's criterion he is precisely what a man ought to be. But in a deeper sense he has lost his self. He has "become an imitation, a number, a cipher in the crowd. " (p. 167)

The task is to live concretely in dialectical relation with the infinite as imaged by the imagination. Kierkegaard understands this dialectic to be a theological one. His proposition, we recall, was this: "The self is the conscious synthesis of infinitude and finitude which relates itself to itself, whose task is to become itself, a task which can be performed only by means of a relationship to God. " (p. 162) By now we have some understanding of what this statement means. The dialectical relationship of the finite immediate self with the projected image of the self, Kierkegaard calls a "God-relationship. " This is not to say that the imaged self is God, but it does clarify the way in which the God-concept functions in human existence. It functions as the transcendent image in relation to which the self has its existence. To be sure, our projected images of the self are not identical with God. Indeed, as we have seen, the imaged self is a "counterfeit" image, a finite image of the infinite, an idol. But existence in relation to the imaged self is a God-relationship in which the imaged self functions as a god. We can now see what Kierkegaard means when he says, "the God-relationship infinitizes" the self. (p. 165) It is by virtue of its relation to the projected image of the self, however imperfect, that the self is enabled to transcend the finitude of its own immediate self. Thus the task of becoming a self is, as Kierkegaard observed, impossible apart from the God-relationship.

One final word is important to the proper understanding of the dialectic of the finite and the infinite. The imaged self itself is always a finite image, though it is made possible by the activity of spirit. Therefore, a self whose God-relationship is defined by a finite image of the infinite is still a self confined to the finite. The process of image-ination is at best an effort of the self to sustain a relation between the finite and the infinite and at its worst a capitulation to the finite. Only that self which relates to the imaged self transparently, is related to the infinite, and is therefore a self.

IV. The Dialectic of Selfhood: Viewed Under the Categories of Causality

The structure of the self, we have seen, consists in a dialectical relation between the finite and the infinite; but the dynamics of selfhood, as we shall see, consist in a relationship between necessity and possibility. Again, the definitive statement of the problem of becoming a self is given in a single complex passage.

> When the self as a synthesis of finitude and infinitude is once constituted, when already it is χατἀξύναμιν, then in order to become it reflects itself in the medium of imagination, and with that the infinite possibility comes into view. The self χατἀξύναμιν is just as possible as it is necessary; for though it is itself, it has to become itself. Inasmuch as it is itself, it is necessary, and inasmuch as it has to become itself, it is a possibility. (p. 168)

Here Kierkegaard is dealing with the difficult problem of freedom and determinism in the dynamics of selfhood. He is insisting upon both factors. It is just as true that man is free as it is that he is determined. Observing the human phenomena, he concludes that "the self . . . is just as possible as it is necessary," just as free as it is determined; "for though it is itself, it has to become itself." Kierkegaard is saying that it is a phenomenological fact that the individual is what he has become, and that his existence is determined by who he is. But he is also saying that this does not exhaust our understanding of that individual. It is equally true that the individual is continually confronted with the task of relating that self he has become to a multitude of possibilities. Thus the self is just as possible as it is necessary; for though it is itself, it also has to become itself. Inasmuch as it is itself, it is determined by what it has become; and inasmuch as it has to become itself, it is free.

Here, even as in the dialectic considered under the aspects of finitude and infinitude, the individual can lose his self if he loses either pole of the dialectic. Selfhood

can be lost in the possible if the self loses its relation to
the self it has become, the necessary self. And conversely,
selfhood can be lost in necessity if the self loses its relationship to possibility. If the necessary determined self
is forgotten in preoccupation with the infinite possibilities
of selfhood, then the self evaporates into abstract possibility.
"Possibility then appears to the self ever greater and greater,
more and more things become possible, because nothing becomes actual. At last it is as if everything were possible
--but this is precisely when the abyss has swallowed up the
self." (p. 169) What is lacking is the willingness "to submit to the necessary in oneself," (p. 169) as Kierkegaard
puts it. The willingness to acknowledge the limit to what
is possible for this concrete, individual, historical self.
Not everything is possible for the particular individual. A
limit is imposed upon him by that history which has given
concretion to the self.

But one can also lose himself through the loss of
possibility. To be sure, there is a stubborn necessity to
the self one has become. The self one has created by his
own historical choices cannot lightly be dismissed. This
self one has created is one's self. He cannot escape it.
It figures determinatively in every subsequent act and choice.
But if the individual becomes totally determined by this
necessary self, if possibility is no more present, then the
self has lost its selfhood. The creative dialectic which
constitutes selfhood has collapsed. The individual is in
bondage to his past. "The determinist or the fatalist is in
despair," Kierkegaard says, "and in despair he has lost
his self, because for him everything is necessary." (p. 173)

Thus selfhood is a dialectical relation between
necessity and possibility. The self in bondage to its past
has lost its selfhood, for selfhood is that mode of being
wherein the individual relates the self he has become to
the spectrum of possibilities which lie before him. But
unless these possibilities are kept in relation to the actualized possibilities which have now become the historical
essence of the individual and are determinative of his actions, selfhood can also be lost in wishful thinking.

Again, Kierkegaard calls our attention to the theological dimension of the dialectic of selfhood. Possibility,
he says, is the very breath of selfhood. Without possibility the self will suffocate. "Personality is a synthesis
of possibility and necessity. The condition of its survival
is therefore analogous to breathing (respiration), which is

100

an in- and an a-spiration. The self of the determinist cannot breathe, for it is impossible to breathe necessity alone,
which taken pure and simply suffocates the human self. "
(p. 173) This spiritual respiration constitutes Kierkegaard's
understanding of prayer. "To pray is to breathe, and possibility is for the self what oxygen is for breathing. " (p. 173)
Prayer, therefore, is the process of relating one's already
determined self to possibility. There is little doubt that
within the dialectic of human existence, possibility is God
for Kierkegaard. Let us cite the key passage here: "In
order to pray there must be a God, there must be a self
plus possibility, or a self and possibility in the pregnant
sense; for God is that all things are possible, and that all
things are possible is God. " (pp. 173 ff.) God is possibility.
Without possibility there can be no such thing as selfhood.
The alternative is fatalism in which selfhood is lost in a
wholly determined existence. "The fatalist, " Kierkegaard
says, "is in despair--he has lost God, and therefore himself as well; for if he has no God, neither has he a self.
But the fatalist has no God--or, what is the same thing,
his god is necessity. " (p. 173) Kierkegaard is insisting
upon the existential reality of God, i. e. possibility. God
is not just the possibility which arises from the imagination
of man; he is the source of possibility. He is the power
which makes possible the imagination of possibilities. He
is the possibility which appears "when a man is brought to
the utmost extremity, so that humanly speaking no possibility exists. " (p. 171) God is the possibility which comes
to man even when his imagination can no longer conjure up
a possibility as his own possibility.

Thus the existential analysis of the self with respect
to its becoming contributes another dimension to our understanding of the existential reality of God. Just as our
structural analysis of the self led us to conclude that God
is the infinite in relation to which the self relates its finite
self, so our analysis of the dynamics of becoming has led
us to conclude that God is the possible to which the self
relates its necessary self.

V.   The Dialectic of Selfhood:
Viewed Under the Categories of Time

We have considered the dialectic of selfhood with
regard to its structure and with regard to its dynamics;
we must now consider it with regard to its reality. By
introducing the term "reality, " Kierkegaard does not intend to take us out of the realm of the existential; he does

101

not intend an ontological judgment here.   He means simply
that the self is qualitatively determined by the kind of
reality to which it relates itself.   Since selfhood is a relation which relates the finite necessary self to its finite
possibilities, it is evident that the character of the self is
dependent upon the character of its transcendent norm.
The importance of this transcendent norm for Kierkegaard
is apparent when we note that in his study of the gradations
of despair or non-being, the criterion is the degree of
consciousness "of having a self in which there is after all
something eternal. " (p. 210)   Thus, considered under the
aspect of reality, the self is a relation between temporal
reality and eternal reality, between an historically con-
ditioned reality and a reality which transcends historical
relativity.

In his treatment of the self as a relation between
the temporal and the eternal, Kierkegaard details the
"stages on life's way" which he later classified as the
aesthetic, the ethical, and the religious.   Though here the
stages are less discrete.

As we have already noted, Kierkegaard's understanding of the self is developmental.   The individual begins his existence as an "it"; he has to become an "I. "
But spirit is present in man, even in his pre-personal
existence.   When spirit manifests itself in man as self-
consciousness, it is of crucial importance what reality the
self-consciousness relates itself to.   If that reality is
exclusively material reality, objects for the gratification
of organic and psychological needs, then the self is the
"aesthetic self. "   The aesthetic self is completely determined by its psychosomatic needs, the material things become its normative reality.   "The sensuous nature and the
psycho-sensuous completely dominate him, " Kierkegaard
says.   "He lives in the sensuous categories agreeable/dis-
agreeable, . . . he is too sensuous to have the courage to
venture to be spirit or to endure it. " (p. 176)   Of course,
the aesthetic self is also a relational mode of being, but
it is a relationship between the self and the temporal objects of its desire.   The aesthetic individual is in despair,
for the dialectic of selfhood has collapsed into the temporal.
Such a man has his being in things.   Thus, when something happens to deprive him of the things in which his
selfhood consists, he despairs.   But actually he was already in despair, for he lacked the eternal.

Of course, there is probably no one who is wholly

without awareness of the eternal dimension of his self. Suppose that this immediate man does have some awareness that his selfhood transcends this finite temporal self, and still he does not become a self. Such a man, Kierkegaard says "has an obscure conception that there might even be something eternal in the self. But in vain he struggles thus; the difficulty he stumbled against demands a breach with immediacy as a whole, and for that he has not sufficient self-reflection or ethical reflection." (p. 188) He is aware that selfhood is more than the acquisition of temporal things, that the object of his longing should transcend the temporal; but he lacks sufficient ethical awareness to make the break with the temporal. This is the despair of weakness to which we have already alluded.

There is a further intensification of this despair when, self-consciously, this man is in despair over his weakness. He has sufficient self-reflection to understand why it is that he is not a self and cannot become a self, namely that he is too weak to make the break. And so, he despairs over his weakness. To be sure, there is present here some hint of ethical awareness, inasmuch as the individual is sufficiently aware of his non-being to feel guilty for it. But he nevertheless remains in the aesthetic mode, for he continues to choose the temporal as definitive of his existence.

The ethical mode of existence, however, fully emerges only when the self relates itself to a reality which transcends his own psychosomatic desires. The emergence of the ethical mode of existence is observed in the child who appropriates the image of his father as the "transcendent" norm of his existence. To be sure, such an image is still a temporal image of selfhood, but it does transcend his own personal impulses as a criterion of truth. The father-image performs the function of communicating the cultural precipitate of truth to the child, thus making possible the ethical dialectic between the individual's desires and the social good. Indeed, Kierkegaard also notes the transition which takes place within the ethical mode of being when the individual transcends the parent's limited comprehension of the good and chooses a more comprehensive social reality as normative for himself. He says, "The child who hitherto has had only the parents to measure himself by, becomes self when he is a man by getting the state as a measure." (p. 210) But the ethical mode of being culminates in the man whose awareness of the eternal is sufficient for him to discern the non-being present in such

103

conformity, and who in desperation wills to be a self. He notes that "in order to will in despair to be oneself there must be consciousness of the infinite self." (p. 201)

This is nonetheless despair, the despair of defiance, for "it acknowledges no power over it, hence in the last resort it lacks seriousness." (p. 202) Such a man does not take seriously the reality of the eternal. He concludes that there is no eternal reality, that man is himself the measure. Not his parents, nor even his culture, but he himself is the measure. He himself is the author of truth. As a consequence he does not succeed more and more in becoming a self. Instead he becomes a "hypothetical self," a self lacking reality, for it is a self which he himself hypothesized.

Now, Kierkegaard wants to insist that there is a qualitatively different mode of existence--the theological. He says: "The gradations in the consciousness of the self with which we have hitherto been employed are within the definition of the human self, or the self whose measure is man. But this self acquires a new quality or qualification in the fact that it is the self directly in the sight of God. This self is no longer the merely human self but it is what I would call . . . the theological self, the self directly in the sight of God. And what an infinite reality this self acquires by being before God!" (p. 210) It should be apparent that the transcendent determinant of selfhood of which Kierkegaard speaks is no mere subjective projection, nor even a cultural image of man, but wholly other than every concrete image we may conjure up. To have man as the "measure" of selfhood, whether in the form of a cultural consensus or in the form of an ideology, or in the form of one's private ideal, is finally to vitiate the dialectic which constitutes the self and to fall into bondage to the temporal. Only when the transcendent pole of the dialectic genuinely transcends every concretion is the dialectic of selfhood sustained. This is the meaning of his often quoted statement that "God and man are two qualities between which there is an infinite qualitative difference." (p. 257) God, therefore, existentially considered with respect to time, is the wholly transcendent telos of man. He is the "eternal" telos, the temporarily unconditioned telos of man.

VI. Conclusions

Within the limits of an existential analysis, then, God

104

is spirit. He is that power which continually projects its own reality before man, creating thereby the structure and the dynamic of selfhood. Structurally considered, he is the infinite pole of the dialectic of selfhood, the non-finite, uncircumscribed "image" of the self. Dynamically considered, he is radical possibility; the projected possibility which is continually beyond actuality and which thereby gives to the self a measure of freedom from the necessary self it has become. And qualitatively considered, is that telos which radically transcends every temporal ideal, every image of the self which has been historically produced. God is therefore the "limit" of man, the absolute limit of selfhood; which is to say the infinite possibility which eternally transcends every historically determined image of the self.

Such an understanding of God poses the problem of indeterminacy. If God is the absolutely transcendent telos of man, how can such a reality function in the dialectic of selfhood, where the problem of the self is to become a concrete self? From our existential analytic we have seen that selfhood is a quest for an "essence" in which the self relates itself to a self-image and seeks to become that self. But if that self-image by which one "measures" himself is radically indeterminate, if it is without attributes so to speak, how can it function concretely in the task of becoming a self?

To be sure, the self is constantly under the necessity of concretizing his God, of giving his God an image, in order that his selfhood not be dissipated in abstraction. And this he does when he adopts the father-image as his Father-God, or when he "becomes a man" and adopts a broader cultural image of the self than that bequeathed him by his father. But the self is equally under the necessity of letting God be God, of acknowledging the historical relativity in every concrete image which he gives to God, of sustaining only a relative relationship to this relative God-- but which is nonetheless a relationship.

In a word, Jesus Christ is Kierkegaard's answer to this dialectical problem. Christ is the paradigm of selfhood. He is the ideal image of the self, the transcendent pole in the dialectic of selfhood. But this answer is still a dialectical one. Kierkegaard does not fall into the trap of absolutizing the historically relative ethic of Jesus as definitive for human existence, thereby collapsing the dialectic into temporality once again. Rather, it is the mode of being which was manifest in Jesus which constitutes the

105

paradigm of selfhood. That mode he understands to be that of sustaining an absolute relationship to the absolute, and a relative relation to the relative. Thus, in adopting Christ as the measure of man, in relating oneself to Christ as the paradigm of selfhood, one is related transparently to the God of Jesus Christ.

Kierkegaard and Politics

Howard A. Johnson

This article last appeared as a chapter in A Kierkegaard
Critique; it is here reprinted with the kind permission of
its publisher, Harper and Row, and of its author, who is
at present Associate Rector, St. Paul's Episcopal Church,
Oakland, California.

No one who is interested in Søren Kierkegaard--or
in politics--can fail to be interested in the year 1848, for
that is the year, said Kierkegaard, whose "actual events,
almighty as they are, have cast light on my thesis. "[1]

The events in question were Germany's war with
Denmark and the whole rash of revolutions in Europe that
year, including Denmark's bloodless revolution by which
its absolute monarchy became a constitutional one.   And
Kierkegaard's thesis was that "the crowd, regarded as a
judge over ethical and religious matters, is untruth. "[2]

Kierkegaard suffered in some respects from an
astonishing political myopia, but coupled with it was an
even more astonishing political far-sightedness.   If the
positive values enshrined in constitutional monarchy and in
democracy were hidden from him, he was fully clairvoyant
of the harm the human race would suffer from that whole
movement which bore the proud device "Liberty, Equality,
Fraternity. " The Kierkegaardian forecast was this: When
men have liberated themselves from God, their struggle
for equality produces only equality in mediocrity, and instead of fraternity we end with convention-ridden collectiv-
ism.   Unless re-won for Christianity, man cannot escape
the descending logic which reads: from monarchy, to
democracy, to communism--i. e. , the abdication of selfhood
and the monstrous standardization and regimentation of
life. [3]

As Kierkegaard saw his century, everything seemed

to converge in a grand conspiracy against the individual human being. "Each age has its own characteristic depravity. Ours is perhaps not pleasure or indulgence or sensuality, but rather a dissolute pantheistic contempt for the individual man."[4]

Behind this puzzling declaration lies Kierkegaard's distrust of the French Revolution, the machine, and Hegel. We shall examine each of these in turn.

Kierkegaard was no advocate of evil kings, and he knew that abuse of power brings upon itself the nemesis of revolution; but he detected that the real evil of his time was its desire to be quit not simply of kings but also of God.[5] What takes the place of God is "a superstitious belief in the saving and beatifying power of the understanding," conjoined with a trust in the future--with a trust, that is, in the power of man, given time, to achieve, by the exercise of his unaided reason, a socio-political Utopia. This, declared Kierkegaard, is "the pretense that the temporal will explain in time what in time must remain a riddle, which only Christianity can solve."[6]

> In these times policy is everything. Between this and the religious view the difference is heaven-wide (toto caelo), as also the point of departure and the ultimate aim differ from it toto caelo, since policy begins on earth and remains on earth, whereas religion, deriving its beginning from above, aims to transcend the earth and thereby exalt earth to heaven.[7]

In this passage Kierkegaard contrasts the Christian outlook with an outlook we have learned to call "secular." Secularism, as James A. Pike, the sometime Episcopal Bishop of California, put it, is this-age-ism, this-age-is-all-there-is-ism. It regards man--his origin, his duty, and his destiny--as completely earthbound. Reducing man to the single dimension of his social value, it eliminates the supernatural altogether. Instead of the ancient and orthodox trilogy, "Nature, Man, and God," we are left with only man and nature. But this man, because he has brains, can harness nature and here on earth build "heaven." "Eternity is done away with, and the stage for the perfection of all is transferred to the temporal":[8] this is Kierkegaard's accurate description of secularism in its optimistic-humanistic form. He makes the same point more devastatingly when he remarks that in our era "committees are

pretty nearly everything."[9]   Since there is no God, no
revealed moral law, no absolute, men are left in sole
possession, and it is up to them, in parliament assembled,
to determine the truth by balloting.[10]   This entire conception rests on "the proposition that the race is the truth and
that this generation is the court of last resort, that the
public is the discoverer of the truth and its judge."[11]   For
"race," however, we must write "crowd" or the "multitude"
or the "masses."   For the majority rules, and vox populi
is vox dei.   This "accounts for the fact that nowadays this
absurdity finds a place in the State: 'the multitude,' an
absurd monster or a monstrous absurdity, which nevertheless is physically in possession of power, and besides that
has an extraordinary virtuosity in making everything com-
mensurable for the decision of the hands upraised to vote
or the fists upraised to fight."[12]

It was the absolute modern man wanted to abolish.
Or rather, he found his absolute in Reason.   But "Reason"
--though spelled with a capital "R" as if it were a god or
goddess, turned out, on closer inspection, to be the autonomous reason of men met together in general assembly to
determine the truth by ballot . . . or by bayonet.[13]   Kierkegaard's opinion was that if this is allowed to have its way,
we may expect sinister results.   "To establish man-made
ethical absolutes must end in the complete denial of absolutes."[14]   For if men acknowledge no law higher than that
of their own creation, and if, out of fear of majority rule,
no one dares to be "angular" enough or "primitive" enough
to rise above "the parrot-wisdom of trivial experience"[15]
(for it always involves a species of martyrdom to break
with the majority), then we have the situation in which a
man finds it "too venturesome a thing to be himself, far
easier and safer to be like the others, to become an imitation, a number, a cipher in the crowd."[16]   But thus the
whole of existence is in danger of sinking down into a gray
mass of "average behavior."   "In Paris," said Kierkegaard,
"they believe in the saving power of mutiny."[17]   If enough
people do a thing, it's right!   And so it comes about that
ethical standards are derived simply by computing the tabu-
lated statistics of what people generally do.   Public opinion
and public conduct--influenced as they are in the twentieth
century by the professional polls, surveys, and reports--
afford fearful confirmation of Kierkegaard's prediction:
Statistics will replace ethics.[18]

Perhaps now we understand Kierkegaard when he
says of his age:

This is what it aspires to: it would build up
the established order, abolish God, and through
fear of men cow the individual into a mouse's
hole. . . . When the established order has
come to the point of deifying itself, then in the
end use and wont become articles of faith, everything becomes about equally important, or custom, use, and wont become the important things.
The individual no longer feels and recognizes
that he along with every individual has a God-
relationship which for him must possess absolute
significance. No, the God-relationship is done
away with; use and wont, custom and suchlike are
deified. But this sort of God-fear is just contempt for God; it does not in fact fear God, it
fears man. [19]

Quite in the spirit of Kierkegaard, Robert M. Hut-
chins, former Chancellor of the University of Chicago, remarks that the Battle Cry of the Republic now is "What
will people say?" Kierkegaard's detestation of "the others,"
the majority, the crowd, is due to the fact that "it renders
the individual completely impenitent and irresponsible, or at
least weakens his sense of responsibility by reducing it to
a fraction."[20]

All of this, thinks Kierkegaard, is a legacy of the
Enlightenment and the French Revolution, and what we can
expect of the Industrial Revolution is a drastic acceleration
of the whole process. Although he stood only at the beginning of the machine age, Kierkegaard feared the coming
mechanization of life with its inevitable concomitants: the
tedium of assembly-line existence, the anonymity of big
cities, the threat of still further depersonalization. In his
many scorching denunciations of "Philistinism" or the
bourgeois spirit (which today we know as suburbiana),[21] we
have the principles of criticism which already Kierkegaard
had begun to apply to the great urban and industrial masses,
although it was left to later men like Ortega y Gasset,
Huxley, Orwell, Gheorghiu, and Heidegger to spell them
out in detail. The desire of the French Revolution, laudable
as it was, that all men might be equal succeeded only in
launching what Kierkegaard called "the leveling process."
But this effort did not level up; it only leveled down. Kierkegaard gave humorous vent to his fear of the leveling
process in a machine age when he scribbled in his Journal
an entry under the heading, "A double leveling down, or a
method of leveling down which double-crosses itself":

110

> With the daguerreotype [which had just been invented] everyone will be able to have their portrait taken--formerly it was only the prominent; and at the same time everything is being done to make us all look exactly the same--so that we shall only need one portrait. 22

The form of expression here is trivial, but if anyone wishes to know how seriously Kierkegaard feared "the leveling process" as a force contributing to the creation of the "faceless multitudes" he has only to read the book called The Present Age.

Whenever this multitude is set upon the throne, says Kierkegaard, "the art of statesmanship will become a game. Everything will turn upon getting the multitude pollinated, with torches and with weapons, indifferent, absolutely indifferent, as to whether they understand anything or no. "23 In a manufacturing age it is, of course, possible to manufacture everything--even public opinion, the mightiest dictator the world has ever known. "Of this public opinion, " writes the great Kierkegaard scholar David F. Swenson, "the modern press is both servant and master, both creature and creator. It gives a tongue to the impersonal impulses generated by the multitude, and so intensifies their power and extends their scope. Press and public are thus a mutual fit, and the essential faults of the one are also the essential faults of the other. "24 Kierkegaard writes:

> If there were only one speaking trumpet on board a ship, and this was in the possession of the pantry-boy, and if everybody looked upon this as a perfectly natural and proper state of affairs: whan then? Everything that the pantry-boy had to say: "mouse in the larder, " "fine weather today, " "Lord only knows what's wrong in the ship's hold, " etc. , etc. , would be published abroad through the speaking trumpet. The captain, on the contrary, would be limited to the use of his own natural voice, for what he had to say was of course not so important. At times he would be reduced to begging the assistance of the pantry-boy, in order that his commands might be made audible. At such times the pantry-boy would feel at liberty to revise the words of command; so that passing through him and trumpet they would become nonsensical and misleading. The captain would then be compelled to strain his

voice in competition, but without success. At
last the pantry-boy would become the master of
the ship, because he had the speaking trumpet. --
Pro dii immortales. 25

And then--if the one and only speaking trumpet
should fall into the hands of the "vested interests," a dema-
gogue, or the Führer . . . !

With these last words we come within sight of what
was, in my judgment, Kierkegaard's most prophetic political
insight. He understood that the real trouble with secularism
is that man can never remain merely secular. Inevitably
man is religious and will turn religious again; and if it is
not the Christian religion to which he turns, it will be
dæmonic religion, religion horribly twisted and distorted.
The trajectory of man's fall is from theism, to humanism,
to materialism. But that is not yet the end. There's no
stopping this thing. The next step, inevitably, is a new
kind of religion. The race which has abolished the old
Absolute will presently invent a new one. And Kierkegaard
knew what the new absolute would be. He learned from
Hegel that it would be the State--a State that demanded of
its citizens uncritical allegiance, unconditional obedience,
religious devotion, and self-immolation.

Kierkegaard perceived that people would give themselves to this wildly, fanatically, religiously, like men
possessed. In his Journal for 1848 he wrote:

> In contradistinction to the Middle Ages and those
> periods with all their discussion of possession,
> of particular men giving themselves to evil, I
> should like to write a book:
>
> On Diabolic Possession in Modern Times
>
> and show how mankind en masse gives itself up
> to evil, how nowadays it happens en masse.
> That is why people flock together, in order to
> feel themselves stimulated, enflamed and ausser
> sich. The scenes on the Blocksberg are the
> exact counterparts of this demoniacal pleasure,
> where the pleasure consists in losing oneself in
> order to be volatilized into a higher potency,
> where being outside oneself one hardly knows
> what one is doing or saying, or who or what is
> speaking through one, while the blood courses

faster, the eyes turn bright and staring, the
passions and lust seething. [26]

Denis de Rougemont asks the question, "What could
Kierkegaard be thinking of when, in his bourgeois, pious
and comfortable Denmark, he wrote these prophetic lines?"
And he answers: "Kierkegaard understood better than anyone and before anyone the creative diabolical principle of
the mass: fleeing from one's own person, no longer being
responsible, and therefore no longer guilty, and becoming
at one stroke a participant in the divinized power of the
Anonymous."[27]

Men who have boasted of their freedom and self-
sufficiency discover presently that they cannot bear the
burden of this autonomy, and so there is a violent swing
of the pendulum to authority and submission. The three
big totalitarian movements of our generation, Communism,
Fascism, and National Socialism, came as political re-
ligions--religions of salvation. So far as I am aware,
Søren Kierkegaard was the first man to understand their
religious character.

French Socialism appeared in the 1830's. The
Communist Manifesto came in 1848. On paper, these movements were outspokenly atheistic, anti-religious. But their
atheism deceived the world into thinking that this was mere
political opposition to any form of religion whatsoever.
The world was fooled by this. Not Kierkegaard. In 1849
he wrote:

> It will become evident, as that which lay at the
> basis of the catastrophe, that it was the opposite
> of the Reformation: then [at the Reformation]
> everything had the appearance of religious move-
> ment but showed itself to be political movement;
> now everything appears to be politics but will
> explicate itself as religious movement. [28]

For all their apparent atheism, Kierkegaard discerned
that Socialism and Communism were essentially religious,[29]
that they were deifications of the State, and that they would
appeal to the masses by their claim to be saviours. Hence,
the struggle to come was to be a struggle between competing
religions of salvation. And with good reason, as history
has shown. Kierkegaard feared that secular man, mechan-
ized man, depersonalized man would easily succumb to the
blandishments of a totalitarian State which offered him secur-

ity but at the price of his freedom.

All of this Kierkegaard saw implicit in Hegel.[30] What he saw there was the philosophical justification, in imposing form, of a State which, since it was the incarnation of Absolute Reason, must bend all individuals to its will--and break those who would not be bent. But with sure instinct, Kierkegaard knew that a society which acts on the assumption that society is everything and the individual nothing always degenerates into the kind of society which destroys individuals and ultimately itself. And when this had happened, then would come the mood of nihilistic despair--this mood which makes our world completely uncertain and completely unpredictable. Anything can happen. For the race, said Kierkegaard, will be so exhausted by the convulsions through which it has passed that people will again be "open." Open, that is, to infection from any quarter. This could be good infection. It could be bad infection.[31] Kierkegaard hopes for the former. The man who anticipated and attacked the foolish doctrine of Inevitable Progress was not himself so foolish as to believe in Inevitable Regress.

> If there is to be real victory, it must happen by means of priests; neither soldiers nor police officers nor diplomats nor political projectmakers will be capable of it. Priests will be required . . . who can break up the "masses" and make them into individual persons.[32]

Kierkegaard is convinced that if only each human being could be helped to become conscious of himself as standing "before God," strictly accountable to God and deeply loved by that God to whom he is precious as a unique and irreplaceable individual, the impersonal thing called "the public" would disappear. Instead of anonymous, irresponsible masses, there would be persons personally related to the personal God, a God of justice and love who demands the transformation of society and provides resources for its renewal. Such people could no longer be stampeded like cattle by daemonic totalitarian movements. Motivated by love of God and neighbor, they would become critical and constructive citizens of the state, not fanatical devotees of the State. "And this is my faith," wrote Kierkegaard, that however much there may be that is confused and evil and detestable in men who have become that irresponsible thing without possibility of repentance which we call "the masses," there is just as much truth and goodness and loveliness in them when one can get hold of the individual. Oh, and in what a high degree would men become--men, and lovable men, if they would become individuals before God!

And therefore he says: "Religion [i. e. , Christian religion] is the true humanity. "[33]

Notes

1. From "'That Individual'--Two 'Notes' Concerning My Work as an Author" in Point of View, p. 122 (XIII, 641). Cp. the "Supplement" bound up in the same book, pp. 159-164 (XIII, 539-543).

2. Point of View, p. 116 (XIII, 637); cf. also p. 122 (XIII, 641).

3. This motif occurs many times--sometimes explicitly, sometimes by inference. Cf. , e. g. , Preface No. 3 and the Postscript to On Authority and Revelation, which is the title Walter Lowrie has invented for his translation of The Book on Adler.

4. Postscript, p. 317 (VII, 344).

5. "The misfortune of our age--in the political as well as in the religious sphere, and in all things--is disobedience, unwillingness to obey. And one deceives oneself and others by wishing to make us imagine that it is doubt. No, it is insubordination: it is not doubt of religious truth but insubordination against religious authority which is the fault in our misfortune and the cause of it. " On Authority and Revelation, p. xviii (VIII B 27, p. 78).

6. On Authority and Revelation, p. xxi (IX B 10, p. 309).

7. Point of View, p. 109 (XIII, 631).

8. Training in Christianity, p. 218 (XII, 247).

9. Point of View, p. 133 (XIII, 649). Cp. The Present Age, p. 17 (VIII, 86).

10. In 1848 S. K. wrote (IX A 4): "Balloting (which is essentially the life-principle in government by the

people; the numerical) is the destruction of everything great and noble and holy and lovable and,
above all, of Christianity, since it is a deifying of
worldliness and an infatuation with this world.
Christianity is the exact opposite. (1) Purely formally. For Christianity is eternal truth, and this
abolishes balloting altogether. As eternal truth,
Christianity is entirely indifferent as to whether
something has the majority behind it or not. But
in the abracadabra of balloting, the majority is
proof of truth; whatever lacks it is not truth, and
whatever has it is truth. Frightful spiritlessness!
(2) Realiter Christianity is directly opposed. For
Christianity, as militant truth, assumes that here
in this wretched world truth is always in the minority. Consequently: from the Christian point of
view, truth is in the minority; according to balloting,
the majority is truth. Indeed!"

11. Point of View, p. 89n (XIII, 614n).

12. On Authority and Revelation, p. 193 (IX B 24, p. 324).
Lest Kierkegaard sound more conservative than he
actually is, let me hasten to note (1) that he fully
acknowledges the competence of parliaments and
people in all purely material and temporal matters
[cf. Point of View, p. 112 (XIII, 634)] and (2) that
by "crowd" Kierkegaard does not imply an invidious
distinction between aristocracy and rabble. "Good
God! How could a religious man hit upon such an
inhuman inequality! No, 'crowd' stands for number,
the numerical, a number of noblemen, millionaires,
high dignitaries, etc. --as soon as the numerical is
involved it is 'crowd,' 'the crowd.'" Cf. p. 114n
(XIII, 635n).

13. S. K. would have agreed entirely with Gordon Keith
Chalmers (in The Republic and the Person) when he
says that we were right in wanting liberty but wrong
in forgetting that "what has really made possible the
liberty of the individual has been not only its root
in truth but the constancy of human agreement about
the relation of man to God, right and wrong, good
and evil." But in "the era of the abolished absolute"
(Chalmers) we are "emancipated from all restraint
(so to call it)," for now there is nothing which "unconditionally stands fast" (S. K.). "Require the
navigator to sail without ballast--he capsizes. Let

116

the race, let each individual, make the experiment of doing without the unconditional--it is a whirlpool and remains such. " Cf. Point of View, p. 163 (XIII, 542).

14. Peter F. Drucker in a brilliant article on "The Unfashionable Kierkegaard" in The Sewanee Review for Autumn 1949: "The ethical position is bound to degenerate into relativism. "

15. Sickness unto Death, p. 64 or Anchor, p. 174 (XI, 173).

16. Sickness unto Death, p. 51 or Anchor, p. 167 (XI, 165). In this way the ground is prepared for men to take refuge in "the collective idea" and "the principle of association" whose logic is: Individually we are nothing, but by the strength of united effort we shall attain the goal. Cf. The Present Age (En literair Anmeldelse). Especially worthy of study is the analysis of envy as "the negative principle. "

17. Stages on Life's Way, p. 433n (VI, 503n). Cp. Sickness unto Death, p. 201 or Anchor, p. 253 (XI, 262).

18. VII A 15 and VII B 213.

19. Training in Christianity, p. 91 and p. 93 (XII, 110, 112). Cf. the whole of VIII[1] A 598, from which I translate only the following: "The communists here at home and abroad fight for human rights. Good; so do I. Precisely for this reason I fight with might and main against the tyranny which is fear of man. Communism leads at best to the tyranny of fearing men (only see how France at this moment suffers from it); precisely at this point Christianity begins. The thing communism makes such a fuss about is what Christianity assumes as something which follows of itself, that all men are equal before God, i. e. , essentially equal. But then Christianity shudders at this abomination which would abolish God and in his place install fear of the masses of the majority, of the people, of the public. "

20. Point of View, p. 114 (XIII, 635).

21. Cf. , e. g. , The Concept of Dread, pp. 83-86 (IV, 400-403); Postscript, p. 486 (VII, 537); Sickness

unto Death, p. 49 ff. and p. 63 ff. or Anchor, p. 166 ff. and 174 ff. (XI, 164 and 173 ff.).

22. Journals, No. 1312 (XI^1 A 118).

23. On Authority and Revelation, p. 195 (IX B 24, p. 326).

24. Cf. Something About Kierkegaard, 1st ed. , p. 151 ff. The long quotation in the next paragraph is taken from Swenson's convenient collection of some of the passages in which Kierkegaard laments that "one great mechanical discovery after the other has made it possible to expound doctrines impersonally in increasing measure," with the result that "there has been collected in modern states a huge inorganic precipitate: the multitude. No one ever really comes to grips with this huge mass. " For a study of the role of the Press in creating the phantom Public see The Present Age, p. 37 ff. (VIII, 98 ff.).

25. VIII^1 A 135.

26. Journals, No. 1063 (X^2 A 490).

27. The Devil's Share, p. 141.

28. X^6 B 40.

29. "The strength in communism is obviously the ingredient of religion, even Christian religion, but dæmonically held. " Cf. X^6 B 41.

30. It would take an entire doctoral dissertation (the world is still waiting for a good one) to document this point properly. Meanwhile, one may consult Dr. G. Malantschuk's article, "Kierkegaard and the Totalitarians" in The American-Scandinavian Review for Autumn 1946--an article still extraordinarily valuable in spite of its having been cruelly abbreviated; one should also read Reinhold Niebuhr's section on "The Loss of the Self in Idealism" in The Nature and Destiny of Man and N. H. Søe's Karl Marx og Marxismen. In S. K. himself, cf. , e. g. , Journals, No. 1050 (X^2 A 426) and Sickness unto Death, p. 102 ff. or Anchor, p. 248 ff. (XI, 256 ff.). Curious that hardly anyone has called attention to the political implications of Fear and Trembling. Cf. Problems I and II.

31. Cf. IX B 10, p. 311 and X^6 B 41; several passages in The Present Age; Preface No. 3 and the Postscript to On Authority and Revelation; and the hilarious letter No. 186 in Breve og Akstykker.

32. X^6 B 40.

33. Point of View, p. 153 ff. and p. 110 (XIII, 533, 632).

Kierkegaard on Capitalism

Werner Stark

First published in the Sociological Review, XLII (1950),
87-114, this·article is here reprinted with the kind permission of its Editorial Board and of the author, who is
at present Professor of Sociology, Fordham University.

In the most concise summary which we possess of
Søren Kierkegaard's system of ideas, in the hundred words
or so contained in Brockhaus' Konversationslexikon, we are
told that his thought was exclusively preoccupied with the
religious destiny of the individual and had no relation to the
social realities of history and culture. Such a statement is
misleading. It is true, of course, that not many pages in
Kierkegaard's voluminous writings are given to a discussion
of the problems of social life: indeed, Kierkegaard cannot even
be called a moral philosopher in the accepted sense of the word.
But that does not mean that he had no social philosophy. His
world-view would have been fragmentary without a definite
opinion on man's relation to his neighbours and the difficulties,
dangers and duties inherent in that relationship. If we look close
enough we are sure to find Kierkegaard's social theory--if not
in his words then behind and beneath them, as a set of convictions implied in all his aesthetic and edifying works. It may
not be easy to lay hands on it, but it is there, and it is definite.

In fact, if anything is surprising about Kierkegaard's
social philosophy, it is the definite character of his dis-
jointed statements, the sureness of touch, as it were, which
he displays when he comes to handle a sociological problem.
On April 6th, 1838, he wrote in his Journal: "There are
on the whole few men who are able to bear the Protestant
view of life, and these, if it is to be truly strengthening
for the common man, must either constitute a smaller society (separatism, conventicle, &c.), or approach Catholicism, in both cases for the sake of developing the social
element, the common bearing of life's burden, which only
the most greatly gifted individuals can get along without."[1]

The modern sociologist will have no difficulty in discerning in this short aperçu an able statement and an implied solution of the main problem of the sociology of religion. What Kierkegaard says is that a church may either be designed as an inclusive society, a guide for all, and then it will tend to assume all the traits exhibited by Roman Catholicism; or conceived as an exclusive elite, a fighting force, and then it will be driven to develop the salient features of a sect, in order to define itself and draw strength from its sense of other-ness, of antagonism to the sinfulness of the world at large. Few sociologists have ever grasped this fundamental alternative, which affords the master-key to the interpretation of the whole institutional development of Christianity, with as much clarity and certainty as Kierkegaard displays in this isolated passage.

Again, Kierkegaard was fully and painfully aware of the grand problem which confronts the modern sociology of knowledge. His essay, "Has a Man the Right to let himself be put to Death for the Truth?", deals with a question which became acute, in sociological discussion, only seventy or eighty years later, in connection with the life-work of Max Scheler and Karl Mannheim. The question is "the relationship between man and man," of between society and society, "with respect to the truth." "What difference," we must ask, "may there be between man and man in their relation to truth?" Can anyone (individual or society) claim to be in exclusive possession of the absolute truth? "Or is not a man, just because he is man, so relative with respect to other men that at the utmost it can be a question of their weakness or mediocrity?"[2] Can we, for instance, claim that our modern order of values is intrinsically better, that is, more valid, than the scale of values current in the Middle Ages, or even among some so-called savages? Kierkegaard clearly realised that we have no Archimedean point from which we can see what is better and worse sub specie æternitatis, in the absolute sense of the term. "Surely," he says, "no man is in this situation, least of all in relation to other men. Every man is himself a sinner. He is related, therefore, not as a pure man to sinners, but as a sinner to sinners,"[3] and so can claim no decisive superiority. Every man, we should say to-day, is himself largely a product of his society: his preferences will be those of the social environment in which he has been reared: he is related, therefore, to other societies not as an unprejudiced judge, but as an uncomprehending stranger to absolute strangers, and thus should not presume to condemn. In a word, "in the relation of man to man, there can be only a relative difference" and "no individual man . . . dare think that he is absolutely in possession of the truth, "4 just as no society can reasonably claim to be in any sense more valuable or more advanced than any other so long as it applies, as the criteria of value and progress, its own relative predilections and preoccupations.

With such ideas Kierkegaard anticipated much of the thought of the later protagonists of the sociology of knowledge who mercilessly unmasked the fallacies of progress and insisted that every society must be measured by its own standards. But Kierkegaard not only anticipated their convictions, he also experienced their uneasiness and despair. Are we not driven when we follow these avenues of thought, to the realisation that our most sacred persuasions may be no more than prejudices, and our most cherished strivings simple obstinacy? Kierkegaard did not flinch from this conclusion, but, he confesses, it made him sad. "It is so sad to have to be separated . . . as from a remembrance which never shall return--to be separated from the thought that a man might hold a conviction so strongly that it would seem natural to him, and that he accordingly would dare to venture, to let himself be put to death for it, to venture, as conviction prompts, to point to this truth by a gesture commensurate to the strength of his conviction. And for me there is something disconsolate in this result. "5 For the purely secular sociologist who is unwilling to give himself to religion, this despair must be the end of the road, unless he veers round and inconsistently assumes that, after all, his own society has forced the iron door to the land of absolute truths. In Kierkegaard we perceive the opposite solution of this great quandary. He realised that the relativity of all human knowledge is an inescapable fact as long as we remain within purely human terms, and that it can only be overcome by a desperate leap, by the acceptance, against the promptings of reason, of a divine revelation which will allow us some insight, however limited, into the realm of the eternal values and realities. The despair is stilled as soon as we raise our eyes to the Saviour Son of God because, "as the Absolute, He must burst the relativity in which men . . . have their being" for the simple reason that "they are merely men. "6

These two examples, chosen at random, must suffice to prove that Kierkegaard's thought was by no means hopelessly blind to the problems and preoccupations of sociology, even if the word is taken in a strict and semi-technical meaning. Nor should it be forgotten that his first publication, the series of articles in the Flyvende Post of 1835/36, was pure political pamphleteering. It cannot perhaps be claimed that what he wrote on that occasion was in any way remarkable or original. His insistence that what is good for one country need not be good for another, that social reform must lead to catastrophe if it follows purely abstract ideas and will pay no heed to the concrete realities, to the traditions and institutions which have grown up for centuries past and are firmly established in a society, that the vagaries of an uprooted mob cannot be a sure guide towards the common good, and so on and so forth--all this was only a retailing of Burke's ideas which Kierkegaard had obviously made his own. Yet the close acquaintance shown here with the great Burke, the forefather of all non-materialistic sociologists, is in itself a noteworthy fact. It is impossible to pass through this school (the best of all at our disposal) without emerging as a man of clear ideas and firm convictions in all matters concerning society and the state.

The social philosophy expressed in these four articles remained with Kierkegaard to the end of his life, even though he never reformulated and expanded it. It is present in all his works, a subterranean stream of ideas, as it were, which we can never see, but whose murmurings are audible all the time. Only once does it come to the surface again, in a chance production of his pen, the literary review of Fru Gyllemburg's novel The Two Ages. We must be glad that, on this occasion, Kierkegaard did what no decent reviewer should ever do: forget about the book he is supposed to discuss and launch out into a general discussion of the things that are on his own mind. Had he been more conscientious, it would be very much more difficult for us to reconstruct his theory of society: indeed, we should know very much less about his whole outlook if it is true, as Lowrie says in his classical study, that this is one of the works in which "all the trends of his thinking find their ultimate and most adequate expression."[7]

With the precision characteristic of all his sociological thought, Kierkegaard opens his discussion of The Present Age with the momentous statement that "our age is essentially one of understanding and reflection," that is, a rationalistic age. The intellect is regarded as the highest endowment of man, reasoning as his finest activity. The mathematician and the physicist, the mass-producer of syllogisms, however empty, is the hero of the hour. Cleverness rather than goodness is the admiration of the day. "If we had statistical tables of the consumption of intelligence from generation to generation as we have for spirits, we should be astounded at the enormous amount of scruple and deliberation consumed by even small, well-to-do families living quietly, and at the amount which the young, and even children, use. For just as the children's crusade may be said to typify the Middle Ages, precocious children are typical of the present age. "[8] Eight hundred years ago people acted without much previous thinking: now they are thinking without much subsequent action. It is the curse of rationalism that it transforms everything into a problem and robs life itself of its immediacy.

To say that an age is an age of rationalism, is tantamount to saying that it is without passion, and consequently without action. Kierkegaard confronts throughout the idea of a passionate age with the idea of a reflective period in which thought acts as a severe check on simple and straightforward behavior. He makes his meaning clear with the help of a splendid simile: "If the jewel which every one desired to possess lay far out on a frozen lake where the ice was very thin, watched over by the danger of death, while closer in the ice was perfectly safe, then in a passionate age the crowds would applaud the courage of the man who ventured out, they would tremble for him and with him in the danger of his decisive action, they would grieve over him if he were drowned, they would make a god of him if he secured the prize. But in an age without passion, in a reflective age, it would be otherwise. People would think each other clever in agreeing that it was unreasonable and not even worth while to venture so far out. And in this way they would transform daring and enthusiasm into a feat of skill, so as to do something, for after all 'something must be done.' The crowds would go out to watch from a safe place, and with the eyes of connoisseurs appraise the accomplished skater who could skate almost to the very edge (i.e., as far as the ice was still safe and the danger had not yet begun) and then turn back. The most accomplished skater would manage to go out to the furthermost point and then do a still more dangerous-looking run so as to make the spectators hold their breath and say: 'Ye Gods! he is mad, he is risking his life.' But look, and you will see that his skill was so astonishing that he managed to turn back just in time, while the ice was perfectly safe and there was still no danger. As at the theatre, the crowd would applaud and acclaim him, surging homeward with the heroic artist in their midst, to honour him with a magnificent banquet. For intelligence has got the upper hand to such an extent that it transforms the real task into an unreal trick and reality into a play. " "Thus our own age is essentially one of understanding, and on the average, perhaps, more knowledgeable than any former generation, but it is without passion. Every one knows a great deal, we all know which way we ought to go and all the different ways we can go, but nobody is willing to move. If at last someone were to overcome the reflection within him and happened to act, then immediately thousands of reflections would form an outward obstacle. Only a proposal to reconsider a plan is greeted with enthusiasm, action is met by indolence. Some of the superior and self-satisfied find the enthusiasm of the man who tried to act ridiculous, others are envious because he made the beginning when, after all, they knew just as well as he did what should be done--but did not do it. Still others use the fact that someone has acted in order to produce numerous critical observations and give vent to a store of arguments, demonstrating how much more sensibly the thing could have been done; others, again, busy themselves guessing the outcome and, if possible, influencing events a little so as to favour their own hypothesis. "9 This is the utmost they will do. They will certainly not overstep the safe borderlines of reflection and prudence. The present age is, as it were, a spectator at its own life-drama. It reminds Kierkegaard of an anecdote he had once heard. "It is said that two English noblemen were once riding along a road when they met a man whose horse had run away with him and who, being in danger of falling off, shouted for help. One of the Englishmen turned to the other and said, 'a hundred guineas he falls off.' 'Taken,' said the other. With that they spurred their horses to a gallop and hurried on ahead to open the toll-gates to prevent anything from getting in the way of the runaway horse. In the same way, though without that heroic and millionaire-like spleen, our own reflective and sensible age is like a curious, critical and worldly-wise person, who, at the most, has vitality enough to lay a wager. "10

Needless to say, an age that is so much enslaved to the intellect and so chary of enthusiasm, the arch-opposite of prudence, will be a bad fostering soil for Christianity. Kierkegaard refused to believe that a man could reason himself into holiness. Like Bergson after him, he was convinced that the intellect could indeed make us see things, but never act--action, the decisive step, will always be born of a vital effort, a kind of enthusiasm, while reasoning will inevitably remain enclosed in its own

125

magic circle. "Viewed from this standpoint," he writes, "philosophy will not serve as a transition to Christianity, for it must necessarily stop with this negative result, and the whole conception of the urge for redemption must necessarily reach man from an entirely different side, that is to say, be first felt and then comprehended . . . The philosopher can very well attain conceptions of man's sin, but from this it does not follow that he recognises man's need of redemption, least of all a redemption which (in correspondence with the universal sinfulness of creation) must be wrought by God, but [at best the concept of] a relative redemption (i. e., the thought that man redeems himself)."[11]

But, unfortunately, rationalism is not only incapable of inspiring the heroic leap into Christianity and redemption, it is positively pernicious and destructive even where purely mundane morality is concerned. The traditional safeguards of decency are hollowed out by it and undermined until they collapse and disappear. Consider how rationalistic discussion has destroyed the moralising power of such a concept as immortality! Under the influence of rationalism "people have completely altered the statement of the case, . . . they have made a question out of immortality, made out of a task a question, out of a task for action, a question for thought. Would not that be the most depraved age," Kierkegaard asks, "which completely transformed its 'duties' into problems for thought? For what is duty? Duty is what one shall do. There must not be any question about duty, but there must be question only whether I do my duty. There must be no question about immortality, as to whether it is, but the question must be whether I live as my immortality requires of me. There must be no question about immortality, as to whether it is, but as to what my immortality requires of me, as to my immense responsibility in the fact that I am immortal."[12] In a reflective age such as ours few will ask what immortality requires of man and many whether it exists: and the more their intellect will make them doubt that it exists, the less will they consider what it requires of them, thus freeing themselves from the uncomfortable thought that they are eternally responsible for their every deed. The more rationalism advances, the further must morality recede. If our age is indeed one of understanding and reflection, it must unavoidably be at the same time "an age of dissolution."[13]

Destructive tendencies, it is true, are always at work in society, in a period of passion as much as in a period of reflection, but there is a significant difference: "A passionate tumultuous age will overthrow everything, pull everything down, but a revolutionary age, that is at the same time reflective and passionless, transforms that expression of strength into a feat of dialectics: it leaves everything standing but cunningly empties it of significance. Instead of culminating in a rebellion it reduces the inward reality of all relationships by means of a reflective tension which leaves everything standing but makes the whole of life ambiguous: so that everything continues to exist in fact whilst by a dialectical deceit, privatissime, it supplies a secret interpretation of the facts--that it does not exist."[14]

In order to understand Kierkegaard's interpretation of modern society, it is essential to penetrate to the deeper content of this passage which is highly characteristic of his thought and style, but somewhat difficult to fathom for the uninitiated. Happily Kierkegaard himself has provided a good illustration which makes his meaning easy to comprehend. The relation of a schoolmaster and his pupil should, in the nature of things, be one of superordination and subordination, of domination and submission: it ought to imply downward-looking sentiments at the one pole and upward-looking sentiments at the other. In an age that is not over-rationalistic, this situation will indeed produce all the feelings and ideas appropriate to its human implications. Not so to-day since rationalism has penetrated every nook and of our social life. "A disobedient youth is no longer in fear of his schoolmaster--the relation is rather one of indifference in which schoolmaster and pupil discuss how a good school should be run. To go to school no longer means to be in fear of the master, or merely to learn, but rather implies being interested in the problem of education."[15] What holds good of the master-and-pupil relationship applies also to other fundamental relations. "A father no longer curses his son in anger, using all his parental authority, nor does a son defy his father, a conflict which might end in the inwardness of forgiveness; on the contrary, their relationship is irreproachable, for it is really in process of ceasing to exist, since they are no longer related to one another within the relationship; in fact it has become a problem in which the two partners observe each other as in a game, instead of having any relation to each other, and they note down each other's remarks instead of showing a firm devotion."[16] But that, surely, merely means that the human bond between father and son has been emaciated by reflection, that it has been destroyed. "What in fact should one call such a relationship?" Kierkegaard asks.

127

And he answers: "A tension is the best description, not, however, a tension which strains the forces to breaking-point, but rather a tension which exhausts life itself and the fire of that enthusiasm and inwardness which makes the fetters of dependence and the crown of dominion light, which makes the child's obedience and the father's authority joyful, the admiration of the subject and the exaltation of the great fearless, which gives recognised importance to the master and thus to the disciple occasion to learn, which unites woman's weakness and man's strength in the equal strength of devotion. As it is the relationships still exist but they lack the tension which makes it possible for them to draw together in inwardness and unite in harmony."[17] From a purely formal point of view, "the relationship continues; something is expressed with an abstract continuity which prevents any real break, but although it must nevertheless be described as an expression of the relationship, the relationship is not only ambiguously expressed, it is almost meaningless."[18]

Thus society is slowly but surely dissolved in the acid of rational reflection. "The established order of things continues to exist but it is its ambiguity which satisfies our reflective and passionless age. No one, for example, wishes to do away with the power of the king, but if little by little it could be transformed into something purely fictitious every one would be quite prepared to cheer him. No one, for example, wishes to bring about the downfall of the eminent, but if distinction could be shown to be purely fictitious then every one would be prepared to admire it. In the same way people are quite prepared to leave the Christian terminology untouched, but are surreptitiously aware that it involves no decisive thought. And so they remain unrepentant, for after all they have destroyed nothing. They no more desire a powerful king than an heroic liberator or religious authority. In all innocence they want the established order to continue, but they have the more or less certain reflective knowledge that it no longer exists."[19] The most frightening aspect of this process of destruction is that it proceeds in the dark, by stealth as it were, undiscovered and unobserved. How different is the situation in a passionate age when the struggle unfolds dramatically in the open! "The demoralisation brought about by autocracy and the decay of revolutionary periods have often been described," Kierkegaard remarks, but "the decay of an age without passion is something just as harmful though, on account of its ambiguity, it is less obvious."[20] Rationalism is like a cancerous growth in the body: once it has taken

hold it will eat on until it has destroyed everything. Thus
we sink without even noticing what is happening. "Reflection
constantly takes only a tiny little bit at a time, and about
this little bit one can constantly say 'Why, in small matters
one may well yield'--until in the end reflection will have
taken everything without anybody noticing it, because it
came about little by little, 'and in small matters one may
surely yield'. "[21] There can be few serious-minded people
to-day who, in the face of the continuous atrophy of our
moral standards, would be inclined to suggest that Kierkegaard has misjudged the situation and misinterpreted its
inward tendencies.

Still, even a society dominated by rationalism is a
sort of society: human relations may be few and empty,
but they continue to exist: there must, consequently, be
some kind of social bond which keeps the herd together.
Kierkegaard, as we have seen, calls a human relation which
has lost its original simplicity and has become emptied
under the impact of rationalisation a tension. "This reflective tension, " he points out, taking his social analysis a
step further, "ultimately constitutes itself into a principle,
and just as in a passionate age enthusiasm is the unifying
principle, so in an age which is very reflective and passionless envy is the negative unifying principle. "[22] In other
words, society continues mainly as an economic entity, for
the sake of the material advantages which it has to offer to
its members: but these members will--not unnaturally--be
supremely watchful that they should each reap as high a
share of these advantages as they possibly can. Thus there
will arise a state of mutual ill-will, or envy as Kierkegaard
terms it, a struggle of all against all, such as we see it
unfolding in the thousand-and-one processes of competition
which have characterized classical capitalism. Here again,
Kierkegaard clearly anticipates a concept which has been
worked out by sociologists later on, and which has cost
them much trouble to develop: the concept of ressentiment
or contravention--that well-known but difficult-to-characterize
state of society in which it is filled by tendencies towards
antagonism and enmity, poisonous tendencies which are all
only too real but which remain latent and to a large extent
disguised.

We see now more clearly why Kierkegaard calls a
relationship that has lost its immediacy and become transformed by reflection, a tension: the term is not ill-chosen
to describe an attitude laden with half-suppressed enmity.
Such states of tension--or of contravention, to use the tech-

nical term--can, of course, develop in any society, a fact
which Kierkegaard fully understood. "Even in the most
enthusiastic ages," he acknowledges, [23] "people have always
like to joke enviously about their superiors." Their ill-will
may at times even have found open expression, as in the
ostracism of a man like Aristides, an act inspired by the
"unhappy love of envy." [24] But such free outbreaks of animosity are not really destructive to the social order: on
the contrary, they are healthy because they clear the air.
(In following these ideas, Kierkegaard is all the time moving
along the paths later travelled by technical sociology.) If,
in a stable society, the lower orders amuse themselves by
joking about the foibles of their betters, "that is perfectly
in order and is entirely justifiable so long as after having
laughed at the great they can once more look upon them
with admiration; otherwise, however, the game is not worth
the candle." [25] The trouble of the modern age--an age, we
must remember, without passion and without action--is that
to-day ressentiment does not find such an open and comparatively harmless and healthy outlet, and that it acts as
a creeping poison in the body social because "it is not
ventilated by action or incident of any kind."

Now, what will happen if a general feeling of ressentiment is not relieved by a violent demonstration of ill-
will towards the eminent, and thereby dissipated and exhausted in action? It will make itself felt as a quiet but
persistent tendency to undermine everything that can be
called distinction: the "unhappy love of envy" expressed
in such an action as the banishment of Aristides will no
longer be followed by the "happy love of admiration": such
changes of attitude are too dramatic for a reflective period:
we shall get instead a grinding attrition which will grind
slowly but surely and exceeding fine. "The ressentiment
which is establishing itself is the process of levelling, and
while a passionate age storms ahead setting up new things
and tearing down old, raising and demolishing as it goes, a
reflective and passionless age does exactly the contrary: it
hinders and stifles all action; it levels. . . . At its most
violent a rebellion is like a volcanic eruption and drowns
every other sound. At its maximum the levelling process
is a deathly silence in which one can hear one's heart beat,
a silence which nothing can pierce, in which everything is
engulfed, powerless to resist. One man can be at the head
of a rebellion, but no one can be at the head of the levelling
process alone, for in that case he would be the leader and
would thus escape being levelled. Each individual within
his own little circle can co-operate in the levelling, but it

130

is an abstract power and the levelling process is the victory
of abstraction over the individual. "[26] Thus out of envy and
contravention arises a powerful drive to abolish the old
distinction of the classes, and indeed every difference between man and man, and we discover and understand one
more of the outstanding features of the modern age, its
demand for social democracy. "The dialectic of the present
age tends towards equality, and its most logical--though
mistaken--fulfillment is levelling, as the negative unity of
the negative reciprocity of all individuals. "[27]

For Kierkegaard democracy--the idea that truth can
be discovered simply by counting heads--is an abominable
stupidity. "Now everyone can have an opinion, " he says
with bitterness. "But they have to band together numerically
in order to have one. Twenty-five signatures make the
most frightful stupidity into an opinion, and the considered
opinion of a first-class mind is only a paradox. "[28] Yet he
realised to the full that nobody and nothing can stop the
march of democracy, not even a counter-movement of
thousands and thousands. "No single individual, " he says,
"will be able to arrest the abstract process of levelling,
for it is negatively something higher, and the age of chivalry
is gone. No society or association can arrest that abstract
power, simply because an association is itself in the service
of the levelling process. Not even the individuality of the
different nationalities can arrest it, for on a higher plane
the abstract process of levelling is a negative representation
of humanity pure and unalloyed. The abstract levelling
process, that self-combustion of the human race . . . is
bound to continue, like a trade wind, and consume everything. "[29] Since these words were written in 1846, much
has happened that has brought them nearer fulfillment: we
cannot but admire the prophetic genius of the man who
wrote them at a time and in a country where the old order
was still standing and the real revolution in social affairs
as yet a long way off.

But Kierkegaard not only realised the future triumph
of democracy: he foresaw quite clearly what the shape and
the life and the expression of the coming mass society
would be, and development has not belied his expectations.
The Present Age anticipates that the power-holders of the
twentieth century would be called the public and the press.
"In order that everything should be reduced to the same
level, " he writes, "it is first of all necessary to procure
a phantom, its spirit, a monstrous abstraction, an all-
embracing something which is nothing, a mirage--and that

phantom is <u>the public.</u> It is only in an age which is without passion, yet reflective, that such a phantom can develop
itself with the help of the press which itself becomes an
abstraction. In times of passion and tumult and enthusiasm,
even when a people desires to realise a fruitless idea and
lay waste and destroy everything: even then there is no
such thing as a public. There are parties and they are
concrete. The press, in times such as those, takes on a
character according to the division of parties. But just as
sedentary professional people are the first to take up any
phantastic illusion which comes their way, so a passionless,
sedentary, reflective age, in which only the press exhibits
a vague sort of life, fosters this phantom. The public is,
in fact, the real levelling-master rather than the actual
leveller, for whenever levelling is only approximately accomplished it is done by something, but the public is a
monstrous nothing. The public is a concept which could
not have occurred in antiquity because the people <u>en masse</u>
<u>in corpore</u> took part in any situation which arose <u>and were</u>
responsible for the action of the individual, and, moreover,
the individual was personally present and had to submit at
once to applause or disapproval for his decision. Only when
the sense of association in society is no longer strong
enough to give life to concrete realities is the press able to
create that abstraction 'the public,' consisting of unreal
individuals who never are and never can be united in an
actual situation or organisation--and yet are held together
as a whole."30

Like democracy, this public appeared to Kierkegaard
as a monstrosity--as "a kind of gigantic something, an
abstract and deserted void which is everything and nothing."31
"The public is a host, more numerous than all the peoples
together, but it is a body which can never be reviewed, it
cannot even be represented, because it is an abstraction.
Nevertheless, when the age is reflective and passionless
and destroys everything concrete, the public becomes everything and is supposed to include everything." "The real
moment in time and the real situation being simultaneous
with real people, each of [them] is something. . . . But
the existence of a public produces neither a situation nor
simultaneity. The individual reader of the press is not
the public, and even though little by little a number of individuals or even all of them should read it, the simultaneity
is lacking. Years might be spent gathering the public together, and still it would not be there. This abstraction,
which the individuals so illogically form, quite rightly re-
pulses the individual instead of coming to his help. The man

132

who has no opinion of an event at the actual moment accepts
the opinion of the majority, or if he is quarrelsome, of the
minority. But it must be remembered that both majority
and minority are real people, and that is why the individual
is assisted by adhering to them. A public, on the contrary,
is an abstraction. To adopt the opinion of this or that man
means that one knows that they will be subjected to the same
dangers as oneself, that they will go astray with one if the
opinion goes astray. But to adopt the same opinion as the
public is a deceptive consolation because the public is only
there in abstracto. "[32] To say, as Kierkegaard does in
these passages, that the public is everybody and nobody at
the same time, is surely more than an idle play with words
and conveys a very definite idea of its essence; in fact, he
could not have better defined it than by saying that it is an
abstract whole which is formed when all participants become
a third party, a party of onlookers. [33] When von Wiese and
Becker, in their Systematic Sociology, speak of the public
as an "abstract crowd"[34] and call it "a mentally formless,
history-less maze--metaphorically speaking, a nebula," they
think in the same terms and move in the same direction as
Kierkegaard long before them.

It is an opinion widely held, and shared even by
quite a few sociologists, that a mass society may be as
well-ordered as a face-to-face society, and that the public
makes, in principle, as good a carrier of the common life
as the more intimate groupings of the past, such as the
clan and the village-community. Kierkegaard ably exposes
the delusionary character of this contention. He shows
convincingly that the sway of the public is detrimental to
the growth of the social virtues, simply because in such an
"abstract crowd" nobody is responsible for anything--even
if all together are responsible for everything. "A generation, a people, an assembly of the people, a meeting or a
man, are responsible for what they are and can be made
ashamed if they are inconstant and unfaithful; but a public
remains a public. A people, an assembly or a man can
change to such an extent that one may say: they are no
longer the same; a public on the other hand can become
the very opposite and still be the same--a public. "[35] "Observe," Kierkegaard points out in another context, "that
there was not one single soldier that dared lay hands upon
Gaius Marius--this was an instance of truth. But given
merely three or four women with the consciousness or the
impression that they were a crowd, and with hope of a sort
in the possibility that no one could say definitely who was
doing it or who began it--then they had courage for it. What

a falsehood! The falsehood . . . is the notion that the
crowd does what in fact only the individual in the crowd
does, though it be every individual. "36 In consequence,
"a crowd--not this crowd or that, the crowd now living or
the crowd long deceased, a crowd of humble people or of
superior people, of rich or of poor, &c. --a crowd in its
very concept37 is the untruth, by reason of the fact that it
renders the individual completely inpenitent and irresponsible,
or at least weakens his sense of responsibility by reducing
it to a fraction. "38 Every mob riot and every lynching bee
is a proof of Kierkegaard's contention. "What I have ascer-
tained, " he says with justice, "is that every man is kindly
when he is alone or when one takes the liberty of talking to
him alone. As soon as men become a 'crowd' they become
odious--oh, never, never anywhere has the worst tyrant
behaved so odiously as does the crowd, or, what is still
more odious, the odiously blameless crowd. "39

Thus a heavy blow is dealt to decency when an
anonymous public comes into existence and becomes all-
powerful. But the demoralisation is still further increased--
and vastly increased--by the influence of the press. A
journalist can hide, and always does hide, behind a wall of
anonymity: he is the irresponsible individual par excellence:
and yet he can pretend, and always does pretend, that he
merely acts as the mouthpiece of public opinion. The press
is at the same time a result and a cause of the demoralisation of society. Kierkegaard calls it a dog which the public
keeps in order to amuse itself. "If there is some one
superior to the rest, perhaps even a great man, the dog
is set on him and the fun begins. The dog goes for him,
snapping and tearing at his coat-tails, allowing itself every
possible ill-mannered familiarity--until the public tires, and
says it may stop. " Yet "the public is unrepentant, for it
is not they who own the dog--they only subscribe. They
neither set the dog on any one, nor whistle it off directly.
If asked they would answer: the dog is not mine, it has no
master. "40 Kierkegaard was soon to experience the truth
of these words which were written in the very days when
the attack on him in the Corsair began. In deep dejection
he calls the press the cause of "the misery of our age"--a
moral misery greater than the greatest material misery of
bygone ages. "The fact that an anonymous author by the
help of the press can day by day find occasion to say (even
about intellectual, moral, and religious matters) whatever
he pleases to say, and what perhaps he would be very far
from having the courage to say as an individual; that every
time he opens his mouth (or shall we say his abysmal gullet?)

he at once is addressing thousands of thousands; that he can get ten thousand times ten thousand to repeat after him what he has said--and with all this nobody has any responsibility . . . nobody, nobody!"41 Can a society such as this where responsibility, the root of all virtues, is cut--can such an anonymous collection of individuals be called good, in any sense of the word, by any stretch of the imagination?

But the levelling process destroys not only public decency, it also undermines personality--even personal intelligence. It makes soulless automata of all. "In our own day," Kierkegaard writes, "anonymity has acquired a far more pregnant significance than is perhaps realised: it has an almost epigrammatic significance. People not only write anonymously, they sign their anonymous works: they even talk anonymously. . . . Nowadays one can talk with any one, and it must be admitted that people's opinions are exceedingly sensible, yet the conversation leaves one with the impression of having talked to an anonymity. The same person will say the most contradictory things and, with the utmost calm, make a remark, which coming from him is a bitter satire on his own life. The remark itself may be sensible enough, and of the kind that sounds well at a meeting, and may serve in a discussion preliminary to coming to a decision, in much the same way that paper is made out of rags. But all these opinions put together do not make one human, personal opinion such as you may hear from quite a simple man who talks about very little but really does talk. People's remarks are so objective, so all-inclusive, that it is a matter of complete indifference who expresses them, and where human speech is concerned that is the same as acting 'on principle.' And so our talk becomes like the public, a pure abstraction. There is no longer anyone who knows how to talk, and instead objective thought produces an atmosphere, an abstract sound which makes human speech superfluous, just as machinery makes man superfluous."42 There is, in a very real sense, a progressive annihilation of man.

There are, of course, as Kierkegaard well knew, some who believe that nothing need be feared on the part of the press because "the truth will always win in the end." But will it? Is it really in its nature more attractive than falsehood? Kierkegaard had not lived, as we have, through a period of propaganda in which lying was raised to the level of a fine art, and yet he saw that any easy optimism in this respect is futile. "O thou who speakest thus," he says to the optimist, "dost thou venture to maintain that men

regarded as a crowd are just as quick to seize upon truth
which is not always palatable as upon falsehood which always
is prepared delicately to give delight?--not to mention the
fact that acceptance of the truth is made the more difficult
by the necessity of admitting that one has been deceived!
Or doest thou venture even to maintain that 'truth' can just
as quickly be understood as falsehood, which requires no
preliminary knowledge, no schooling, no discipline, no
abstinence, no self-denial, no honest concern about oneself,
no patient labor?"[43] It is vain to believe that in this world,
among unregenerate men, the scales are ever even between
good and bad, and doubly vain to expect goodness where
there is no responsibility, as in the public and in the press.

If we now survey Kierkegaard's social theory as it
is set out in the foregoing pages, we see that it rested on
a double hate: hate of rationalism, and hate of "the crowd."
Both these hates had very deep roots in his personal experience. He thought of himself when he said that precocious children--children who are intellectual before their
time--were as characteristic of the modern age as the
children's crusade was typical of the Middle Ages:[44] he
had been a precocious child himself, and an over-early
assumption of the burden of thought had spoilt his life. "I
have possessed no immediacy," he complains, "have therefore, in the ordinary human sense, never lived. I began
straight away with reflection, not as though I had acquired
in later years a little reflection, but I am sheer reflection
from first to last. In the two ages of immediacy (childhood and youth) I was able, with the dexterity spirit always
possesses, to help myself, was compelled to help myself,
with some counterfeit of youthfulness; but without being yet
clear in my own mind what the gift was that was granted
me, I lived through the pain of not being like others."[45]
The hate of the mass went, if possible, still deeper with
him. "It was related to me when I was only a small child,
and with the utmost emphasis," he tells us in one of his
most beautiful passages, "that they spat upon Christ, who
yet was the truth, that the crowd ('they that passed by')
spat upon Him and said, 'Hold thy peace.' This I have
treasured deep in my heart (for though there have been
moments, yea, hours, when that has been for me as if
forgotten, yet have I constantly returned to this my first
thought), and so, the better to treasure this under the most
opposite outward appearance, I have hidden it in the deepest
recesses of my soul; for I was fearful lest it might early
escape me, lest it might trick me and become like a blank
cartridge. This thought . . . is my life, . . . and though

I were to forget everything, yet would I not forget that they told this to me when I was a child, and the impression it made upon the child. "[46]

Passages like these allow us to divine how earnestly Kierkegaard thought, and how deeply he felt, about the problems of society, and how much his social philosophy meant to him, connected as it was with the nethermost layers of his personal existence. Yet if it was personal, it was not for that reason the less levelheaded and realistic. Indeed (as has already been indicated) if anything is surprising about his sociology, it is the fact that it so clearly grasped the salient features of the capitalist order of society which was then slowly establishing itself in the western world. It is true to say that rationalism and levelling are the most characteristic traits of "the present age," the capitalist epoch--rationalism whose triumph can be seen in the progress of science, more particularly physics, the science of sciences of the modern world; and levelling which is still at work, and which has not only brought forth the liberal democracy of Britain and the United States, but also tends to create a mass man and a mass mind in keeping with the mass products of the rationalized industries. There is more than a superficial resemblance between Kierkegaard and Marx, the greatest analyser of the capitalist world. "Capital" proves on every page that capitalism is above all a rational and eternally rationalising system of economy; and it describes the processes by which the manifold status-groups of the past are inexorably being reduced to the common status of proletarianism. Sometimes the two thinkers come so close to each other that they seem to occupy the same point of view. [47] When Kierkegaard says that "finally, money will be the one thing people will desire" and that, moreover, money is only "an abstraction, "[48] he expresses ideas and uses language which could just as well have come from Marx. For Marx, money is in the first place the great rationaliser of life, and the agency which blots out all qualitative differences and reduces everything to a mathematical equality, and it is for this double reason that he regards it as the symbol of modern life, thus revealing a very real kinship to his Danish contemporary.

This spiritual kinship between Kierkegaard and Marx may seem surprising if we think of Marx as a rabid revolutionary and of Kierkegaard as a religious genius. But our surprise is bound to evaporate as soon as we remember that both men faced the same enemy--the French Revolution and its offspring, the capitalist order, in which the love of

137

the common man was as little at home as the love of God.
Kierkegaard may have hated the modern age for a very
different reason than Karl Marx, but he hated the same
age, the age of which "enrichissez-vous, messieurs, " was
the joyfully repeated slogan, a slogan equally repulsive to
the communist and the Christian. But Kierkegaard and
Marx shared even more than this. They were also linked
by a common dependence on, and a common antagonism to,
their master Hegel. Both began as Hegelians and both
broke away from the Hegelian philosophy without ever rid-
ding themselves completely of its influence. Thus nothing
is more natural than that they should have travelled together a good way on the same road.

The common starting point and the ultimate diver-
gence of Kierkegaard and Marx are best seen in a comparison of their theories of development. As true Hegelians,
both used the dialectical triad of thesis, antithesis, and
synthesis, but whereas Marx thinks of the future in economic terms, Kierkegaard is engrossed in religious categories. When Kierkegaard says "that everything creative
is latently polemical, since it has to make room for the
new which it is bringing into the world, "[49] he is as yet
fully in step with the great communist. Perhaps Marx
would even have approved of the following sentences which
outline as it were the scheme of Kierkegaard's idea of the
historical process: "The present age is essentially one of
understanding lacking in passion . . . . By comparison
with a passionate age, an age without passion gains in
scope what it loses in intensity. But this scope may once
again become the condition of a still higher form, if a
corresponding intensity assumes control of the extended
field of activity which is put at its disposal. "[50] What Kierkegaard is saying in this somewhat dry and abstract passage
which is fully understandable only to him who knows the
Hegelian jargon, is this: that if an age of enthusiasm is
followed by a rationalistic and calculating age, this must
not be regarded as pure retrogression; the rationalistic and
calculating generation will have the virtues of its vices; it
will gain knowledge and clarity and thus raise humanity to
a higher level, notwithstanding the fact that it lacks what
is most important of all, namely immediacy; if then, in the
end, a new enthusiasm sweeps over the race, a new state
will be reached which will be finer than the original state,
than the starting point, precisely because the intervening
era of rationalism will have left its mark. As Kierkegaard
himself expresses it: "It must always be remembered that
reflection is not in itself something harmful, that, on the

contrary, it is necessary to work through it in order that one's actions should be more intensive. The stages of all actions which are performed with enthusiasm are as follows: first of all comes immediate enthusiasm, then follows the stage of cleverness which, because immediate enthusiasm does not calculate, assumes with a calculating cleverness the appearance of being the higher; and finally comes the highest and most intensive enthusiasm which follows the stage of cleverness and is therefore able to see the shrewdest plan of action, but will disdain it and thereby receive the intensity of an eternal enthusiasm. "[51] We are here patently still on common ground with the Marxians, whose triad of historical development bears a strong family likeness to Kierkegaard's scheme in that it teaches that the period of class war and general disharmony which lies between the original communism of the clans and the coming communism of world society was a necessary and useful interlude, because without it the latent productive powers of the human race could never have been developed. But this is as far as the agreement goes: from now onward the two paths of thought are seen to diverge, until they end in diametrically opposed conclusions.

For Kierkegaard now throws a religious light on the process which, for Marx, is a purely human affair: he interprets it in Christian terms. "The servants of the levelling process are the servants of the powers of evil," he says, "for levelling itself does not come from divinity and all good men will at times grieve over its desolation, but divinity allows it and desires to bring the highest into relation with the individual, i. e., with each and every man. "[52] The dialectical process is not driving towards a community of goods, but towards communion with God. "When the generation, which itself desired to level and to be emancipated, to destroy authority and at the same time itself, has, through the scepticism of the principle of association, started the hopeless forest fire of abstraction; when as a result of levelling with this scepticism, the generation has rid itself of the individual and of everything organic and concrete, and put in its place 'humanity' and the numerical equality of man and man: when the generation has, for a moment, delighted in this unlimited panorama of abstract infinity, unrelieved by even the smallest eminence, undisturbed by even the slightest interest, a sea of desert; then the time has come for work to begin, for every individual must work for himself, each for himself. No longer can the individual, as in former times, turn to the great for help when he grows confused. That is past; he is either

139

lost in the dizziness of unending abstraction or saved for
ever in the reality of religion . . . For the development
is, in spite of everything, a progress because all the individuals who are saved will receive the specific weight of
religion, its essence at first hand, from God himself. Then
it will be said: 'behold, all is in readiness, see how the
cruelty of abstraction makes the true form of worldliness
only too evident, the abyss of eternity opens before you,
the sharp scythe of the leveller makes it possible for every
one individually to leap over the blade--and behold, it is
God who waits. Leap, then, into the arms of God'. "[53]
The end of the way is not plenty, but redemption; not redemption according to the flesh, but redemption according
to the spirit. Like Marx, Kierkegaard could express a
desire "to help on the levelling process" in the knowledge
that this would bring nearer the moment of destiny. But
the moment of destiny is not the nationalisation of the means
of production: it is the reconciliation of man with the Cre-
ator- and Redeemer-God.

It is an interesting but idle speculation how Kierkegaard would have reacted to Marx's interpretation of social
development: his own forecast is not necessarily at variance
with what has been called historical materialism so far as
description and interpretation of reality are concerned,
though, of course, its political aim and endeavour would
have filled him with horror. He is inclined to admit that
"the principle of association" may be "valid where material
interests are concerned"[54] and that "with respect to all
earthly and material goods . . . it is far more likely that
many, by the strength of united effort, should attain the
goal"[55] than each man fending for himself, however much
it may be true that, on his spiritual pilgrimage, the individual must go alone. The main and decisive difference
between Kierkegaard and Marx consists in the simple fact
that they are concerned with different sectors of existence:
Marx with this nether world, Kierkegaard with the higher.
Perhaps Kierkegaard would not have quarrelled with Marx
at all but simply have insisted that "that which in politics
and in similar fields may be justifiable, wholly or in part,
becomes untruth when it is transferred to the intellectual,
the spiritual, the religious fields. "[56] He is surprisingly
emphatic on this point. He calls it "a thing that goes without saying and which I never have denied, that in relation
to all temporal, earthly, worldly matters the crowd may
have competency, and even decisive competency as a court
of last resort. "But" he goes on to say, "it is not of such
matters I am speaking, nor have I ever concerned myself

140

with such things.   I am speaking about the ethical, about
the ethico-religious, about 'the truth,' and. I am affirming
the untruth of the crowd, ethico-religiously regarded, when
is treated as a criterion for what 'truth' is. "[57]

Still, we must not conclude from passages such as
these that Kierkegaard thought of the higher and the lower
realms as divorced realities which may conceivably follow
divergent routes.   It is true that there is a difference
"since policy begins on earth and remains on earth, whereas
religion, deriving its beginning from above, aims to transcend the earth and thereby exalt earth to heaven. "[58]   But
the great question is, which of the two fields of endeavour
should have the primacy--policy or religion?   It is only
here that the whole contrast between the Christian and the
communist critic of capitalism becomes manifest.   Marx,
pursuing the ancient dream of his race, wanted his para-
dise on earth.   For him, the primacy of politics is a fore-
gone conclusion.   But to Kierkegaard that is a grotesque
conception, a contradiction in terms.   In fact, he saw in
this very idea the curse of the nineteenth century.   "The
misfortune of our time is just this," he says, "that it has
become simply nothing else but 'time,' the temporal, which
is impatient of hearing anything about eternity; and so would
make eternity quite superfluous by means of a cunningly
devised counterfeit, which, however, in all eternity will not
succeed; for the more one thinks oneself to be able, or
hardens oneself to be able, to get along without the eternal,
the more one feels the essential need of it. "[59]   No, in a
higher sense religion and politics must be seen as one, and
as a unity in which the religious element predominates: it
must be recognised, he insists, "that the religious is the
transfigured rendering of that which the politician has thought
of in his happiest moment. "[60]   If the abolition of the class
regime is the grand end of all revolutionary movements,
these movements can only fulfil themselves by means of
the religious.   "No politics ever has, no politics ever can,
no worldliness ever has, no worldliness ever can, think
through or realise to its last consequences the thought of
human equality . . . It is only religion that can with the
help of eternity, carry human equality to the utmost limit--
the godly, the essential, the non-worldly, the true, the
only possible human equality.   And therefore (be it said to
its honor and glory) religion is the true humanity. "[61]

Kierkegaard was firmly convinced that in a materialistic medium equality can never be established: that it can
only be realised among those who have opened their hearts

to the Gospel-spirit. Once more we are amazed to see how
closely he knew and how shrewdly he observed reality. He
understood already in his day that the proletarian movement,
even while it was clamouring for equality, was already developing an upper class of its own, a new elite, which was
by no means in love with the broader masses. He recognised that the soap-box orator of to-day is the commissar
of to-morrow, a new master no better than the old. "What
they call the common people have hardly had many in
Copenhagen who loved them . . . more sincerely than I do, "
he writes in bitterness, "--naturally enough, for I have been
neither a journalist nor an agitator. "62 It is not true that
"none has more contempt for what it is to be a man than
they who make it their profession to lead the crowd"63--
they who see humanity always in hundreds, as an anonymous
mass, and have nobody whom they could justly call a loved
one?

It would not be true to say that Kierkegaard desired
equality as much as Marx did: he desired it in fact much
more fervently. The difference does not lie there. It lies
rather in the fact that Kierkegaard refused to see the individual as a number, a non-entity, and to conceive ideal
society as a collection of non-entities, as a human ant-hill.
Individualism and egalitarianism are in his thought fused
into a higher unity. An ideal society presupposes both:
the stronger the individuals, the firmer also the social
bond. "It is only after the individual has acquired an ethical outlook, in face of the whole world, that there can be
any suggestion of really joining together, " he writes.
"Otherwise the association of individuals who are in themselves weak, is just as disgusting and as harmful as the
marriage of children. "64 According to Kierkegaard, the
antithesis "personality--community"--"individuality--collectiv-
ity" is a thoroughly false one. There is, in truth, no
contrast: as a man elevates his very own soul, he develops
at the same time his social self. And Kierkegaard empha-
sises on every possible occasion that every human being,
however low-born, however poor in spirit, has it in him
"to acquire an ethical outlook, " to become an individual in
the highest sense of the word. Many passages illustrate
this conviction which is as firmly established in Kierkegaard's mind, and as fundamental to it, as the opposite
conviction that the "crowd" is the "untruth. " "Any man
who finds himself, religiously speaking, " we read in The
Present Age, "has only achieved what every one can
achieve. "65 Or again, in The Point of View for My Work
as an Author: "Eternity which arches over and high above

142

the temporal, tranquil as the starry vault at night, and God
in heaven who in the bliss of that sublime tranquility holds
in survey, without the least sense of dizziness at such a
height, these countless multitudes of men and knows each
single individual by name--He, the great Examiner, says
that only one attains the goal." Yet "that means, every
one can and every one should be this one."[66]

Throughout this discussion, Kierkegaard makes a
silent distinction between equality according to the spirit,
and equality according to the flesh. In the materialistic
sense absolute equality is no more than a chimera because
in this world men are born with differing needs and endowments; but in the religious sense it is an undeniable fact,
for all are one before the throne of Almighty God. "From
[religiously] becoming an individual no one, no one at all,
is excluded, except he who excludes himself by becoming a
crowd. To become a crowd, to collect a crowd about one,
is on the contrary to affirm the distinctions of human life."[67]
This duality of meaning in the word "equality" is fully ex-
emplified in Kierkegaard's own literary work, and he draws
our attention to this point, so supremely characteristic of
the difference between a worldly and a godly approach to
the problem of ideal society. "In every one of [my] pseudonymous works this theme of 'the individual' comes to evidence in one way or another; but there the individual is
predominantly the pre-eminent individual in the æsthetic
sense, the distinguished person, &c. In every one of my
edifying works the theme of 'the individual' comes to evidence, and as officially as possible; but there the individual
is what every man is or can be. The starting-point of the
pseudonyms is the difference between man and man with
respect to intellect, culture, &c.; the starting-point of the
edifying works is the edifying thought of the universal human.
But this double meaning is precisely the dialectic of 'the
single individual.' 'The single individual' can mean the one
and only, and 'the single individual' can mean every man."[68]
Kierkegaard, a great lover like his Divine Master, always
meant "every man." "Thou plain man!" he writes, a few
days before his end, in The Instant, in the very last number which was ever to be written, "The Christianity of the
New Testament is something endlessly high, but note that it
is not high in such a sense that it has to do with the difference between man and man with respect to intellectual
capacity, &c. . . . No, it is for all. Every one, unconditionally every one, if he unconditionally wills it, if he
will unconditionally hate himself, will unconditionally put
up with everything, suffer everything (and this every man

can if he will)--then is this endless height attainable to
him . . . Thou plain man! I do not hide from thee that,
according to my notion, the thing of being a Christian is
endlessly high, that at no time are there more than a few
that attain it--as Christ's own life attests when one considers the age in which He lived, and also His preaching
indicates if one takes it literally. Yet nevertheless it is
possible for all. "69

It is hardly unfair, in view of these pathetic words,
to say that the difference between the egalitarian ideal of
Marx and the egalitarian ideal of Kierkegaard is the difference between a levelling down and a levelling up. That,
anyway, is how he himself understood the difference. Destruction of distinction in the purely secular sense is to
him "the levelling process at its lowest, for it always
equates itself to the divisor by means of which every one
is reduced to a common denominator. Eternal life is also
a sort of levelling, and yet that is not so, because the
unity is that every one should really and essentially be a
man in a religious sense. "70 Now, how can that unity be
achieved, that egalitarianism which is the very "idea of
religion?"71 It is in the answer to this salient question
that the discrepancy between the two thinkers reaches its
maximum and becomes an unbridgeable gulf. For Marx it
was a matter of course that ideal society was a problem of
economics, and that it could be secured by a re-distribution
of wealth. For Kierkegaard it is an axiom that nothing--
absolutely nothing--can be achieved by economic methods
and means. Indeed, according to Kierkegaard, "the equali-
tarian order" conceived in the spirit of religion cannot even
be materially attractive: he says that it is bound to be
"severe and the profit seemingly very small. " And why?
Because it implies duties rather than rights, abnegation
rather than indulgence. The individual will have to learn
"in the reality of religion and before God to be content with
himself, and . . . instead of dominating others, to dominate himself"; he will have to be satisfied "with that as the
highest, because it is the expression of the equality of all
men before God. "72 Clearly, Kierkegaard was willing to
make the greatest sacrifices at the altar of equality, while
Marx expected to get it for nothing, and unlimited plenty
into the bargain. It is not very difficult to see who was
the dreamer and who the realist in this matter. People
will never be ready to share and share alike until they
have vanquished, in the depth of their hearts, that urge
towards self-preference which is the very hallmark of un-
regenerated man.

Yes, Kierkegaard was in the last analysis much more of a realist than Karl Marx. Marx believed that human selfishness was not an eternal trait of human nature, but just a passing feature, born of the institution of private property and bound to fade away with it. He had not fathomed the abysmal depths of the human soul and seen the eternal necessity of a saviour from beyond: he laboured under the "illusion of temporal existence that we are a lot of us, pretty much the whole of humanity, which in the end can . . . be itself the Christ."[73] Kierkegaard, on the other hand, faced the fundamental fact of our fallen state, namely that we can only advance towards the good, alike as individuals and in society, if we overcome ourselves and follow the Cross. "Complete human equality would be attained, in case every one were in truth to love his neighbour as himself."[74] That, Kierkegaard says, is simple enough, but we have got to understand that to love our neighbor is to deny ourselves, and self-denial is the bitter chalice of which we all desire that it should pass. Indeed, the divine love, out of which alone a truly good society can grow as a flower grows from its mother soil, the love which Saint Paul, in the Epistle to the Colossians, calls the bond of perfection, implies sacrifice and suffering, and that is the greatest lesson of the Christian faith, the essential message of Mount Calvary.

Notes

1. Walter Lowrie, Kierkegaard, 1938. p. 162.

2. The Present Age, Engl. transl. 1940, p. 126 seq.

3. Ibid., p. 127.

4. The Present Age, pp. 131, 135.

5. Ibid., p. 128.

6. Ibid., p. 88.

7. Lowrie, p. 293.

8. The Present Age, p. 3.

9. The Present Age, pp. 8 seq., 60.

10. Ibid., pp. 60 seq.

11. Lowrie, p. 163.

12. Ibid., p. 377.

13. The Point of View, &c., Engl. transl., 1939, p. 132.

14. The Present Age, p. 15.

15. Ibid., p. 18.

16. The Present Age, pp. 17 seq.

17. Ibid., p. 19.

18. Ibid., p. 20.

19. The Present Age, pp. 20 seq.

20. Ibid., p. 43.

21. The Point of View, p. 136.

22. The Present Age, p. 21.

23. The Present Age, p. 24.

24. Ibid., p. 26.

25. Ibid., p. 24.

26. The Present Age, p. 27.

27. Ibid., p. 28.

28. Ibid., p. 62.

29. The Present Age, p. 32.

30. The Present Age, pp. 37 seq.

31. Ibid., p. 41.

32. Ibid., pp. 38 seq.

33. The Present Age, pp. 43 seq.

34. Loc. cit., p. 477.

35. The Present Age, p. 40.

36. The Point of View, pp. 114 seq.

37. Kierkegaard appended a footnote to this statement which
    he would, no doubt, have wished to see reproduced
    wherever this passage is quoted. It is necessary in
    order to forestall a misunderstanding which is apt to
    arise because the word "the crowd" is ambiguous
    and may by some be taken to mean "the lower
    classes," "the proletariat." That is not Kierke-
    gaard's meaning. He bids the reader to "remember
    that here the word 'crowd' is understood in a purely
    formal sense, not in the sense one commonly attaches
    to 'the crowd' when it is meant as an invidious quali-
    fication, the distinction which human selfishness ir-
    religiously erects between 'the crowd' and superior
    persons, &c. . . . 'Crowd' stands for number, the
    numerical of noblemen, millionaires, high dignitaries,
    &c. --as soon as the numerical is involved, it is
    'crowd,' 'the crowd'."

38. The Point of View, pp. 114 seq.

39. The Present Age, p. 115.

40. Ibid., pp. 45 seq.

41. The Point of View, p. 118.

42. The Present Age, pp. 58 seq.

43. The Point of View, p. 119.

44. The Present Age, p. 3.

45. Lowrie, p. 49.

46. Lowrie, p. 42.

47. Cf. what Berdyaev says about this fact in his book
    The Russian Idea, p. 94 et seq., where the Marxian
    doctrine of the fetishism of goods is rightly inter-
    preted as "an existential sociology." Cf. also
    Solitude and Society by the same writer.

48. The Present Age, pp. 12 seq.

49. The Present Age, p. 56.

50. The Present Age, p. 48.

51. Ibid., pp. 67 seq.

52. The Present Age, p. 66.

53. Ibid., pp. 64 seq.

54. The Present Age, p. 61.

55. The Point of View, p. 113.

56. Ibid., p. 117.

57. Ibid., p. 112.

58. Ibid., p. 109.

59. The Point of View, p. 110.

60. Ibid., p. 109.

61. Ibid., pp. 109 seq.

62. Ibid., p. 130.

63. The Point of View, p. 115.

64. The Present Age, p. 62.

65. Ibid., p. 41.

66. The Point of View, pp. 113 seq.

67. The Point of View, p. 121.

68. Ibid., p. 126.

69. Lowrie, pp. 581 seq.

70. The Present Age, p. 47.

71. Ibid., p. 34.

72. Ibid., p. 35.

73. The Point of View, p. 137.

74. Ibid., p. 120.

The Anthropology
of Søren Kierkegaard

William A. Johnson

First published in The Hartford Quarterly, IV (Summer 1964), 43-52, the article is here reprinted with the kind permission of the Publications Committee of the Hartford Seminary Foundation and of the author, who is at present Visiting Professor of Religion, Princeton University.

Søren Kierkegaard attempted in his lifetime to "re-introduce Christianity into Christendom." At the same time, however, he found it necessary to introduce Christianity to the thought-world of his time. In the development of a rapprochement between the Christian faith and the world, Kierkegaard developed an anthropology. The basic components of this anthropology are:

I

"Spirit" and "Self" expressive of God's will in creation:

It is important to recognize at the outset that Kierkegaard used the same terminology as that of the anthropological position he so intensely fought against. When he defined man as the unity of "Spirit" and "Self,"[1] he was using these terms as they were used in German Idealism. [2] Kierkegaard's definition of man began with a conception of the "Self," which he equated with individual self-consciousness. He critized, however, a conception of the Self which did not give a content to the Self. In his dissertation, The Concept of Irony, he criticizes Kant's "Ding an sich" because it was an "empty" category.

The concept of "choice" is of major significance for Kierkegaard's anthropology. Assessor Wilhelm in Either-Or[3] asserts that the major objective of man's life is to gain something for himself. Man is faced with an "either-or" situation--he must choose what is to be the objective

151

for his life.[4]   However, as Kierkegaard shows, the choice
is not between good and evil, but between the aesthetic and
the ethical "modes" (or "stages") of life.   Man's native
abilities are proximate to his existence, Kierkegaard maintained.   If man permits that which is proximate to comprise
the whole meaning of his life, then man is living aestheti-
cally.   If, on the other hand, man seeks to find meaning in
his life on the basis of a decision, a projection into the
future, then he is living ethically.   "To choose," therefore,
is necessarily related to the ethical stage of life.[5]   "To
choose," insists Assessor Wilhelm, means that man consciously chooses himself in relation to his "eternal validity."[6]

However, when one chooses oneself, the result may
be despair.[7]   Despair is the realization that man has based
his life upon transitory values.   Man must "choose himself" as he is in reality, but must do so with the awful
possibility that his life does not have a relationship to
eternal validity.[8]   The man who has not chosen to live
decisively is filled with despair, whether he realizes it or
not.   The aesthetic way of life is constructed upon transitory features of existence, and therefore has no relationship to eternal validity.

The Self which man chooses is not an abstraction
from reality, but is always a concrete Self.[9]   The Self
that exists in the aesthetic stage is the finite Self, the
Self that lacks eternal validity.   The Self which man chooses
in the ethical stage is the Absolute Self, the Self in relation to its "eternal validity."   When man is conscious of
his eternal relationship, he assumes responsibility for himself.   Man, however, can only "choose himself" in his
eternal validity when he chooses himself as guilty.[10]   Repentance and remorse are the forms by which man expresses this guilty state.   Man chooses himself concretely
as "this specific individual," with definite abilities, dis-
positions, which is influenced by a particular environment.
There remains at all times tension between man as he is
in himself and his present state in life.   Kierkegaard speaks
of this tension as the "encounter" with the Absolute.   The
form of this encounter is a judgment and a demand upon
the individual.   Man's present life is filled with despair
because he has constructed it upon something transitory.
Man can never avoid the act of repentance.   He must choose
himself in his specific "existential" situation.

In Concluding Unscientific Postscript, Kierkegaard
introduced the concept of divine assistance which enables

man to live the ethical life. [11]   To choose oneself is not to
create a new Self; rather, it means the relating of oneself
to the active will of God.   The choice of the Self "in despair" means to repent and to love God anew.   To love God
is only possible, says Kierkegaard, because God has first
loved us. [12]   The choice, therefore, becomes a re-birth
and an absolute abandonment of the Self.   The Self is transformed, and is now related to God. [13]

        Kierkegaard equates man's eternal validity with the
immortality of the soul.   Man's ethical consciousness leads
directly to the consciousness of his eternal being.   The
concept of the immortality of the soul, as it is employed
by Kierkegaard, refers to the eternal validity to which man
is bound forever.   Through the choice, man becomes conscious of the demand eternally upon.   Johannes Climacus
can speak, therefore, of the impossibility of a metaphysical
interpretation of immortality.   The ethical demand receives
its eternal validity first through the concept of immortality. [14]

        The Absolute Self cannot be conceived of in terms of
the highest values which are common to mankind.   Man can
never attain the Absolute Self by reference to the exemplary
"normal" human.   Neither is the Absolute Self to be thought
of in terms of "duty to a multitude of moral propositions." [15]
The Absolute Self is rather the Self that is part of God's
will in creation.   The Self becomes Absolute when the
Absolute (God) chooses to love man.   Man is, however, at
all times, responsible to the historical context of his life,
and must make his choice while immersed in concrete
reality.   The mystic, on the other hand, says Kierkegaard,
chooses himself, but does so not in relation to the world. [16]
The mystic relates himself to the eternal, but without a
concomitant "concrete" relationship to his historical situation.   His life, says Assessor Wilhelm, is a "deception";
he has not chosen himself ethically.   His despair is illusory
because point of contact with reality is superseded by his
unity with the eternal. [17]

        Man's Absolute Self has been created by God.   God
gives man individuality in his creation.   Every man has a
particular task to perform in creation. [18]   The fulfillment
of this task, therefore, is an expression of God's will in
creation.   The meaning man receives from the fulfillment
of his task is derived from the relationship which exists
between God and man.   Man must constantly be reminded
that this relationship is the primary relationship--all other
relationships are relative to the specific historical situation

in which man finds himself. Man, who very readily forgets this fact, is reminded of the relativeness of his situation by the despair which he experiences. This enables man to recognize again that he stands before God in an eternal relationship.

Assessor Wilhelm uses the term "Spirit" interchangeably with "Self."[19] Man's spiritual nature distinguishes him from all that is in creation which cannot live in relationship with God. Man's Spirit is defined also in terms of the "Infinite Self," which is also related to God's will in creation. The Infinite Spirit "realizes" God's will in the finite world. The finite world is not the evil world, but is the earthly sphere upon which the infinite makes itself "concrete."[20] Man's Absolute Spirit must be concerned with the historical situation in which he finds himself. Man must be responsible to this situation. Man's finite existence can never be absolutized, however, for his whole life must be placed in relation to God's will in creation. Man worships the Creator, never the created.[21]

The difference between good and evil, right and wrong, appears to man first in the "choice." First, man is ethically responsible, then he is able to discern the difference between good and evil. The choice is always a singular one, however. The choice is the choice of the Absolute Self. When man chooses himself, he also chooses the good.[22] The good is defined by Kierkegaard in a similar way to the Eternal Self. When man is conscious of himself in relation to his Creator, then he receives insight into the nature of the good, and consequently, into what is evil. The "good" Kierkegaard defines as that which is identical with God's will in creation; "evil" is that which stands in opposition to God's will in creation.

When man chooses himself absolutely or in the absolute relationship, he also chooses freedom. "Freedom" is defined by Kierkegaard as man's awareness of the responsibility he has for himself. Man is free when he relates himself responsibly to that in life which possesses absolute validity. Freedom, as such, is identified with the Absolute Self, and subsequently with God's will in creation.

II

"Spirit" and "Self" as bearers of the human synthesis.

"Spirit" and "Self" function in Kierkegaard's anthro-

154

pology as the "bearers of the human synthesis." In The Concept of Dread,[23] man is described as a "synthesis of soul and body, which is united by the spirit." However, body, soul and spirit are not three different levels or strata of the nature of man. Body and soul make up the human, that is, they "form the human synthesis." The human synthesis is thereby maintained by the spirit. Through the spirit man is "related to himself and to the conditions of his existence," as well as to the Infinite Spirit and the Creator. Man is therefore conceived of unity; the total man stands in relationship to God.

Man is also defined (in The Sickness unto Death[24]) as the synthesis of the finite and the infinite, the temporal and the eternal. Kierkegaard was extremely critical of Hegel's conception of time in terms of the past-present-future continuum. Time, as Hegel's infinite progression, offers for Kierkegaard no fixed point for the relationship of past to future. Only the eternal can provide this point of contact between past and future. The eternal is defined by Kierkegaard as the present filled with the infinite.[25] The eternal is also defined by Kierkegaard in terms of God's relationship to man in creation. He can also speak of the eternal as righteousness; as that which distinguishes right from wrong. As such, the eternal has relevancy to the ethical task.[26]

For Kierkegaard, the present is always defined in terms of specific ethical categories, and these terms are designated as being related to the will of God in creation. God's will is raised above all of the changes of time and belongs to a perfection that has no past or future. The relationship between eternity and time is realized in "the moment."[27] The moment, however, is located in time, not above it; it is not "an atomistic abstraction," nor is it to be identified with pure being. The moment is "filled with destiny" and, as such, is the point of contact between time and eternity. Christianity, said Kierkegaard, recognizes the eternal in the moment, but also recognizes the present and the past. The "fulfillment of time" is the central category for Christianity. This is the presence of eternity in time. The "fulfillment of time" also includes the presence of eternity in the past and in the future.[28]

Man as "Spirit" stands in relationship to the Absolute or Eternal Spirit. Man, therefore, as a temporal being, is related directly to the eternal, as the eternal is related to time. Man lives in a temporal continuum which

is characterized by the "eternity-filled" moment. Man also
has a history. The moment is decisive for man's history.
In the moment man is placed before the eternal. The
moment is a moment of decision. Man cannot eradicate
the demands of the moment any more than he can the record of his past. [29]

Man, as an existing being, is confronted by the
eternal in his specific historical situation. Eros is characteristic of existence. [30] Man is never Being, but is
always becoming. Man's life is characterized by a cease-
less struggle for development and expression. Life is
always a struggle for existence. Infinity and eternity are
never fully possessed by man. Man "struggles" to grasp
and express them in his life. [31]

Through the Self, man is related to God. Despair,
which is the "sickness unto death," appears in the relationship to God when the relationship is out of order. Despair
is always found in man totally; that is, man as the synthesis of mind, soul, and spirit. If man were independent
of the relationship to God, despair would be only a formal
category--man simply would not be himself. [32] However,
a man who experiences despair can also will himself. For
this reason, it is apparent, said Kierkegaard, that man
must be dependent upon the Creator for his existence.
Despair indicates that man creates a god of himself at the
same time that he negates God and his creation. Another
form of despair may be evidenced, that is, when man wills
not to be himself. This is also expressive of man's attempt
to flee from the will of God. [33]

Man must choose to be himself. However, man as
the synthesis of the finite and the infinite must be involved
in his historical situation. The finite in the synthesis is
the delimiting factor in man's existence. The infinite is
the expansive. [34] Only when both of these factors are related correctly does man "choose himself." When there is
a disparity between the finite and the infinite within man,
the result is despair. Despair means that man lacks either
the finite or the infinite characteristic of his existence, or
it means that they are maintained in a disproportionate way
within man. In finite despair, man has lost the sense of
the origin and meaning of his life. He has become anonymous. In infinite despair, man's emotions, reason and
will are "fantasy"-filled. [35]

Spiritlessness

Man can never search for God, said Kierkegaard,
because God always remains hidden. It is rather God who
seeks man. Man cannot ever break away from his relationship to God. God unremittingly attempts to make
himself known in man's life. Whether man is conscious of
it or not, he is a created being and, as such, is bound to
his Creator. The relationship between God and man expresses itself most clearly in Kierkegaard's conception of
man as Spirit and Self. The question is posed by Kierkegaard whether man can be defined as Spirit and Self before
the choice; that is, before man is <u>conscious</u> of his eternal
validity.

According to Kierkegaard's anthropological principles,
man at all times must be described in terms of Spirit and
Self. Kierkegaard uses the figure of Nero as an example. [36]
He describes Nero's refusal to be decisive and pictures the
Spirit within him as a "dark cloud"; "his wrath broods over
his soul. " This, for Kierkegaard, is Nero's despair.
Nevertheless, he is defined in terms of Spirit, even though
he had <u>not</u> chosen himself, nor was conscious of himself,
nor wished to understand what is the meaning of his despair.

In another reference, Kierkegaard speaks of the
heathen (both within Christianity and outside of it!), who is
<u>spiritless</u>. The experience of dread makes the heathen
<u>conscious</u> of his relationship to Spirit. [37] The moment man
discovers this relationship, he feels his guilt.

The aesthetic man will not recognize the God-relationship because he has embraced the transitory and the immediate and magnified these to a position of absoluteness. He
is, therefore, not conscious of himself in his eternal validity,
as Spirit, although in reality, he exists in this relationship. [38]

IV

Man created in the image of God-conscience and "the Individual. "

Man, said Kierkegaard, has been created in the
image of God. Man, as Spirit and Self, stands inextricably
in relation to the will of God. As Spirit and Self, he is

distinguished from every other creature in creation. Furthermore, man, because he is _free_, is able to respond to God. He can acknowledge in every moment of his life his dependence upon God, the Creator. [39] Man, however, who does not acknowledge his dependence upon God remains the "natural" man. Man has the responsibility to make the will of God in creation a reality in his life. However, between created man and Creator God there is a distinction regardless of the level of man's God-likeness. An "infinite qualitative distinction" remains between God and man at all times. [40]

It is only the man of faith, said Kierkegaard, who expresses God's creation in his life, and who acknowledges everything as a gift from God. [41] The "natural man" is separated from infinite spirit because of his guilt. Guilt effects a radical disharmony between himself and his Creator. From man's standpoint, an insurmountable chasm is built up which separates man from God. Only Christ can "bridge up the gap" between God and man. However, even after sin is forgiven, the qualitative difference between God and man remains, [42] God is Creator and man the created.

Man is related inextricably to the will of God. This relationship is revealed to man through his conscience. Conscience is characteristic of man as personality. [43] Man thereby recognizes his dependence upon his Creator. [44] Conscience makes God contemporaneous, and by so doing defines the limits of man's existence.

"The Individual" is a term used by Kierkegaard which means Spirit, Self and Conscience. Man's recognition of his individuality is identical to the recognition of his relationship to God. "The Individual" is therefore the category which most clearly defines the nature of Christianity.

Man's relationship to God is intimately tied up with his immortality. Immortality can never be demonstrated, said Kierkegaard, for this would destroy the God-man relationship. Man must remain distant and distinct from God. Man's position in relationship to God must be one of humility and penitence. [45] Man's knowledge of God, furthermore, is always _negative;_ God remains the "unknowable" God. [46]

Kierkegaard criticized Idealistic philosophy because it did not attribute any content to the Self. Over against the speculative "pure" selfconsciousness, Kierkegaard advo-

cated the Socratic "Know thyself." The Self is related to
God. By means of the "choice," the "leap of faith," man
recognizes himself as a concrete individual, responsible to
God's will in creation. Man's relationship to God does not
exclude his relationship to society. Man must be responsible
to himself, but at the same time, he is responsible to his
neighbor. Only then is it possible for man "to find himself in God."[47]

Notes

1. Hermann Diem, Philosophie und Christentum bei Soren
   Kierkegaard (Forschungen zur Geschichte und Lehre
   des Protestantismus). Zweite Reihe. Band 1.
   Munchen 1929, p. 10.

2. Cf. Soren Kierkegaard, Samlede Vaerker, udgivne af
   A. B. Drachmann, (Kobenhavn, J. L. Heiberg og
   H. O. Lange, 1920-1936), Bind I-XV. Anden Udgave.
   XIII, p. 372ff.

3. II, p. 193.

4. II, p. 182ff.

5. II, p. 182.

6. II, p. 192.

7. II, p. 223, 230.

8. II, p. 226.

9. II, p. 233.

10. Ibid.

11. Cf. Diem, op. cit., p. 32, 37; T. Bohlin, Soren
    Kierkegaard's etiska åskådning (Stockholm, Diss.,
    1918); Fr. Petersen, Soren Kierkegaard's Christen-
    domsforkyndelse, (Christiania, 1877).

12. Samlede Vaerker, II, p. 233ff.

13. II, pp. 233, 238, 241.

14. II, p. 292.

15. II, p. 274ff.

16. II, p. 279; cf. also Emanuel Hirsch, Kierkegaard-Studien I-II, (Gütersloh, 1933), p. 623, "Das Gott der Schöpfer ist, der mich setzt, und der Heilige vor dem ich mich als schüldig weiss, sobald ich mich zu ihm verhalte, wird mit dem Grundakte der ethischen Lebensanschauung eine den Menschen innerlich bestimmende wahrheit, und alle ethische Sinnhaftigkeit des Lebens quillt aus dieser wahrheit. "

17. Samlede Vaerker, II, pp. 260-270.

18. II, p. 318.

19. II, p. 204.

20. II, p. 270.

21. II, p. 236.

22. II, p. 236.

23. IV, p. 391.

24. XI, p. 167 etc.

25. Cf. T. Bohlin, Kierkegaards dogmatiska åskådning (Stockholm, 1925), p. 113ff.

26. Samlede Vaerker, VII, p. 332ff.

27. IV, p. 348.

28. IV, p. 395. Cf. Martin Heidegger, Sein und Zeit (Jahrbuch für Philosophie und phänomenologische Forschung. 8. Halle, a. d. s. , 1927), p. 338, where Heidegger reprimands Kierkegaard for what he calls "a vulgar interpretation of time. " Heidegger is criticized for this generally; cf. Annemarie Vogt, Das Problem des Selbstbewusstseins bei Heidegger und Kierkegaard (Giessen, Diss. , 1936), p. 18ff.

29. Samlede Vaerker, IV, p. 393.

30. Cf. VII, p. 71ff. , p. 76ff.

31. VII, p. 70.

160

32. XI, p. 143.

33. XI, p. 146ff.; cf. VIII, B p. 168, 5.

34. XI, p. 161.

35. XI, p. 161ff.

36. II, p. 179.

37. VII, p. 544, cf. also II, p. 196.

38. Cf. Elisabeth Niessen, Der anthropologische Geist-
    begriff bie Soren Kierkegaard (Philosophisches
    Jahrbuch der Goresgesellschaft 52; Fulda, 1939),
    p. 64.

39. Samlede Vaerker, cf. XI, p. 152.

40. V, p. 190.

41. XI, p. 289, cf. X, p. 85.

42. XI, p. 289, cf. X, p. 85.

43. VII, A p. 10.

44. IX, p. 166.

45. XI, p. 259.

46. XIII, p. 279.

47. II, p. 233, cf. II, p. 278ff.

The Demonic in Mozart

Geoffrey Clive

First published in Music and Letters, XXXVII (January 1956), 1-13, the article is here reprinted with the kind permission of its editor and of the author, who is at present Chairman of the Department of Philosophy, University of Massachusetts-Boston.

I

In an extensive footnote to his Dogmatik Karl Barth pays this tribute to the genius of Mozart:

> Why and in what sense can this man be called
> unique? Why has he, for him who can under-
> stand him, almost with every measure which
> passed through his mind and which he wrote down
> on paper, created music for which "beautiful" is
> an inadequate expression; music which for the
> "just" is not entertainment, nor pleasure, nor
> edification, but flesh and blood; music full of
> consolation and admonition, as they need it,
> never reduced to mere technique and never senti-
> mental, but music "moving," free, and liberating,
> because wise, virile, and sovereign? Why can
> one maintain that he has a place in theology
> (especially in eschatology and cosmology) although
> he was no church father and not even a particu-
> larly devout Christian--and beyond that Catholic!--
> and, when not busy composing, according to our
> notions leading a somewhat fickle life . . . He
> has heard the harmony of creation as providence
> in coherent form of which darkness is also a
> part, but in which darkness is no eclipse, also
> the deficiency which is no flaw, the sadness which
> cannot lead to despair, also the gloomy which is
> not transformed into the tragic, the infinite sorrow
> which nevertheless remains unconstrained to posit

162

itself absolutely--precisely therefore also joyous-
ness, but also its limits, the light which is so
radiant precisely because it breaks through the
shadows, sweetness which is also pungent and
therefore does not carry satiety in its wake, life
which is not afraid of death but knows it well
. . . In the music of Mozart--I ask whether one
also finds this in any of his successors?!--we
are dealing with an illuminating, I should like to
say with a compelling proof that it is a slander
of creation to ascribe participation in chaos to
her because she includes a YES and a NO within
herself, because one side of her is turned toward
NOTHINGNESS and the other toward GOD.   Mozart
makes audible that the creation praises the Lord
also in its negative aspect and thus in its totality
. . .[1]

Undoubtedly the father of modern dialectical theology
would have taken his most prominent disciple in the twentieth century to task for connecting the unintelligible holiness
and omnipotence of God in a partially evil world with Mozart's
peculiar affection for the demonic mode of providence--that
is to say, the mode in which God speaks to us through
seeming self-travesty or denial.   Søren Kierkegaard, who
discusses Mozart's music in the context of the "aesthetic
stage on life's way," took a singularly profound but negative
view of it[2] inasmuch as he sought to become worthy of
serving God rather than beauty, his first love.   This paper
attempts to clarify Kierkegaard's criticism of Mozart and
especially the demonic element so characteristic of his
compositions.

The central theme in Don Giovanni is the inter-
mingling of freedom and dread.   Don Juan glides through
the world like a god radiating irresistible charm and suffused with seemingly inexhaustible energy.   His main objective in life is the seduction of desirable women, but he
pursues it with such devotion and uninhibited feeling that
self-indulgence appears invested with beauty.   Demonic
about Don Juan is his unwillingness to sleep or rest, his
indefatigable loyalty to the sensual principle.   God created
man in His own image.   This means that even though creatures we are to some extent endowed with divine energy.
Don Juan has chosen to utilize this precious gift for the
fulfilment of his sensual pride rather than for the perfection of his nature.   In this connection it must be noted that
unlike his subsequent heirs he is not an especially calcula-

ting or despairing lover. He does not dream of the un-
attainable and then discard on having found it. Nor does
he show any particular interest in experimenting with women
in order to gain greater self-knowledge. Nor, as far as
the libretto of the opera is concerned, is he a crass pragmatist solely motivated by the recurring taste of success.
There is an ironic contrast between his 1003 conquests in
Spain alone and the absence of a single triumph in the
whole course of events Mozart set to music. Mozart's
hero-villain is still somewhat of a preface to the age of
frustration and aberration he helped to make famous. [3] All
he desires is the immediacy of satisfaction heightened by a
fast turnover. His single-minded application to the preser-
vation and regeneration of a single value could under other
circumstances easily be mistaken for religious martyrdom.
If we could think of God as consistently and patiently as
Don Juan thinks of womanhood many of us would indeed be
saved. Giovanni is a fine illustration of Reinhold Niebuhr's
seminal theological insight: man is free to destroy his own
freedom. This possibility, I feel, points to the threat of
the demonic in human existence.

But man is also in dread. By what stroke of genius
does Mozart towards the end of the catalogue aria introduce
the bassoons with a sharply rhythmic, unexpectedly brood-
ing and ominous phrase to remind us that all is not purely
laughable even in a comic situation. At this point in the
opera the accented bass figuration is but a shadow of darkness briefly beclouding the prominent light into which Leporello casts his master. With the progress of the action
it assumes spiritual significance. Leporello relishes the
master-slave relationship thrust upon him. For survival
he is at the mercy of Don Juan's pleasure, but he prefers
this state of affairs to any alternative position in life requiring a greater degree of responsibility. In spite of his
intermittent threats to break with his master, he bathes
contentedly in the dazzling sunshine of Juan's glory until
and unless danger to his life becomes imminent. He pre-
tends to be entirely in on Juan's career though it is clear
from the start that he lacks not only his master's animal
magnetism but his faith and recklessness as well. Again
and again where Don Juan is prepared for decisive action
Leporello pines to cower in a corner hoping against hope
that the association which enables him to shine will not be
held against him once its radiance is eclipsed. Whereas
Don Juan successfully reduplicates intention in action, however frustrating its consequences may turn out to be, Leporello can only be himself as an annex attached to the main

building.

His dread, of course, is patently human and therefore intelligible. Like most of us he finds evil more enticing than good, especially when another is held to account for so ingeniously manipulating it. But he has a conscience which troubles him at times and a fear of physical annihilation which throttles any total involvement in the irregular, however scintillating to the curiosity. Whereas Juan represents the sensual superman aloof from freedom's attendant restraints, Leporello is his dialectical opposite, a willing slave to convention trembling to preserve his necessary bondage. In The Sickness Unto Death Kierkegaard contrasts these two types of despair: the despair of infinitude as being due to the lack of finitude and the despair of finitude as being due to the lack of infinitude. [4] Don Juan's will is "fantastic," "limitless," virtually unrelated to his general humanity. He is capable of creating hell on earth because the world means nothing to him beyond being a source of unending pleasure. The fanaticism of a religious mystic who professes to despise mere finitude in order to please God has a good deal in common with this non-morality, which respects no personal obligations, immunizes itself to vicarious suffering and acts according to the maxim that concrete particulars matter little. "Generally the fantastical," writes Kierkegaard, "is that which so carries a man out into the infinite that it merely carries him away from himself and therewith prevents him from returning to himself." Leporello, on the other hand, is unaware of his true condition:

> While one sort of despair plunges wildly into the infinite and loses itself, a second sort permits itself as it were to be defrauded by "the other." By seeing the multitude of men about it, by getting engrossed in all sorts of worldly affairs, by becoming naïve about how things go in this world, such a man forgets himself, . . . does not dare to believe in himself, finds it too venturesome a thing to be himself, far easier and safer to be like others, to become an imitation, a number, a cipher in the crowd . . . . What is called worldliness is made up of just such men, who (if one may use the expression) pawn themselves to the world.

Mozart spiritualizes this drama through music which can only be described as heavenly. The principal characters

as a rule sing melodies transfiguring even their negative
moods into transparent loveliness, though not without occasional suggestions of the despair lurking beneath superficially healthy-looking, robust and cheerful countenances.
The masterly score reflects the interplay of external
sparkle and inner uneasiness throughout the opera. I would
call special attention to the trio following the death of Donna
Anna's father. Suddenly the tremendous excitement generated by Giovanni's nocturnal intrusion dies down as the participants join in the kind of song which, as the Germans
would put it, can tear the soul asunder. It is a genuine
sublimation of Zerrissenheit. Then there is the pointed
change of mood from "Fin ch'han dal vino" to the masked
trio wherein the victims soberly pledge themselves to joint
revenge before accepting Don Juan's bold invitation to his
ball. And the ball itself! Where else in art or literature
can one find ananalogous synthesis of the licentiousness and
formalism so harmoniously interfused in Enlightenment life?
To the strains of the conflicting dances played by different
orchestral groups on and off stage Mozart allows tremendous
tension to build up. For a moment we are disarmed by
the brilliance of the setting--lights, velvet, shining metal
and glass, the graciousness of Don Juan as host. We are
almost persuaded by his intrinsic goodness, if only it were
permitted lasting expression in congenial surroundings such
as these when Zerlina's scream breaks the spell. The
dances are interrupted. Mozart's music at once plunges us
into the ensuing turmoil. It is as if on the spur of the
moment we turned from Rousseau's 'Social Contract' to a
chapter in his 'Confessions' or from Kant's 'Introduction
to the Metaphysics of Morals' to his discussion of radical
evil in 'Religion Within the Limits of Reason.'

Don Juan remains unrepentant, insolent and impervi-
ous to change even when confronted by the statue of the
Commandatore. It is sensualism militant and resentful of
interference which informs his whole bearing in the face of
impending disaster. As if nothing were amiss he sits down
to a table worthy of the highest humanistic refinement
Europe had cultivated since the Renaissance. So revealing
is the contrast between his lack of humanitarianism and
the sprightly melodies improvised by himself to enhance the
conviviality of the setting that, especially to the modern
listener, it conveys a Dostoyevskian insight into God-re-
pudiating defiance posing as pious equanimity. There is no
question about Giovanni's having the best of times. He goes
so far as brazenly to invite his judge to share it with him.
Whereas so many composers choose to represent the horribly

fascinating through dissonance, crescendi or leaping fifths and sevenths signifying nothing, Mozart, a wiser psychologist to say the least, envelops Don Juan's presumptuous indifference in merry reminiscences from Figaro and snatches from minor operas. For him the last supper becomes an occasion of infectious merry-making.

But the illusion of a humble place beyond moral good and evil at Don Juan's table proves quite ephemeral. Accompanied by running scales simple enough for children to practise on the piano--Mozart's irony here is simply sardonic--Don Juan makes a fiery entrance into hell. Reminiscent of Dante's great sinners in the Inferno, he does not despair of his personality even after the ghastly consequences of his way of life have been fully spelt out for him. Leporello still possesses enough of man's animal fear of the bizarre to desist from openly challenging the transcendent powers. Ethically he is less unrepentant than Don Juan, dialectically he lacks his religious irreligiousness to be damned by deliberate choice. Leporello's physical survival serves to underscore the Christian notion of charity for those too weak to help or hang themselves. Seeking a master more appreciative of his talents of servility he joins in the controversial final chorus celebrating the Enlightenment faith in requited virtue.

What kind of a comedy or tragedy is Don Giovanni? At one moment Mozart confronts us with the terror of underworld flames, at the next he pours forth gentle, directionless melody. What sense, if any, the listener asks himself in this connection, do human fortunes make? Instead of suggesting any unambiguous answer to that question Mozart lets the first violins play a final maddeningly quick theme--a detached commentary on the whole previous action. So long as we can view our follies with a suspension of emotion we need not despair of ourselves altogether. The very fact that the human race does not merely consist of Don Juans, Leporellos, Masettos and Zerlinas, but also includes an occasional Mozart to sing about them is in itself a reaffirmation of human dignity and self-transcendence. What are the last strains of Don Giovanni but genius rejoicing in existence, however confused, however baffling? Because the world for Mozart never lost its fundamental goodness he was able to express the dialectic between light and darkness without courting fate.

The ending of Don Giovanni has been the subject of considerable speculation and criticism. A good deal of this,

167

I feel, rests first of all on a superficial acquaintance with
Mozart's music in general and secondly on the indiscriminate
application of essentialist criteria for dramatic and emotional consummation to a profoundly concrete work of art.
Naturalism as well as romanticism in its undialectical forms
insists on seeing a visible consistency in events which form
a finite perspective they rarely disclose. Thus it is mor-
ally satisfying that a villain like Don Juan should become
the victim of his own unbridledness, but to stress his undeniable charm in spite of his character is painfully dis-
tracting from his merited doom. Or, if Mozart had intended to conceive his theme comically, why does his music
express numerous tragic overtones? So contiguous are the
depths of human depravity and greatness that reason aims
to keep them apart whereas passion blurs their respective
particularity through fusion. The love-death of Tristan and
Isolde and the triumph of freedom in Fidelio illustrate these
possibilities on the highest level of artistic realization.
There is nothing obscure or ambiguous about the forces of
evil being overcome by the good in Beethoven's delineation
of abstract justice; on the other hand Wagner's lovers literally lose themselves in a womb of sheer subjectivity. Mozart successfully avoids both the hypostatization as well as
the cancellation of opposites by allowing his situations to
retain their existential confusion. As in real life the death
of a great public enemy is attended by manifestations ranging
from gratefulness to morbid mirth, so the destruction of
Don Juan releases mixed feelings of tranquil expectation and
recollection.

II

If the composer of Don Giovanni and the author of
The Diary of a Seducer had ever had occasion to meet it is
interesting to speculate how they might have influenced each
other. Certainly Kierkegaard's spiritual attraction to Mozart
is more consistent though no less deep than his criticism
of Mozart's operas. Reacting against the confounding of
cultural with Christian values generally characteristic of
the educated middle class in nineteenth century Europe
Kierkegaard set out to re-establish the autonomy of God-
centered inwardness. What he found so questionable in reflective intellectuality conceived as an end in itself was the
tacit acknowledgement of human self-sufficiency by all its
enthusiasts. They were convinced that by virtue of being
sensitive or talented every man might theoretically participate in the liberating effects of aesthetic experience while
by virtue of God's grace only those can attain salvation who

168

choose to accept Him and have been chosen as acceptable
by Him. If man could understand himself through cultural
activity alone Biblical revelation would be superfluous at
best. But Kierkegaard's objections to the religion of humanism have a wider basis than his corrective approach to
the meaning of the Cross. Being a romantic himself both
by temperament and the "sentimental education" he had
absorbed so readily, Kierkegaard gained an uncanny insight
into the rapture-let-down-boredom-melancholy pattern of
just listening to music or indulging religiously in some other
variety of "higher pleasure." With Schopenhauer and
Baudelaire he was one of the first searching critics of self-
realization dispensing with a superseding goal. Nobody else
has so perspicaciously analysed man's infinite tolerance for
despair precisely when the mind, having conquered the body,
claims recognition of absolute sovereignty. Furthermore,
he clearly saw the paralysing ethical implications of any
ultimate human concern with introspective enjoyment. Music,
for instance, is especially prone to beguile us into states of
euphoria during which the least demand for concrete service
becomes a disturbing burden. Indeed it is not only in bo-
hemian circles that one encounters a striking lack of corre-
lation between self-fulfilment and self-renunciation.

While from Kierkegaard's understanding of the "offence" of the Cross the ideational vagueness and amoral
immediacy of musical experience as a substitute for faith
in things definite, invisible and transcendent can readily be
grasped, 'it is less clear why he singled out the music of
Mozart rather than that of Beethoven or Goethe's lyrical
poetry to illustrate his phenomenology of the aesthetic mode
of existence. Perhaps it is just a coincidence that the
spread of existentialist philosophy since the first world war
has been accompanied by a great Mozart revival. Without
having to stress his place of honour in the long-playing
record catalogues or his popularity, superior to Wagner's,
in present-day Germany, few would disagree, I believe,
that next to Bach he has become the most esteemed of
serious composers, certainly in the eyes of the intelligentsia.
Is it too far-fetched to imagine a vital connection between
the instability and anxiety of thinking people to-day and their
preference for the kind of music which reveals and partly
overcomes these negative characteristics? Kierkegaard was
so unerringly prophetic in his philosophical and theological
preoccupations that his choice of Mozart, a comparatively
underplayed and misunderstood composer in the nineteenth
century, fits in with his overall critique of that age. It
would have been odd for him to meditate, say, on the "Ode

to Joy," inasmuch as its respectability to his own generation
made the text, at any rate, already spiritually suspect. I
imagine that it was precisely the deceptive uncomplicated-
ness of Mozart's art, its lack of a message and extraordinary clarity which helped to arouse Kierkegaard's interest.
In saying this I do not intend to be unjust to Stendhal and
E. T. A. Hoffmann, or to imply that one had to break with
Wagner to see the point, though Nietzsche went so far.

Quite likely Kierkegaard sensed the religious appeal
of Mozart's music which it exercises particularly on those
who have striven for dogmatic neutrality and uncompromis-
ing honesty. If not concretely Christian like Bach, this
music, negatively speaking, neither was inspired by nor
perpetuates an alternate myth such as the teleological conception of nature among the romantic composers or over-
riding love of national tradition ranging from Wagner's
remythologizing of Teutonic deities to Smetana's intoxication
by Czech woodlands and meadows. Mozart, Moerike tells
us, asked the blinds to be drawn on his way to Prague
though the scenery outside was undoubtedly beautiful; moreover, there isn't a trace of ideological claptrap--The Magic
Flute completely transcends its libretto, not to mention the
fact that the Requiem was composed at about the same time
--determining the flow of his genius. To be sure, he was
never, on the other hand an apostle; the still aristocratic
orientation of his life and work kept him immune from the
music for . . . something or other crusades that swept so
many nineteenth-century composers off their feet and continues to play havoc with the creative process even now.
Mozart's music bears witness to an absence of illusions
which makes it dialectically less irreligious, perhaps ethically more profoundly idolatrous, than the diluted piety of
nationalist composers. No wonder that Kierkegaard's attitude towards the Salzburg Wunderkind was highly ambivalent:
the foreboding that in Mozart's music the aesthetic and the
religious, the genius and the prophet, are almost indis-
tinguishably one.

Only Bach, whose Christianity in opposition to Kierkegaard's is explicitly cultural, has been as successful in
giving joint expression to love of human and divine through
music. And it is worth while to ask how Kierkegaard
would have approached his fellow-Lutheran, for in him he
encounters a kind of non-nominal Christian genius he himself possessed without ever doing justice to it in his self-
interpretation. I think Bach disconfirms Kierkegaard's
case against Mozart by virtue of having written relatedly

oriented music without feeling any great threat or contradiction to his faith on that account. Why was Kierkegaard
so uneasy about being a Christian humanist on the plane of
Bach or Milton when ostensibly this is what he could have
been and was by inclination in spite of himself? Superficially it is true that Mozart's operas concern themselves
above all with the interplay of natural feelings--everything
gratuitous, ephemeral, moody and uncertain appearing in
unabashed prominence as if life consisted of a series of
seductions and preparatory erotic gymnastics. In this
connection Kierkegaard was more than justified in calling
attention to the decadent aspects of unbridled aestheticism.
But it is one thing to criticize the make-believe world of
opera (as Plato had criticized the poetry of Homer), another
to perceive the consequences of an exclusive preoccupation
with beauty (witness Rimbaud, Stefan George, Oscar Wilde,
and their circles whom Kierkegaard was disillusioning
seventy years in advance), and yet a third to evaluate justly
the total impact of a Mozart opera. Even if one should
have to grant (which one doesn't!) that Mozart's operatic
music is devoid of ethical-religious moments, it does not
follow that the behaviour of Mozart's characters on the
stage is to be taken as a reliable guide as to the conduct
of men and women on earth. To insist, as Kierkegaard did,
on the existential reduplication of rational insights is not to
be committed to the proposition that art is the mirror of
actuality.

No doubt the eroticism of the natural against the
blessedness of the twice-born man receives preferential
treatment in Entführung, Figaro, Don Giovanni, Cosi and
Magic Flute, where most of the time none of the characters
aspires to any state other than the satisfaction of impulses.
Like Kierkegaard himself Mozart was too realistic to create
morality plays, the limitations of the ethical point of view
being crystal-clear to both. Besides, the conventions of
opera were not designed to justify the ways of man to God.
Mozart was certainly a master at representing the dodges,
vagaries, concealments and white lies of frail and mis-
chievous human nature. But it would be patently false to
credit him with the view that this is all there is to being
an animal walking on two legs. The delineation of attraction and repulsion between the sexes, to use Kierkegaard's
own phrase, is coming to terms with one of life's "critical
situations. " How could the diarist of a seducer in Either/
Or or the narrator of the banquet in Stages on Life's Way
take issue with the eroticism of, say, Don Juan? Was not
Mozart in fact doing something quite similar in illuminating

the depths of human degradation and worth through an analysis of passion? Is there not an element of "indirect communication" in the haughtiness of the Countess, the servility of Leporello, the rages of Osmin and the cynicism of Don Alfonso, so that their inner life confronts us two-dimensionally the moment we make their acquaintance?

The merely aesthetic (if there is such a pure type) in 'Don Giovanni' is but a preface to the aesthetic-religious or irreligious. Underlying the surface themes of the opera --intrigue, murder and seduction--is Mozart's intense preoccupation with the dialectic between hybris and nemesis, grace and damnation, redemption and punitive suffering. It is hard to find a major ethical or religious issue which is not touched on in the course of the drama: Juan's unmerited length of life to inflict pain on the comparatively innocent, his seemingly successful defiance of providence, Zerlina's reckless affection ("batti, batti, bel Masetto") oblivious of consequences, Leporello's boot-licking, Masetto's wellmeaning but wellnigh destructive stupidity and Donna Anna's hysterical righteousness are but a few examples. The reconciliation scene in The Marriage of Figaro is ethical in import, not to mention the letter duet in which Susanna and the Countess epitomize genuine communion between two members of their sex or Barbarina's air which inexplicably breaks off in the middle after intoning an unexpected, excruciating air of sadness that, for want of a sounder term, could be called metaphysical.

It goes without saying that Idomeneo is an ethical drama though its religious origins are pagan. In Fear and Trembling Kierkegaard's admiration for self-sacrifice as portrayed by the Greek tragedians is second only to his uncomprehending awe in the presence of Abraham's faith "by virtue of the absurd." Mozart's Idomeneo, as far as I know, is an unparalleled translation of pre-Christian occidental religiousness into a modern musical idiom. It is miraculously free both from Gluck's leanings towards the mannered and the romantics' sentimental idealization of the past. As to Cosi fan tutte, it is among other things a profound study in irony which Kierkegaard in his Concluding Unscientific Postscript linked with the ethical mode of existence in so far as any distinction between pretence and reality presupposes a transcendence of and detachment from immediacy. Finally, a brief word about the Entführung. The Pasha music in Act I exposes the presumptuousness attending worldly power by literally laughing it out of existence; and when the would-be abductors are caught by Osmin after having misused all their elaborate preparations Mozart, by dint of a few interpolated measures before the action continues, opens up a yawning abyss, the nothingness not only of disappointed lovers but potentially, ever threatening to envelop us, of mankind at large. [5]

III

Before these discontented times, in which so many of us have become predisposed to discern uneasiness and torment in each profound expression of the human lot, Mozart was commonly regarded as a cheerful composer who contrary to his own basic inclinations gave vent to private sorrows in a few late works. According to this view the outstanding characteristics of Mozart's scores (on the whole) are complete mastery of sonata form, restraint, lightness of touch, brilliance and, most important, geniality. Occasional clouds may damp without dispelling the underlying gay, rhythmic pulse of his compositions. Children should practise them at an early age not only on account of their technical simplicity but because they will be spared a while longer the disillusionment and sadness implicit, let us say, in Beethoven, Schubert and Brahms. Exposure to these masters, some would argue in order to make an impression, requires a certain familiarity with the facts of frustration and satiety mercifully confined to adult experience. Thus Mozart is seen to have possessed a remarkable gift for evoking the moods of childhood without falling into sentimentality or condescension. He is the composer of eternal youth from whose genius emanates a flood of beautiful sound --singable, harmonious and full of good spirits. He is a favourite son of the gods, the same gods whom Hölderlin in Hyperion vainly strove to reaccommodate to the western tradition about ten years after Mozart's death.

An opposing school of thought which, as indicated above, has gained strength in the twentieth century, maintains that Mozart's music is problematical and soul-searching from the early Symphony in G minor (K. 183) through the "dissonant" Quartet of the middle period to the clarinet Concerto. The representatives of this standpoint share with many existentialists a pronounced aversion to the happier moods of mankind. Without necessarily going so far as to deny the affirmative quality of Mozart's works they tend to interpret it as an incidental feature, a kind of relief from the composer's hidden preoccupation with the decline of western civilization. "Indeed," they will tell you, "there is a Mozart for our children, but he did not mean to ad-

173

dress us who know all the horrors of life." Meticulously
they will divide the works into ordinary eighteenth-century
stuff, youthful experiments, bread-and-butter divertimento
writing and so on, until they have isolated the quintessence
of the real Mozart who is to be found in approximately a
hundred compositions each of which either has tragic overtones, anticipates Beethoven's last quartets or plunges us
into the depths of melancholy suggestive of Chopin. These
people can hardly get over the fact that the "Incarnatus est"
in the Requiem is so outspokenly exhilarating, trills within
trills, ascribing this fault to Mozart's weakened faith in
the Christian scheme of redemption. Thus he is seen as a
musical prophet of contemporary doom and gloom. He is
the composer of Dionysian passion from whose genius emanates a flood of beautiful sound resigned, sorrowful and
filled with ill forebodings. He is the last aristocratic humanist in music who had gleaned the meaninglessness of it
all but kept the secret locked in a few select compositions
until Sir Thomas Beecham and the first world war provided
the catalyst which released it to the present generation.

The demonic in Mozart's music is the coexistence
and mutual interplay of the joy of Hyperion dancing at the
dawn of history and the anxiety of Kierkegaard, Amiel and
Jacobsen face to face with nothingness. No discursive mediation of these two elements is possible, yet Mozart's music,
without destroying the authenticity of either, expresses joyful affirmation always on the edge of profound nihilism.
Just because music is capable of saying more than words,
of expressing the inarticulate double feelings of the inner
life, Mozart succeeds in confronting us with a major paradox as a unified experience. Philosophers, historians and
poets since the seventeenth century have analysed and be-
moaned the split soul of occidental man. Painters like
Rembrandt, Goya and van Gogh have movingly depicted the
visible effects of this schism on a man's face or in his
apprehension of ordinary objects. Music alone, among the
arts, and Mozart's music par excellence, can encompass at
once (for the right listener!) as they go hand in hand the
most dreadful doubts and a persisting obligation to carry on
in spite of them.

The thought of a circular square, a benevolent devil
or a loving hate is absurd. Our language stipulates that
these are incompatible concepts even though, taking the last,
we have such an experience without being able to put it into
words. Mozart actually turns this kind of unintelligible con-
junction into concrete recognizable music events with a logic

174

of their own. Comparable to a mystic he penetrates the
core of anomalies to a unity of opposites which, being
musical, continues to be temporal.[6] Composing towards
the end of the eighteenth century between the "pre-established
harmony" and the "ages of anxiety," no longer totally committed to the one, not yet enamoured of the other, but
cognizant of both, Mozart's music gives unique expression
to this spiritual crisis still unresolved to-day.   Demonically
in Mozart the depths of hope and hopelessness interfuse as
in redemptive suffering extremes of non-correlation continue
to reveal the glory of God.   Throughout his life Luther felt
tempted to confound the will of God with the voice of Satan.
Listening to Mozart it is always hard to tell whether the
heavens have opened up or the ground beneath our feet is
about to cave in, or both.   It is regrettable that Kierkegaard neglected to develop his insight further into the affinity of the aesthetic with the religious.   If he had he
would very likely have revised his estimate not only of
Mozart's music but also of becoming a Christian.   While
Mozart takes irrepressible delight in illuminating the subtlest
transitions of the inner life his music expresses beyond
them our unstable lot on earth: at once ludicrous and pitiful,
trying and uplifting, wretched and great.   An age such as
ours reawakened to the bestial potentialities of civilized
communities may still find an element of regeneration in
him who, on his two hundredth birthday, confronts us,
demonically, with what we were at the outset and what we
hope again to become at the end of time.

Notes

1.   Karl Barth, Die kirchliche Dogmatik, III, 3 (Zürich,
     1950), pp. 337-39.   (My translation.)

2.   Cf. Either/Or; a Fragment of Life, trans. by David F.
     and Lillian M. Swenson, I (Princeton, 1949), pp.
     35-111.

3.   Lenau's Don Juan, for example, kills himself out of
     ennui when on the verge of final success.   Don Juan
     in Don Giovanni does appear a failure in his ama-
     tory exploits, yet it would contradict his essential
     nature to despair of tangible accomplishments, for
     then he would have ceased to be authentically de-
     monic or single-mindedly dedicated to the quest and
     realization of one aim only.   Girls had good cause
     to be afraid of him, but not of his "Hamlet-like"

successors as the romantic poets drew them.

4. Cf. <u>The Sickness Unto Death</u>, trans. , with an introduction, by W. Lowrie (Princeton, 1946), pp. 46ff.

5. In fairness to Kierkegaard it must be emphasized that his category of the purely aesthetic was intended as a tyoplogical abstraction which as such may exist only in infants or irresponsibles. But if most forms of the aesthetic mode of existence are reflective as well as sensual how can music fail to have ethical-religious content, being so closely tied to the inner life of Man?

6. The piano Fantasy in C minor, for example.

William Styron's Don Juan

Kenneth A. Robb

First published in Critique, VIII (Winter 1965-1966), 34-46, and is here reprinted with the kind permission of its editors and of the author, who is at present Professor of English, Bowling Green State University.

Critics have ranged far afield trying to find comparisons for William Styron's Set This House on Fire. To Robert Gorham Davis, Mason Flagg is "a Cavigliostro, a Svengali."[1] To Richard Foster, he is a Jay Gatsby; Peter Leverett is a Nick Carraway, Francesca is a Silvana Mangano, Cass Kinsolving is "like Holden Caulfield grown up," and the novel is a pastiche of Fitzgerald, Nabokov, Conrad, Salinger, Faulkner, Hollywood, etc.[2] In a more perceptive article, Lewis Lawson studies Cass Kinsolving, "Kierkegaardian man of despair," from Kierkegaard's religious view of life as it is expressed in The Sickness Unto Death.[3] Certainly Cass Kinsolving is this man. And we need go no further than Kierkegaard to find the source for much of the characterization, structure, and action of Set This House on Fire, for the novel is in large measure a complex translation, into prose and into the contemporary world, of Mozart's version of the Don Juan legend as it is discussed in the Either part of Kierkegaard's Either/Or. Thus Cass Kinsolving is successively Cherubino, Papageno, Leoprello, Masetto, and the Commendatore. Mason Flagg is Don Giovanni and Francesca is Zerlina.

References to his recordings of The Magic Flute and Don Giovanni key Cass' progress through the stages of his despair up to the moment when he kills his Don Giovanni, Mason Flagg. At that point he takes the Kierkegaardian leap from the aesthetic stage to the ethical stage.[4] In this stage he pleads with Luigi Migliori, the Italian policeman, to arrest him for murder. But Luigi does not defer to the absolute moral standard of the ethical stage as an ordinary policeman would. Instead, he tells Cass, "You

sin in your guilt! . . . Consider the good in yourself!
Consider hope! Consider joy!"[5] His refusal to arrest
Cass forces him to take the second Kierkegaardian leap--
from the ethical stage to the religious stage--and it is in
this last stage he exists at the end of the novel and in the
narrative present, when he and Peter Leverett try to piece
the whole story together. Of course these "stages on life's
way" that Kierkegaard describes should not be considered
always temporally successive and mutually exclusive. [6]
Nevertheless, investigating what may be loosely called the
aesthetic aspects of the novel in terms of Kierkegaard's
aesthetic discussion of Mozart illuminates important areas
of a novel critics seem to have had a hard time with.

In "The Immediate Stages of the Erotic or the
Musical Erotic" Kierkegaard, disguised as Victor Eremita,
editor of the papers of a young aesthete called A, asserts
and defends the proposition that "Mozart's Don Juan takes
the highest place among all classical works."[7] In an argument too long to be summarized here, A finds the absolute
subject of music to be the sensuous-erotic in its immediacy
(69). Language, on the other hand, is "the one absolutely
spiritually qualified medium; therefore it is the proper
vehicle for the idea" (65), and since "language becomes
the perfect medium just at the moment when everything
sensuous in it is negatived" (66), its absolute subject cannot be the sensuous-erotic. Furthermore, A says:

> . . . if I imagine this [sensuous-erotic] principle
> concentrated in a single individual, then I have
> the concept of sensuous-erotic genius . . . which
> in its immediacy can only be expressed in music.
> . . . In its mediacy and as reflected in some-
> thing other than itself, it comes under language
> and becomes subject to ethical categories (63).

In terms of Mozart's operas, the sensuous-erotic genius is
best expressed in its immediacy in Don Giovanni. The
immediate expression of this genius is found in Set This
House on Fire in the playing of Cass' recordings of Don
Giovanni; its mediate and reflective expression is found in
the character Mason Flagg, who "becomes subject to ethical
categories. " Cass kills him as the Commendatore kills
Don Giovanni. Viewed in the light of A's aesthetics, the
death of Mason Flagg is a logical consequence of Styron's
having expressed the Don Juan legend in prose.

According to A, the three stages of the immediate or

178

musical erotic are desire defined as <u>dreaming</u>, desire defined as <u>seeking</u>, and desire defined <u>as desiring</u>. Instead of <u>stages,</u> A says, he might better have <u>used</u> the word <u>metamorphosis</u> because:

> The different stages taken together constitute the immediate stage, and from this we may perceive that the individual stages are rather a revelation of a predicate, so that all the predicates rush down into the wealth of the last stage, since this is the real stage. The other stages have no independent existence; in and of themselves they exist only as parts of a conceptual scheme, and from this one may see their accidental character as over against the last stage (73).

Desire defined as dreaming is represented by the mythical Cherubino in The <u>Marriage of Figaro;</u> desire defined as seeking, by the mythical Papageno in The <u>Magic Flute</u>; and the whole opera <u>Don Giovanni</u> represents the last, the "real" stage, desire defined as desiring.

In <u>Set This House on Fire,</u> there are no references to Cherubino or <u>The Marriage of</u> Figaro, but in telling Peter of a youthful affair he had with Vernelle Satterfield (259-65), Cass describes his state at that time in terms remarkably similar to A's description of Cherubino (74-77). From Kierkegaard's religious point of view, Cass then experienced "The despair which is unconscious that it is despair, or the despairing unconsciousness of having a self and an eternal self."[8]

The second stage, desire defined as seeking, is fully presented in the novel to the accompaniment of the relevant aria sung by Papageno in The <u>Magic Flute.</u> As Lawson has shown, in Paris Cass experiences immediacy and in his "moment of rapture" Cass is an immediate man in Kierkegaard's religious terminology.[9] From his later perspective, Cass describes his problem at that time as "Kinsolving pitted against Kinsolving," and he describes himself then as "a regular <u>puddle</u> of self" (250, 254). Suddenly enraged by the efforts of his wife, Poppy, to make him "do something," he drove her and the children from the apartment. Left alone, he says,

> --I opened another bottle of this crummy brandy and got my <u>Magic Flute</u> out and put it on and staggered around the joint for a while, hating

myself, hating Poppy and my own glands and the
life-force or whatever it was that caused me to
produce such a useless, snotty-nosed, colicky
tribe. . . .

Then, Cass continues, ". . . I began to simmer down--
gradually, I guess--most likely the music was stealing into
my bones . . . " (255). In his discussion of Papageno, A
comments:

Music can effectively banish thoughts, even evil
thoughts, just as we say about David that his
playing exorcised Saul's evil spirit. On the other
hand, there is a great delusion in this idea, for
it is true only in so far as it carries consciousness back into immediacy, and lulls it therein.
The individual may therefore feel happy in the
moment of intoxication, but he only becomes the
more unhappy (81).

This lulling of the individual, this carrying of the consciousness back into immediacy, is precisely what happened to
Cass as he looked out the window while the music was playing.

After the moment of rapture, Cass blacked out, he
says, and when he came to, "the woman singing Mozart was
still soaring off on the same aria, the same measure, in
fact" (258). This probably refers to the third aria in the
opera, the Queen of Night's "O zittre nicht, mein lieber
Sohn," which would reinforce Cass' temporary and illusory
feeling of well-being. Papageno's aria is the first in the
opera, and presumably Cass "staggered around the joint"
through the overture and the first few minutes of the opera
to arrive at the window when Papageno sang "Der Vogel-
fänger bin ich ja!" A says of the aria:

As you know, Papageno accompanies his light-
hearted cheerfulness on the flute. Every ear has
certainly felt itself moved in a strange manner by
this accompaniment. But the more one considers
it, the more one sees in Papageno the mythical
Papageno, all the more expressive and characteristic one will find it; one does not tire of hearing
it again and again, because it is an absolutely
adequate expression of Papageno's life, whose
whole life is such an incessant twittering; who,
always carefree, chirps on in all idleness, and

180

who is happy and satisfied because this is his
life-content, happy in his work and happy in his
song (80-81).

But in mediacy and in life viewed from Kierkegaard's religious position, this everlasting, immediate expression of
eroticism is illusory and cannot be sustained, as Cass and
Kierkegaard's immediate man discover.[10] A detail of the
scene seems to support the identification of Cass and the
bird-catcher Papageno. As he looked out the window, Cass
says, ". . . there were pigeons up there, a great flight of
sun-flecked wings, all wheeling around in space" (257).

The Magic Flute is not played elsewhere in the novel,
but there are two allusions to it. Peter Leverett calls
Saverio, the village simpleton, "my bedeviled, lustful,
gifted Papageno," and after he talked to him, he says, "I
got up, thinking that I heard a faint toy piping sound in the
air around us, the sorrowful scamper of naked feet, long
ago pursued, long made still" (69-70). This passage probably refers to Papageno's pursuit of Papagena, his Täubchen.
From Saverio's identification with Papageno, we may conclude that he is Cass' alter ego: he represents the potentially dangerous stage of the immediate man that Cass
ultimately and fortunately passes beyond. Cass is suspected
of murdering Francesca, while Saverio is the actual mur-
derer; Cass comes close to going insane, while Saverio is
placed in a Salerno madhouse.

The second allusion occurs at the end of the novel,
after Luigi sets Cass free. Cass returns to Poppy and
stands by their bedroom window, looking down at his children who are "sort of strutting face to face and soundlessly
clapping their hands together, like some vision of Papageno
and Papagena . . ." (500). From the window, Cass looks
back and down on the earlier stage of immediacy he has
passed through, a stage that is naturally childlike.

Like the predicates of the first two stages of the
immediate erotic in A's discussion, all events of Set This
House on Fire "rush down into the wealth of the last stage,
since this is the real stage"--the fateful night at Sambuco.
The first part of the novel is Peter's narration; he tells
Cass of his relations with Mason Flagg and all he knows
about the night in Sambuco. But Peter's knowledge is only
fragmentary and tantalizing; he sets up a number of predicates and the reader is led on by his desire to know who
murdered Mason Flagg. When Cass begins his narration in

Part II, he immediately announces that he killed Mason; with this, the reader's attention shifts to Cass, "the Kierkegaardian man of despair," and to his condition before, during, and after the murder.   Motivation becomes paramount.   The first part of his narration--particularly the depiction of his moment of immediacy--is dependent on the later part, for in Cass' spiritual history the critical moment is that in which he takes the first Kierkegaardian leap, from the aesthetic stage to the ethical stage, by killing Mason Flagg.   During the night before the murder, Cass plays records of Don Giovanni, and references to the opera indicate Cass' progressively changing relationship to Mason.

Styron has more than adequately established Mason Flagg as a psychological Don Juan through Peter's description of Mason's relationship to "Wendy-dear," his mother (77-93), his constant discarding of his mistresses, his maltreatment and discarding of his wife Celia (165), and through Cass' depiction of his desire for and rape of Francesca.   A final touch is supplied when Cass suspects Mason of repressed homosexuality (414, 441), a component that is often associated with the Don Juan psychological type.

But more important to seeing Mason as Don Giovanni is the fact that all of the people in Sambuco live an existence derived from Mason Flagg's.   A says of Don Giovanni:

> Don Juan is the hero of the opera, the chief interest centers in him; not only so, but he lends interest to all the other characters.   This must not be understood, however, in a merely superficial sense, for this constitutes the mysterious in this opera, that the hero is also the animating force in the other characters . . . he is, so to speak, the common denominator.   The existence of all the others is, compared with his, only a derived existence (118).

In the novel, Rosemarie De Laframboise is Mason's mistress and lives off him; Francesca steals food from him; Windgasser has a stroke of luck when Mason arrives in Sambuco and rents an apartment from him; Peter goes to Sambuco because Mason invites him; the movie people leave the village the morning of his murder because of his murder.   Cass Kinsolving is absolutely dependent upon the man who becomes his master, Mason Flagg.   The sole exception is Luigi, who stands outside of the analogy with the opera and who, in letting Cass go free, shares implicity

182

with him the ethical judgment of Mason.

By strict analogy to the three stages of A's discussion, it might be expected that Cass would be the Don Giovanni since he has already gone through the Cherubino and Papageno stages. But the third stage is represented, strictly speaking, not by Don Giovanni, but by the whole opera Don Giovanni. The part of the novel analogous to the opera takes Cass only to the first Kierkegaardian leap, where the opera ends. Beyond that, Cass has other ordeals to undergo. But Don Giovanni, of course, never escapes the first stage; he is condemned within it. Therefore, although he is the central character of the novel as a whole, Cass is quite properly not the Don Giovanni of this version of the legend.

In retrospect, the most ironic passage of the book is that in which the overture to Don Giovanni is played (97). [11] As Peter and Rosemarie approached Mason's apartment on the way to his party, the noise of an orgy resounded through the courtyard: "From the region upstairs, muffled yet distinct behind the alabaster walls, came the noise of a tinkling piano, feet thumping, a high falsetto voice singing above it all, then wave upon wave of hysterical laughter." A suitable prose description, perhaps, of Don Giovanni's last party. But then, Peter says, as the two passed Cass Kinsolving's apartment on the lower level: "Close by us, from a doorway at the level at which we were standing and so loud that each crashing bass note had the effect of the tread of elephants, a phonograph erupted the opening bars from the overture to Don Giovanni." The opening bars of the overture are the same bars that announce the arrival of the statue of the Commendatore to render ethical judgment on Don Giovanni in the last scene of the opera. The reference to these bars signifies the beginning of the climactic events of the novel and forecasts the death of Mason Flagg-Don Giovanni. As the music blasts through the noise of the party it seems figuratively to pronounce judgment. Yet the most ironic touch is Peter's reaction: "Together, none of the sounds made any sense; I felt deafened, and I had the childish urge to stick my fingers in my ears."

The second reference to Don Giovanni occurs as Peter and Crips stand on the balcony looking down on the other guests at the swimming pool. They talk about Mason, and then all at once, "Out of some window now on the level directly below us Don Giovanni came again," says Peter (120). The phrases heard are those of Leporello at the beginning of I, v. "Ehi! caffe!" is sung by Don Giovanni, but Leporello's "Rinefrescatevi! . . . Bei giovinotti!" dominates: "I heard Leporello boom above the flutes and strings." The opera scene in which the phrases are sung is the one in which Don Giovanni attempts to complete his seduction of Zerlina while Leporello keeps Masetto, her bridegroom, occupied. The Don has already mentally seduced her in the duet "La ci darem la mano" (I, ii).

Now occurs a place where the events of the opera and those of the novel merge significantly. A moment after the phrases are heard, Peter says, the record is taken off the player (121). Crips goes off to bed; Peter is left alone at about 1:00 in the morning (126). Suddenly Francesca stumbles through the room with Mason in pursuit. Later it is learned that Francesca has been raped (436). In terms of elapsed time, Francesca probably enters the room at about the time that Zerlina would have cried out "Oh, Numi! son tradita!" if the record has not been turned off. Zerlina cries these words when Don Giovanni makes his second attempt on her.

But more important in terms of Cass' spiritual development is the fact that shortly after these events he is summoned to the party by Mason to entertain the guests (182-89). In other words, Cass plays the role of Leporello soon after the phrases sung by Leporello are heard coming from his apartment. Moreover, he has played this role to Mason's Don Giovanni almost from the time Mason appeared in Sambuco; he has been Mason's toady, fool, and servant. He has been sexually attracted toward Francesca, as Leporello is attracted toward the women of the village in the third scene of the opera's first act. While he originally agreed to employ Francesca himself, he had no money, and therefore Mason "appropriated" her: ". . . after all, he could pay; Cass couldn't . . . ." At the time, Mason made his intentions toward Francesca clear, but Cass threatened him. When Mason apologized, Cass, "--in deathly outrageous panic lest his harsh words cause Mr. Big to withdraw the bambini's fresh milk, plus Life Savers, bubble gum, frankfurters, bacon, liverwurst, booze (not the least)--had been soft, conciliatory, deplorable" (408). Like Leporello (II, i), Cass is repelled by the sexual activities of his Don Giovanni, but his repulsion is overcome by the power of money. He is Mason's "man" (426). At the time he performs for the guests, Cass knows Mason has raped Francesca. But Cass is drunk and he needs to get the pills for Michele from Mason. He dares not revolt; he still stands in the Leporello relationship to his Don Giovanni.

Cass hears the phrases from Zerlina's aria "Batti, batti," at 5:00 a. m. (450). He has made the trip to Tramonti and administered the medicine to Michele. He knows Francesca has been raped, but not that she has been attacked again and left to die. He lies in bed listening and thinking, and the words come to him although there is no indication that his recording of the opera is playing. Zerlina sings her aria to Masetto after she has been mentally seduced by Don Giovanni. As Cass puts it, "Fair bare-legged barefooted Zerlina imploring her country lover patience, patience, asking him to forgive" (450).

In raping Francesca, Cass says, Mason was "raping me." He goes on to say that after having been a slave to Mason, he had "moved closer to a condition of freedom, and Mason knew it even if I didn't, and this he couldn't bear" (444). Cass had been working toward freedom through his love of Francesca and through obtaining medicine for Michele. [12] But just as Don Giovanni violates the relationship between Masetto and Zerlina by mentally seducing her, so Mason destroys the pure relationship between Cass and Francesca in his attempt to squelch Cass' bid for freedom. Cass says: "No . . . I never made love to Francesca, ever. I wanted to, God knows. So did she, I know. We would have sooner or later, I know. But we never made love" (439). Similarly, Don Giovanni attempts to seduce Zerlina on the day she marries Masetto, during the festivities. Cass goes on to describe what it was he found in Francesca: "Joy you see--a kind of serenity and repose that I never really knew existed" (440). When he hears the words from Zerlina's aria, Cass' relationship to Mason corresponds to Masetto's relationship to Don Giovanni. Because of his love for Francesca, Cass is not quite the slave to Mason that he had been when he was in the Leporello relationship, but like Masetto's, his opposition to his Don Giovanni is ineffectual and not very vigorous. Yet the relationship undergoes another change signaled by reference to Don Giovanni.

Cass falls asleep and when he awakens, he puts on a Mozart record. Whether or not it is the one containing the next aria he hears is not indicated in the novel, but that is unimportant. For the aria is so altered as to make it apparent that the opera and Cass' situation have fused. Cass hears a voice, "slyly suggestive now above the flutes and strings, and seeming to emanate not from the outside but from a point much closer, close to his ear" (454). The words that the voice speaks are variations on portions of Leporello's "List Aria," I, ii. In his essay A waxes enthusiastic over the aria as an "epic moment." Leporello sings the aria to Donna Elvira, but A points out that although Leporello sings it when Don Giovanni is not physically present, the music "lets us hear Don Juan, lets us hear the variations in him, evokes the effect which the spoken word or the dialogue is not able to do." He continues:

> The faithless lover . . . is not present . . .
> Since it is general knowledge that he is away, it might seem queer that I mention him, and in a way, draw him into the situation; on second thought we might find this quite proper and see here an example of how literally the statement must be taken that Don Juan is omnipresent in the opera (131).

Styron transmutes this aria from Leporello's enumeration of Don Giovanni's conquests into the direct voice of Mason Flagg-Don Giovanni.

The first group of words is "Let me tell you something Cash, old Cassius, my boy . . ." and in effect they correspond to Leporello's opening words:

> Madamina!
> Il catalogo è questo,
> Delle belle, che amò il padron mio!
> Un catalogo egli è ch'ho fatto io . . .

"Cassius" is a jocular, but from a later point of view rather ironic, nickname Mason applies to Cass (414). The second group of words is "Let me tell you something, old Cash, virgin tail can be the very best in . . . ," corresponding to Leporello's "Sua passion predominante /E la giovin principante." The third group of words is:

> I've had French stuff and I've had Spanish stuff in fact you might say I've sampled the whole broad spectrum pole to pole but they say that until you get yourself between the thighs of one of the little guinea girls and by guinea I only mean the joking generic term for . . .

These words correspond to Leporello's catalogue:

In Italia sei cento e quaranta,
In Alemagna due cento trent'una;
Cento in Francia, in Turchia novant'una,
Ma, ma in Ispagna, son già mille e tre!

Throughout the entire aria, Leporello lists Don Giovanni's sampling of "the whole broad spectrum pole to pole."

The voice firmly establishes the identity of Mason Flagg as Don Giovanni. It is clear that Cass hears his Don Giovanni's list of conquests under the influence of his knowledge that Mason has raped Francesca: she was a virgin, she is the "guinea" referred to. Cass has passed through two relationships to Mason Flagg, submission (Leporello) and ineffectual opposition (Masetto). The voice of the sensuous-erotic genius, who operates within Cass' own world, destroying the one he loved and attempting to destroy him, leads Cass to carry out the operatic situation to the end and fulfill the role of the Commendatore's statue, who actively opposes, condemns, and executes Don Giovanni. Cass does this when he learns that Francesca has been attacked a second time and lies dying; he believes Mason Flagg has assaulted her again, just as Don Giovanni twice tries Zerlina in the opera.

But it should be emphasized that Cass is neither drunk (as he usually is) nor hypnotized by the music when he murders Mason. His cold sanity is shown by his clear thinking and planning when he stands outside Mason's door and when he pursues Mason up the path (457-65). The Kierkegaardian parallel holds here too, for as Lowrie has said, the leap ". . . is indeed a decisive choice, and as such it is an expression of the will. But this does not imply an antithesis between intellect and will, for the whole man, intellect, feeling and will, is involved in the choice."[13] Whichever approach to the murder is taken--through the opera recordings and Either or through The Sickness Unto Death--it must be regarded as a reflective, sane act, and that is the way it is depicted.

A major discrepancy between the opera and the novel is that Don Giovanni remains insolent toward the statue of the Commendatore up to the moment of the handshake, but Mason cringes under his bed behind a locked door. Cass' own account of the situation as Peter tells it provides the best explanation:

. . . he was in basic command of the situation

> . . . after months and days of limp and ineffectu-
> al bondage when he was unable to break through
> to prick the cowardice at Mason's core, he was
> at last on top--he felt Mason's fear of his venge-
> ance now even before grappling with him--and he
> knew that by that terror alone he could imprison
> Mason within the room (458).

There is no cowardice at the core of the opera's Don
Giovanni, but he operates in music, outside the sphere of
ethics, while Mason Flagg, created in prose, "becomes
subject to ethical categories. "

A few details in the description of Cass' pursuit and
murder of Mason are reminiscent of the condemnation of
Don Giovanni by the statue of the Commendatore. When
Don Giovanni shakes hands with the statue in pledge that he
will dine with him, he is frozen in its grasp. In the novel,
as Cass groped for Mason under the bed, "very slowly now
he put forth his hand to grasp Mason's wrist . . ." (460),
as though he expected that Mason too would be frozen in
the grasp. Again, after Cass killed Mason with a stone,
he stopped and looked down at him: "Then in his last
grief and rage he wrestled Mason's body to the parapet,
and wearily heaved it up in his arms and kept it for a
moment close to his breast. And then he hurled it into
the void" (465). There is no "chorus from below" here,
drawing Don Giovanni down into hell. There is only a man
acting within the human sphere. But the downward movement and the word void are suggestive parallels.

It is possible to see many details in which Styron
has followed the suggestions of A. For example, one
critic of Set This House on Fire has accused its author of
intensifying the Fitzgeraldian money mystique almost to the
point of parody. 14 However, A points out that if an author
grants his Don Juan the means of existence, "then Don
Juan comes under the category of the interesting. " But "if
the poet denies him this means, then the interpretation
falls under the category of the comic. " Molière followed
the latter course: "If I allow Don Juan to be in financial
straits, harassed by creditors, he at once loses the ideality
he has in the opera, and the effect becomes comic" (108).
Mason Flagg, no comic character, is conspicuously rich;
the extent of his wealth is never really defined. For this
Don Juan, in this society, money is the means by which
passion can achieve its satisfaction, and since Mason Flagg
has money, he may well "come under the category of the

interesting."

Styron's use of the Don Juan legend via Mozart via Kierkegaard informs Set This House on Fire with a coherence and unity that correlates well with his depiction of Cass Kinsolving as a "Kierkegaardian man of despair." Like many other modern writers, Styron is tapping basic traditions of Western culture, but to perceive this, the reader must go beneath the surface of Mason Flagg's obvious affluence and Cass Kinsolving's unconventional, apparently erratic behavior.

Notes

1. Robert Gorham Davis, "Styron and the Students," Critique, III (Summer, 1960), 39.

2. Richard Foster, "An Orgy of Commerce: William Styron's Set This House on Fire," Critique, III (Summer, 1960), 58-70.

3. Lewis A. Lawson, "Cass Kinsolving: Kierkegaardian Man of Despair," Wisconsin Studies in Contemporary Literature, III (Fall, 1962), 54-66.

4. See Marjorie Grene, Introduction to Existentialism (Chicago, 1959), pp. 30-31.

5. William Styron, Set This House on Fire (New York, 1960), pp. 494, 495. All further citations in the text are to this edition.

6. James Brown, Kierkegaard, Heidegger, Buber and Barth (New York, 1962), p. 32.

7. Søren Kierkegaard, Either/Or, trans. David F. and Lillian Marvin Swenson, rev. Howard A. Johnson (Garden City, New York, 1959), pp. 56, 63. All further citations in the text, except where otherwise footnoted, are to this edition. Walter Lowrie (A Short Life of Kierkegaard, pp. 92-93) states that A's views are those of Kierkegaard when he was in the aesthetic stage.

8. Søren Kierkegaard, The Sickness Unto Death, trans. Walter Lowrie (Princeton, 1941), p. 44.

9. Lawson, p. 57.

10. Ibid., p. 57.

11. See A's discussion, pp. 125-27.

12. Lawson, pp. 65-66.

13. Walter Lowrie, A Short Life of Kierkegaard (Princeton, 1942), p. 174.

14. Foster, pp. 60ff.

Søren Kierkegaard and
Educational Theory

Brian V. Hill

First published in Educational Theory, XVI (October 1966), 344-353, the article is here reprinted with the kind permission of its editor and of the author, who is at present Senior Lecturer in Education, Wollongong University College, Australia.

Introduction

In 1952 a collaborative essay was published on "Existentialism and Education"[1] in which Kierkegaard was represented through the selections of his writings in Bretall's anthology. [2] As an essay it misrepresented both Existentialism and Kierkegaard. The analysis of Existentialism centered on Kierkegaard and Sartre, stressing the antisocial elements that one can admittedly find in both, without conceding that Existentialism might also be represented through Nietzsche, Buber, Dostoevski, Jaspers and many others. It thereby lacked an awareness of the profundity and pertinency of the Existentialist protest. The study of Kierkegaard was more understandably limited by the scope of the essay, but it resulted in caricature, for it is difficult to do justice to the sweep of Kierkegaard's thought without dutifully plodding through the corpus of his writings and acknowledging the master plan which his successive publications followed. Subsequent investigations by professors Morris and Kneller[3] have grasped the nettle more firmly and made insightful attempts to get inside the Existentialist mode of thought, while theistic Existentialism has been ably expounded in Britain by professors Niblett and Jeffreys. [4] However, because their treatments are synoptic, one does not encounter the full thrust of Kierkegaard's thought as such. This article attempts to suggest some issues affecting educational theory which would profit from more extended study of the Kierkegaard corpus.

191

Biographical Note

Fulsome biographies are available in English, [5] but some reminder of the circumstances of his life is necessary because it is a key with which to unlock many of the important implications of his writing. Born in Copenhagen in 1813 to a prosperous but melancholy merchant with a guilt complex aggravated by an austere brand of Lutheranism, Kierkegaard went up to university rebelling against his father's religion. His studies were dominated by Hegelianism until in 1838 he experienced a personal religious conversion which for him provided the frame of reference through which he looked critically at Christendom and Hegelianism. After a swift and successful courtship he became engaged to be married but the singularity of his family and personality led him to break the association in 1841 and thereafter to plunge into an amazingly productive writing schedule. In 1843 he leapt to fame in Denmark with the publication of Either/Or, but fell from favour two years later through being lampooned by a fashionable scandal-sheet The Corsair, an experience which hurt but did not surprise him. In later years he began a sustained attack on the state church on grounds of formalism and hypocrisy, and died at the age of 42 from sheer nervous exhaustion.

The extraordinary intensity of his introspection led him to focus on the significance of the human individual, and this preoccupation resulted in attacks on three flanks of nineteenth century thought. For Kierkegaard the primary foe was formal Christendom; he described his literary corpus as the product of uniformly religious authorship, [6] and the solution he proposed to man's existential dilemma was a religious one--the leap of personal faith. Yet it is superficial to dismiss Kierkegaard on this ground if one happens to be an opponent of religious points of view, as is evident from the thinkers of very different persuasion who have taken their cue from Kierkegaard. A secondary foe was current philosophical method, epitomised in Hegel but stemming from Descartes and continuing, say the neo-Kierkegaardians, into modern positivism and Philosophical Analysis. It may seem absurd to bracket Hegel with, say, Wittgenstein, but the point we owe to Kierkegaard is that both approaches are objective and abstractive, and lose sight of the existing person. In one sense speculative and analytic philosophy are at opposite poles, but viewed existentially they are of a kind. The third foe was the conformist society of Copenhagen, ruled by public opinion and the press, content to leave truth to the mercy of noisy social consensus.

Kierkegaard's mode of combat was existential rather than academic. While his intellect was powerful and his reflection disciplined, he did not seek to prove his point by tempered logic, but provoked the reader into self-examination by striking phrase and literary device. Thus it is as easy as it is illegitimate for the casual reader to extract slogans like 'truth is subjectivity' and 'the absurd is the object of faith,' and compose dispassionate academic rebuttals of them. To dissent from Kierkegaard one must first discover his true purpose in writing the way he did, and read enough to 'receive'--if only temporarily--the point of view. He was not seeking to found a school of thought or to recruit disciples[7] but to awaken in others an awareness of the datum of their own personal existence as a fact too real to be melted down into logico-scientific abstractions. One, but not the only consequence, that he expected from such an awakening would be the discovery of that infinite anguish which pervades every human individual because of the ambiguity of his situation as a self-conscious being in a finite jacket.

Kierkegaard and Philosophical Method

Philosophy of education is a vexed discipline, seeking to chart a course between the Scylla of Hegelian-type speculation and the Charybdis of barren linguistic analyses. But the challenge which Kierkegaard presents is of a different order altogether. Morris has done us a disservice in putting 'Existentialism' alongside other traditional 'isms' in his Philosophy and the American School, [8] in that one is not dealing with an ideology in the sense that, say, Idealism is one. Kierkegaard insists that "an existential system cannot be formulated,"[9] for the existential way of looking at things is an alternative to the logico-scientific way, and is just as likely to lead to any number of speculative constructs. The important thing is that while one may view some datum from a standpoint of detachment and objectivity, one may also view it from a standpoint of personal appropriation, of being involved in its consequences.

It is not true, as is often claimed, that Kierkegaard disregards scientific endeavor. All honor, he says,

> . . . to the pursuits of science, and all honour
> to everyone who assists in driving the cattle
> away from the sacred precincts of scholarship.

> But the ethical is and remains the highest task
> for every human being. [10]

That is, the kind of knowledge which has most bearing on human conduct qua human is that related to ethical decision. We are de-humanising man when we insist that all data must be considered in scientific categories.

> If a man occupied himself, all his life through, solely with logic, he would nevertheless not become logic; he must therefore himself exist in different categories. [11]

Swenson warns us that we are not likely to be able to grasp the significance of Kierkegaard's thought if we approach him via the "time honoured antitheses between Realism and Idealism, between Empiricism and Rationalism . . ." for they seem "somewhat lame and in need of revision"[12] when viewed existentially.

This finding squares with the growing conviction in philosophy of education that the 'isms' approach in inadequate. The stalemate which Wegener discerned in 1959[13] was only the fruition of the tradition inherited from Hegel through Dewey of endeavoring by rational speculation to encapsulate human behavior. The smug self-assurance of the 'ismatics' is exactly what Kierkegaard found so objectionable and unwarranted in Hegel.

But lest those who re-define philosophy of education purely as analysis of educational language become prematurely gleeful about support from so unexpected a quarter, it is necessary to emphasise that they too are under fire from Kierkegaard. Their criticism of the 'isms' approach is on the ground of the impossibility of logical or experimental verification. But Kierkegaard's is on the ground that rational categories cannot accommodate the existing individual, and this objection holds also for the analytic mode of philosophising. It is not faulty, but it is insufficient.

> Had not Pilate asked objectively what truth is, he would never have condemned Christ to be crucified. Had he asked subjectively, the passion of his inwardness reflecting what in the decision facing him he had in truth to do, would have prevented him from doing wrong. [14]

Philosophical analysis is after all a sophisticated Rationalism,

194

based on the assumption that the clarity afforded by reason
is the soundest guarantee of human advance. Kierkegaard
rejects this view at several points. He sees in it a per-
petuation of the intellectualist optimism of the Greeks, who
defined sin as ignorance, thereby ignoring the force of will.

> The Greek intellectualism was too . . . naive
> . . . to be able to get it sinfully into its head
> that a person knowingly could fail to do the good
> . . .[15]

Secondly, he attacks at the root the Cartesian emphasis on
the thinking being, as others have done, by pointing out the
logical error in Descartes' cogito, ergo sum. But instead
of merely refuting it, he demonstrates that the very tautology which vitiates it proves something else. 'Cogito'
means not 'thought' but 'I think, am thinking.' Kierkegaard
comments: "I am thinking, ergo I am; but if I am thinking
what wonder that I am."[16] Thought is subsequent to existence, and reality is located not in objective reflection but
in subjective decision. I do not live in the past, with
which the reflecting philosopher has to do, but in the present, where decision and involvement are mandatory. If
anything, "I choose, therefore I am," or better, having
regard to a point made later in this article, "In choosing,
I become what I am." The universe of discourse which
copes with this aspect of human-ness is ethical and dialectical.

Hence one may confidently predict that Kierkegaard
would be impatient with the Philosophical Analyst's way of
working, especially in the field of ethics. His would be
the concern of Heinemann, when he says:

> Is the analysis of ethical statements really the
> only function of a moral philosopher? Is it not
> more important to clarify the condition of man,
> . . . to appeal to them to make their own de-
> cision and to take the responsibility for their
> actions, and to discuss the criteria on which the
> rightness of an action is based?[17]

Substitute 'educational statements' for 'ethical statements'
and 'philosopher of education' for 'moral philosopher,' and
one has a new contract for the educational theorist. Whereas O'Connor[18] seeks to remove normative elements from
educational theory and Paul Hirst carefully refutes him by
demonstrating that knowledge fulfils a different function in

educational 'theory' from that in scientific 'theory,'[19] and therefore some dealings in normative judgements are unavoidable, the Kierkegaardian viewpoint insists that in matters which, like education, deal with human behavior, the normative elements are the lynch-pin of the whole investigation.

Education needs philosophers who will expose and analyse the anthropologies assumed by scientific and educational theories, and check their adequacy against existential insights into the nature of man. The norms we seek are not merely concepts or standards but stimuli to personal appropriation.

Kierkegaard and the Social Sciences

It is often claimed that the discipline of education is purely social science, hence Experimentalist and Analytic attempts to equate educational and scientific theory. Kierkegaard's commentary on such attempts may be seen in his rebellion against the Hegelian endeavour to 'mediate' between unlike phenomena (e. g. facts and values) until all are brought into harmony with a total rational synthesis.

This has three consequences. The first is the absorption of the particular. Dangerous from a purely logical point of view, this is disastrous when the particular is a human being.

> The systematic Idea is the identity of subject and object, the unity of thought and being. Existence, on the other hand, is their separation. [20]

Kierkegaard ironically describes the thinker who erects an immense building, "a system which embraces the whole of existence and world-history," but who, when we investigate his personal life, does not live in the palace but "in a barn alongside of it, or in a dog-kennel, or at the most in the porter's lodge."[21] He resembles the behavioral scientists who seek universal laws and models by which to explain man's actions, but continue to live as though they controlled their own personal fortunes. [22] The uniqueness of individuals for Kierkegaard consists not merely in their bio-social differentia but in the selfhood they develop through ethical decisions.

This invokes Kierkegaard's second objection. Hegel's system neglects ethics. [23] This is because ethics operates

196

at a different level from universal ideas. One may describe ethical standards and behavior, but this does not
supply motive or stimulus, the constraint of obligation within the individual. Jeffreys makes a similar point when he
deplores the reductionist methodology in the social sciences
which 'explains' beliefs and attitudes in terms of "basic
social, or even biological, needs," blithely ignoring the
problem of validity in a loaded quest for origins. [24] Valuable as scientific endeavor is, the study of man has a different locus from the study of any other entity. One may
study the bio-social aspect objectively for certain purposes,
but to do justice to man <u>qua</u> man another frame of reference
is called for. This is because he is a choosing being.

Hence the third objection. Hegel's system is a
necessary one and therefore deterministic. So likewise is
modern social science. But existence precedes essence
and decision the explanation of that decision. "Life can
only be explained after it has been lived"[25] and man is the
only creature who attempts explanations, for he lives in
the 'present' and is capable of looking along the time continuum.

> Time is infinite succession. The life which is in
> time and is merely that of time has no present
> . . . On the other hand if time and eternity are
> to touch one another it must be in time--and with
> this we have reached the instant . . . Only in the
> instant does history begin . . . and now begins
> spirit. [26]

Hence Kierkegaard's discontent with the orientation which
Cartesianism has given to research about man. Hence his
defence of our common belief that we possess an area of
genuine freedom of choice. Causal determinism is the
product of hindsight, but man exists in the present. The
kind of discourse which suits this aspect of the study of
man is ethico-religious; without it we are failing to discuss
man.

Note that Kierkegaard is quite prepared to concede
that "every individual begins in a historical nexus, and the
consequences of natural law are still as valid as ever,"[27]
but he insists that human personality is the measure of the
degree to which the self outstrips such factors and functions
as an autonomous agent. Because of this the study of man
requires special concepts not applicable to lower levels of
existing life. [28] "The choice itself is decisive for the content

of personality. "29

Here indeed is a fundamental cleavage between Experimentalist and Existentialist, such as no attempted rapprochement[30] can mend. It looks so hopeful--both highlight the category of 'becoming.' But whereas the Experimentalist relates 'becoming' to the stimulus-response cycle of problem solving, and views the individual behaviorally, Kierkegaard speaks of becoming a self, a 'being,' and views the individual inwardly and ethically. For one, man is a re-agent of change; for the other man is man as he becomes agent of change.

Of course the social sciences were scarcely afoot in Kierkegaard's day and he no doubt undervalued the power of heredity and environment, yet he did forsee, through the inherent assumptions of Hegelian rationalism, trends which have arisen in the social sciences and threaten the status of the individual. Moreover in one field he has had a continuing impact, despite the changes that have occurred in it since he referred to it as 'psychology.'

Kierkegaard and Psychology

It is frequently claimed, more especially in the Old World, that one of Kierkegaard's achievements is to have formulated an introspective depth psychology capable of providing significant insights that are neglected by those positivistic psychologies which presuppose that mental life is a peripheral phenomenon. [31] To those who superficially dismiss Kierkegaard's psychology as disguised theology, Rohde replies that it makes a genuine contribution as psychology per se, because of the way in which it makes the 'individual' and his introspection the focus of concern, averting that absorption of his uniqueness which occurs when behaviorist sciences concede no basic difference between human beings and animals. [32]

For Kierkegaard the individual is an existing, knowing spirit or 'self.' Man is differentiated from other entities because he knows he exists; indeed, he knows that he knows he exists. In a double act of reflection he outdistances them by his capacity not merely for consciousness but for self-consciousness. Self is a "derived, constituted relation"[33] arising from the interaction of the finite body and infinite spirit. Man's advantage over the beast, and his despair, is to be a paradoxical synthesis of "the infinite and the finite, of the temporal and the eternal, of freedom and necessity. "[34]

Hence it is Kierkegaard's conviction that in studying the existential states of mind he is engaged in a reality-quest more basic where man is concerned than behavioral descriptions. In the book Either/Or he presents the contrast between a variety of postures based on an aesthetic approach to life, and the views of a practising ethicist. It emerges that the aesthetician strives to be a spectator, detached from moral involvement with, or commitment to, other people. He takes his pleasures as they come, but is not able to rise above an inward melancholy. In this book the aesthetician is simply a hedonist, whether by inertia or design. However, taking Kierkegaard's views overall, he obviously regards the academic researcher as an aesthetician too, insofar as he concentrates on speculative wissenschaft and practises as a life-pose the attitude of objectivity and rational detachment.

A book published two years later, Stages on Life's Way, takes the analysis a step further by postulating an existence-level beyond the ethical, that is the religious. The mark of this stage is that the ethicist has come to realise the impossibility of attaining his moral ideals, and has lost his erstwhile sense of achievement in a dawning sense of estrangement and despair. It is of the essence of being human that he cannot take the pragmatist's easy way out, and tailor the ideal to the actual.

Finally, four years later in The Sickness Unto Death he differentiates religiousness A from religiousness B. The first is a state of despair in which one realises the continuity of one's spirit with the eternal, but is shackled by the finitude of the body. The second is paradoxical and specifically Christian, because it is the despair of a sin-consciousness on which has dawned the knowledge that God is transcendentally different. At this point the psychological analysis shades over into theology. The fully enlightened despair of man can only be lifted by personal faith in, and creaturely submission to, God.

The lynch-pin of Kierkegaard's analysis is the claim that all men experience a nameless despair or dread, and that therefore no psychological investigation is adequately aligned which does not employ this existential insight. He defends this thesis throughout his works but especially in Sickness Unto Death. Here he begins by showing that even the mass of men, who are not conscious of despair because of the immediacy of their living, are sick, just as one may find people who think they are healthy when their physician knows they are not. However with a

> . . . certain degree of self-reflection begins the act of discrimination whereby the self becomes aware of itself as something essentially different from the environment, from externalities and their effect upon it. [35]

and then the fat is in the fire--"the more consciousness the more intense the despair. "[36] When a man probes the enigma of his existence he exposes a sense of alienation and estrangement. This is a truth fundamental for psychology and yet a truth only personally discovered, hence Kierkegaard's reiteration to the point of overstatement: "Truth is subjectivity. "[37]

Examples of despair and its practical effects are given in one place, and relate to death, immortality and marriage. Of the last he gives a most unsatisfactory account, but his comments on death are acute. We have in common with animals that we will one day die. Yet unlike them, we know that we shall die. This is not merely objective speculation but subjective truth. "All men die" is a logical premise, but "I will one day die" is an existential contingency. As such it can impart a new seriousness to the life we live, and it is this dimension of consciousness to which Kierkegaard seeks to call us. [38] The influence of What Jaspers from a psychiatric background has termed 'boundary situations' like death, guilt and suffering is a major component of the 'existential psychology' which Europeans have developed, and to which Kierkegaard in common with Freud may be said to have contributed.

Kierkegaard and Politics

While his profoundly introspective nature equipped Kierkegaard admirably for the investigation of the individual, it worked against an equally searching analysis of society and social interaction. Bretall calls him an 'unpolitic man'[39] and in a letter he once said "I have never concerned myself with Church and State, these things are too high for me. "[40] The political revolutions of 1848 only invited his comment insofar as they caused the devaluation of some of his investments and the conscription of his man-servant. [41] Even in the Works of Love which expounds the command to love one's neighbor, no practical program of group action

200

emerges.

However he did discern signs in his own age of
social malaise, and some of his most pungent remarks retain their relevance today. His encounters with a fluctuating
public opinion moulded by the popular press produced proph-
ecies of woe that have been dreadfully fulfilled this century
and partly account for his popularity in Europe.

> Wherever there is a crowd there is untruth, so
> that (to consider for a moment the extreme case),
> even if every individual, each for himself in
> private, were to be in possession of the truth,
> yet in case they were all to get together in a
> crowd . . . a voting, noise, audible crowd--un-
> truth would at once be in evidence. [42]

Elsewhere he speaks of the "abstract, levelling process"[43]
in which press, philosophy, psychology and society are
involved, robbing the existing individual of autonomy and
worth. His remedy, the personal challenge of evangelical
religion, is not congenial to many, but his diagnosis has
been repeated a thousand times in the present age, as when
Morris refers scathingly to "the well-known massman, conformist patterns of contemporary life"[44] and Robert Beck
draws together the findings of recent sociological studies in
"Perception of Individualism in American Culture and Education. "[45]

Kierkegaard's failure to face squarely the need for
the individual to exist in a socio-political nexus was after
all a reflection of his personal flight from creative social
involvement, particularly in the intimacy of marriage. Perhaps it was necessary that his plea on behalf of the unique
individual should be so starkly presented, in order that in
the subsequent 'century of the common man' it might resist
facile amalgamation with the doctrines of sociality so current.
Undoubtedly it has been partly responsible for Reinhold
Niebuhr's new light on the social problems of America's
'great society. '

Conclusion

Kierkegaard has been too easily dismissed by slight-
ing references to his radical slogans and the lack of an
integrated social dimension in his thinking. Alternatively
he has been discussed through his interpreters, and the
cumulative power of his main argument missed. This article

cannot have presumed in so short a space to remedy these defects, but the endeavor has been made to hint at the profundity and relevance of his philosophising. Educational theory is obviously dependent upon the tools of philosophy and the social sciences, in view of its central concern with the human learner growing up in society. For this reason it stands in need of Kierkegaard's shock-treatment, especially in relation to that awkward, primitive and divine datum, the existing human person.

Notes

1. Educational Theory, II, No. 2, April 1952, pp. 80-91.

2. Robert Bretall, (ed), A Kierkegaard Anthology, London: Oxford University Press, 1947.

3. Van Cleve Morris, "Existentialism and Education," Educational Theory, IV, No. 4, Oct. 1954, pp. 247-258: "Existentialism and the Education of Twentieth Century Man," Educational Theory, XI, No. 1, Jan. 1961, pp. 52-60; and George F. Kneller, "Education, Knowledge and the Problem of Existence," Harvard Educational Review, 31, Fall 1961, pp. 427-436; Existentialism and Education, New York: Philosophical Library, 1958.

4. W. R. Niblett, "On Existentialism and Education," British Journal of Educational Studies, II, No. 2, May 1954, pp. 101-111; and M. V. C. Jeffreys' several books especially Mystery of Man, London: Pitman, 1957, and Personal Values in the Modern World, Harmondsworth, Middlesex: Penguin, 1962.

5. Especially Walter Lowrie, Kierkegaard, 2 vols., New York: Harper and Bros., 1962, and David F. Swenson, Something About Kierkegaard, Minneapolis: Augsburg Publishing House, rev. ed., 1956, chaps. 1-3.

6. The Point of View for my Work as an Author . . ., trans. Walter Lowrie, London: Oxford University Press, 1939, pp. 15 and 92.

7. He humorously points up the absurdity of such an intention by describing the man who for religious reasons believes that having disciples is wrong.

The conviction with which he promotes this view
earns him a following--of disciples! He has made
the mistake of lecturing on it as a proposition instead of living by it as subjective truth. Through the
latter he may acquire secret disciples who learn
maieutically, but they will not be his courtiers in
public. See Concluding Unscientific Postscript to
the Philosophical Fragments, trans. David F. Swenson and Walter Lowrie, London: Oxford University
Press, 1945, p. 70.

8. Boston: Houghton Mifflin, 1961.

9. Concluding Postscript, p. 107.

10. Ibid., p. 135.

11. Ibid., p. 86.

12. Swenson, op. cit., p. 35.

13. Frank C. Wegener, "The End of an Educational Epoch:
What Next?" Educational Theory, IX, No. 3, July
1959, p. 129. Wegener's article is still within the
epoch however, because he attempts to introduce yet
another 'ism' in the grand tradition, which he calls
the Organic Philosophy of Education.

14. Concluding Postscript, p. 206.

15. The Sickness Unto Death, trans. Walter Lowrie,
Princeton: Princeton University Press, 1941, p.
145.

16. Concluding Postscript, p. 281.

17. F. H. Heinemann, Existentialism and the Modern Predicament, London: Adam and Charles Black, 1953,
p. 171. Heinemann overshoots his mark in the last
clause, which is surely the point at which Analytic
method is most helpful and essential.

18. Thus D. J. O'Connor, An Introduction to the Philosophy
of Education, London: Routledge and Kegan Paul,
1958, p. 109.

19. "Philosophy and Educational Theory," British Journal
of Educational Studies, XII, No. 1 Nov. 1963, p. 60.

20. <u>Concluding Postscript</u>, p. 112.

21. <u>Sickness Unto Death</u>, p. 68.

22. Gordon Allport's work on personality is a well-known exception to the rule, but note his acknowledged debt to European 'existential psychology.' His discussion of "Scientific Models and Human Morals" is exceptionally relevant to the point here being made. See <u>Personality and Social Encounter</u>, Boston: Beacon Press, 1964, chap. 4.

23. <u>Concluding Postscript</u>, p. 99.

24. Jeffreys, <u>Mystery of Man</u>, p. 65. Also p. 19: "The sociological method tends to eliminate from the picture the distinctively human quality of behavior. The approach is one that highlights the irrational elements in behavior; the more irrational the behavior, the more easily can it be accounted for in terms of social pressure. "

25. Bretall, <u>op. cit</u>., p. 10.

26. <u>The Concept of Dread: A Simple Psychological Deliberation Oriented in the Direction of the Dogmatic Problem of Original Sin</u>, trans. Walter Lowrie, London: Oxford University Press, 1946, pp. 77-80.

27. <u>Ibid</u>., p. 65.

28. Again Jeffreys echoes Kierkegaard: "We shall never make sense of human behavior if we use sub-human categories to describe it--alongside the physico-chemical and biological categories, we need categories that are 'personal' in the sense that they provide the appropriate terms in which to discuss the behavior of rational and moral beings. " (<u>Mystery of Man</u>, p. 17). See also Allport's report of an analysis of terms employed in psychological research, which showed heavy stress on reaction to stimuli, little on the initiation of action by the person. (<u>Op. cit</u>., pp. 40-41).

29. Bretall, <u>op. cit</u>., p. 102.

30. E. g. Walter Cerf, "Existentialist Empiricism and Education, " <u>Harvard Educational Review</u>, XXVII,

Summer 1957, pp. 200-209.

31. Thus Kneller, "Education, Knowledge and the Problem of Existence," p. 429, and Allport, op. cit., p. 44.

32. Peter Rohde, Søren Kierkegaard: An Introduction to His Life and Philosophy, trans. Alan Moray Williams, London: George Allen and Unwin, 1963, p. 153.

33. Concluding Postscript, p. 135.

34. Ibid., p. 17.

35. Sickness Unto Death, p. 86.

36. Ibid., p. 65.

37. Concluding Postscript, pp. 169ff.

38. Op. cit., p. 150.

39. Bretall, op. cit., p. 259.

40. Swenson, op. cit., p. 31.

41. Lowrie, op. cit., vol. 2, p. 393.

42. Point of View, p. 112.

43. The Present Age . . ., trans. Alexander Dru, London: Fontana, 1962, p. 61.

44. Van Cleve Morris, "Existentialism and the Education of Twentieth Century Man," p. 52.

45. Educational Theory, XI, No. 3, July 1961, pp. 129-145.

Kierkegaard's Theory of Communication

Raymond E. Anderson

First published in Speech Monographs, XXX (March 1963),
1-14, the article is here reprinted with the kind permission
of the Speech Association of America, and of the author,
who is at present Professor of Speech, Augsburg College.

A speech may be analyzed and evaluated from many
points of view, such as logic, psychology, aesthetics, or
ethics. Each discipline is a domain of inquiry, a frame of
reference, and a realm of meaning; each has its own concepts, generalizations, and principles which pertain to the
management of discourse. All appropriate disciplines have
something to offer the rhetorical critic, but which should
supply the referential framework for a particular speech
depends upon the nature of the enterprise in which the
speaker is engaged and upon the context in which this undertaking has meaning and value.

The thesis of the first five sections of this article is
that existential philosophy, particularly the thought of Søren
Kierkegaard (1813-1855), brings to rhetoric a point of view
which is not only useful but also necessary to the proper
understanding and evaluation of ethical and religious discourse. The development of this thesis encompasses the
following topics: (1) the existential point of view, (2) "subjectivity" as a general end of discourse, (3) limitations of
traditional forms of discourse, (4) "indirect communication,"
and (5) "edifying discourse." In the sixth and concluding
section the writer analyzes the significance of Kierkegaard
for rhetoric in general.

The Existential Point of View

Beginning with each person's consciousness of himself, the existentialist approaches his analysis of the mental
life by using the standpoint of the experiencing person.
Each individual has a knowledge of himself which is so inti-

mate, so concrete, so immediate, and so kaleidoscopic
that no author, not even the most skillful delineator of
character, can describe it. In a scientific age, this self-
knowledge is disparaged, of course, as subjective, illusory,
or unreal, but Kierkegaard insists that each person's experience of himself has a reality more concrete than "hard
facts" stated in terms of the abstract entities of science.
The domain of the subjective life, within whose boundaries
all the decisive ethical and religious battles are won or
lost and in whose counsels the destiny of each individual is
decided, is not less real for the fact that it cannot be observed by an outsider.

One should not be surprised if Kierkegaard's way of
thinking seems unscientific. Kierkegaard had great respect
for science and was himself something of a psychologist,
but he felt that science as a way of understanding a human
life, particularly one's own, is inherently limited by its
method and point of view. Life itself forces us to adopt
an existential approach in the practical ordering of affairs,
for the forward movement of life forces us to evaluate, to
choose, to act, to determine our destiny, and to view ourselves as human beings capable of doing these things.

Existentially, a person is always seen as being in a
particular situation. Here he often is facing alternative
courses of action, and he always is in process, moving
forward in time and in a sense coming into being every
moment. Of particular interest to the existentialist is the
individual's way of dealing with the various factors given
in his existence--impulses, motives, and feelings he discovers within himself as well as people and situations in
his environment. Kierkegaard observed that men differ
greatly in their way of dealing with themselves and others;
some yield heedlessly to the impulses and inclinations of
the moment, while others make decisions thoughtfully with
reference to a lofty standard or a long-range goal. Thus,
there are different ways of living--different styles of valu-
ation--and a person's characteristic style may be called
his "mode of life."

In his doctrine of the "modes of life" Kierkegaard
sets forth a philosophy of values in which he describes the
fundamental alternatives open to every human being. He
identifies the modes of life as aesthetic, ethical, and religious and contends that this set of categories covers the
entire range of possibilities.

In his vast and complex authorship, Kierkegaard analyzes human values from several standpoints: As a philosopher, he surveys the realms of value, defines and classifies values, and discusses questions relating to their nature and grounds. As an existential psychologist, he explores the personality dynamics involved in various value orientations and in shifts from one "mode of life" to another. As a writer of imaginative literature, he creates fictitious authors, each of whom gives prolific literary expression to his particular view of life. The end of these diverse studies is a theory of aesthetic values, a theory of ethics, and a theory of religion--all brought together in a theory of values, the unifying feature of which is the existential point of view.

"Subjectivity" as a General End of Discourse

While there are three modes of life in Kierkegaard's classification, the basic division actually is twofold, since the most fundamental separation is between "aesthetic immediacy" and "ethico-religious subjectivity." Essentially, the former has to do with the enjoyment of sense experience without regard to ethical or religious considerations, and the latter with the stouthearted earnestness needed in keeping oneself in check and with the making of decisions in terms of an ethical a religious ideal.

The concept subjectivity is basic to an understanding of Kierkegaard's theory of communication, because it identifies the "essential ingredient" of ethicality and religiousness and poses, therefore, the general end of ethical and religious discourse. In the Kierkegaardian literature, this concept has a richness of meaning that is difficult to appreciate. Roughly, subjectivity designates seriousness of moral purpose--". . . the will to be and to express perfection (ideality) in every-day reality . . .";[1] more precisely, it is "An objective uncertainty held fast in an appropriation-process of the most passionate inwardness . . .[2] The psychological unity which characterizes subjectivity as a quality or an activity of the inner life tends to be obscured as one describes it. Nevertheless, one may identify in Kierkegaard's use of the term subjectivity the following dimensions of meaning: a break with immediacy--a passionate resolution by which one renounces the life of thoughtless impulse and inclination and chooses instead to live by consciously relating himself to an ideal conception of what it is to be a man; "inwardness"--a turning of attention toward the quality of one's relation to this ideal; "passion"

--wholehearted commitment; "self-awareness"--a daily
watchfulness over oneself; striving--an intensification of
the volitional aspect of personality in willing, deciding,
choosing, and renouncing; "existential dialectic"--the interplay of thought, will, feeling, and imagination in striving to
reach the ideal; acceptance of freedom and responsibility--a
willingness to endure the anxiety of freedom and to be held
responsible for one's actions; ethical maturity--a willingness
to forego immediate satisfactions in favor of long-term
commitments, and the capacity to apprehend a unifying view
of life and to follow out its declension into its manifold particulars. 3, 4

Kierkegaard's analysis of subjectivity is significant,
for the central problems of communication in the ethico-
religious sphere, as Kierkegaard sees it, are related to
the nature of the goal. Merely to list these dimensions of
meaning is to call attention to the magnitude and the com-
plexity of the problem of communication that subjectivity
poses. In fact, Kierkegaard insists that it cannot be communicated and that it, therefore, should not be regarded as
an effect of discourse but rather as an independent self-
activity.

In speaking of these matters, Kierkegaard often
points to Socrates, whom he describes (as did Plato) as a
"midwife. " Socrates, he says, did not give truth to the
learner but merely presided at its "birth"--a birth occasioned
by a series of questions designed to "bring forth" what was
within and thus to stimulate the learner into self-discovery. 5
This is Kierkegaard's conception of the relation between
subjectivity and communication. The task of "bringing
forth" subjectivity he calls "edification, " and the form of
public address used for this task is named "edifying discourse. "6

Limitations of Traditional Forms of Discourse

According to Kierkegaard, subjectivity cannot be
communicated by lecturing, arguing, or persuading, for it
is neither an idea to be explained, a proposition to be
proved, a feeling to be aroused, or a pattern of conduct to
be incited. Thus, if the edifying speaker begins to lecture,
to argue, or to persuade, he is likely to obtain a result
other than the one intended. [The issue involves the relation between content and form, and Kierkegaard insists that
the form of edifying discourse be consistent with its content
and goal. He carries this analysis further by showing specif-

ic ways in which the purposes and the methods of edifying discourse should differ from those of informative, argumentative, and persuasive presentations.

1. The basic distinction between informative and edifying discourse is that the former deals with "objective truth" whereas the latter is concerned also with "subjective truth." Objective truth is a quality of propositions; subjective truth, a quality of persons. The latter pertains only to ideality, and truth in this context is the seriousness with which a person strives to make his life conform to an ethical or a religious ideal. Thus, objective and subjective truth are separate dimensions of ethico-religious truth. 7

This difference between the two types of truth is reflected in the forms of communication suitable to each. The objective type may be communicated in a lecture, since it is transmitted directly through language symbols by a process of coding and decoding. Subjective truth, however, involves a more complex process, since its apprehension requires a "double reflection." In the first stage the listener grasps the ideal requirement in its abstract form and understands what is required of him. In the second stage he applies this understanding to himself by asking, "How is it with me?"8

Kierkegaard noted that the clergymen of his day often were lecturing when they should have been preaching. What they said usually was correct enough, but they encouraged their listeners only to reflect upon religious themes --a process which implies an attitude of personal remoteness quite proper for a lecture but not for an edifying address. In contrast, the most important thing in the edifying speech is the "thou and I," the speaker and the person addressed. Such discourse ought to be personal and subjective, and its nature is altered fundamentally if it becomes a cold analysis of ethical or religious subjects. 9

2. In discussing the relationship of edifying discourse to argumentative communication, Kierkegaard concerns himself primarily with two issues: (a) What can be demonstrated through evidence and reasoning? (b) What is likely to bring about subjectivity in the listener? His stand on both of these issues is negative, for he insists that an edifying speaker cannot possibly prove the truth of his ethical or religious life-view and that, even if this were possible, the logical demonstration would not lead the listener closer to a decisive personal commitment. 10

210

The position that proving the truth of an ethical or religious position is impossible rests upon the basic assumption that primary values are grounded not in empirical evidence or in reflection but in human interests. As a case in point, Kierkegaard analyzes the difficulties involved in any attempt to prove the truth of Christianity. He notes the element of objective uncertainty present in all historical claims, the difficulties involved in the use of miracles as proofs, and the impossibility of proving that God exists or that any event in the natural order is an act of His. [11], [12]

The claim that logical proof is ineffective as a means of winning ethico-religious conviction rests upon Kierkegaard's conception of belief. Belief is defined as the product of a volitional act in which one chooses to risk asserting a particular position even though he realizes that its truth is objectively uncertain. [13] Logical demonstration, thus, tends to prevent credence by removing the occasion for choice. What people ordinarily call belief, on the other hand, is intellectual assent to propositions; and proofs, of course, can bring this about. Ethico-religious faith, however, is a complex phenomenon involving the total personality and necessitating personal choice and continuing appropriation. Intellectual conviction regarding the objective certainty of ethical or religious propositions is inherently inconsistent with the all-consuming nature of ethico-religious belief, for thinking that one has knowledge removes the possibility that the personality of the listener can constitute itself in a decisive act of commitment. [14], [15]

3. Persuasion and edification, likewise, differ in important respects. The analysis of differences is complicated, however, by the fact that these terms are drawn from different frames of reference: persuasion is a psychological concept; edification is an ethico-religious concept.

At the risk of oversimplification, one may identify certain differences in method. The persuasive speaker seeks to capitalize on ethos; the edifying speaker seeks to minimize it. The former channels existing desires; the latter confronts the listener with an ultimate value which may require the renunciation of existing desires. The one employs techniques of suggestion; the other fears that the use of suggestion may short-circuit the very process of valuation he hopes to cultivate. [16], [17], [18]

Before we leave this discussion of the limitations of the traditional forms of communication, several observations should be made. First, the line between edifying discourse and the other forms probably cannot be drawn as sharply as these contrasts seem to suggest; the difference in most cases, indeed, is a matter of degree. Second, the principle that self-actualization (of which subjectivity appears to be an instance) cannot be produced directly by lecturing, convincing, or persuading, has long been accepted in the field of psychological counseling, and it would seem to have far-reaching significance for the theory of discourse. Third, if one is to take a humanistic view, one must agree with Kierkegaard's contention that, when discourse deals with the ultimate questions of life, the use of persuasion reveals a fundamental disrespect for human personality. In regard to the "leap"--the choice which determines one's destiny--a man has a right to risk his own life, but not that of another.

Indirect Communication

Kierkegaard's analysis of the problem of communication posed by the nature of subjectivity led him to develop and to employ a technique of "indirect communication." Considering himself to be something of a Socrates in this respect, he often describes his own approach as maieutic.

A direct form of discourse is useful, according to Kierkegaard, if one is communicating objective content or if the listener already has a serious interest in the ethical or religious quality of his life. Indirection, however, becomes necessary if the objective content is known and accepted while inwardness is lacking. [19] Thus, to arouse inwardness in a person who has an essentially correct understanding of what it is to be religious, who is not earnestly striving to live up to this understanding, and who does not notice the contradiction but continues to think of himself as a religious person, requires indirection; for such a person lives in an "illusion" which is immune to the frontal attack which characterizes the traditional forms of discourse. Few men, according to Kierkegaard, have understood this problem or have known how to deal with it as well as did Socrates. The presence of ethico-religious illusions, for both Socrates and Kierkegaard, indicates the need for an indirect method of communication. [20, 21]

What is the nature of the illusion which a communicator must dispel if he is to succeed in the ethico-religious sphere? Although there are as many forms of ethical and religious illusions as there are modes of behavior which superficially seem to be genuinely ethical or religious, a threefold classification of these illusions is possible--the poetic, the practical, and the speculative. In each of these types the individual confuses subjectivity with the more apparent correlates: in the poetic, with moods and feelings; in the practical, with respectability and practical accomplishment; and in the speculative, with reading, thinking, and talking about ethical and religious matters. [22]

Such misconceptions, of course, are subtle and stubborn--so formidable that the task of dispelling ethico-religious illusions requires an entirely new "military science":

> Here I cannot develop further the pressing need Christendom has of an entirely new military science permeated through and through by reflection. In several of my books I have furnished suggestions about the principal factors of such a science. The gist of it all can be expressed in one word: The method must be indirect. But the development of this method may require the labour of years, alert attention every hour of the day, daily practice of the scales, or patient finger-exercise in the dialectical, not to speak of a never slumbering fear and trembling . . . All the old military science, all the apologetic and whatever goes with it, serves rather--candidly speaking--to betray the cause of Christianity. At every instant and at every point the tactics must be adapted to a fight which is waged against a conceit, an illusion. [23]

Nor is the need for a "military science" without specific application to the problems of the clergy, many of whom, although convinced that the apparent religiousness of their membership was illusory, did not know what to do about it. The need for a new type of discourse was urgent. With no better method at hand, the usual course was a direct attack, the sort of assault which arouses defensive reactions, sets the will in opposition, and ends by strengthening the listener in his illusion. [24] If the listener happens to be in an agreeable mood, the effect of directness is that he not only agrees with everything the speaker says but also affirms that he has always believed the same. [25] Such an outcome, of course, is as useless as outright rejection.

This, then, is the situation which calls for an indirect method. What is meant by "indirect communication?"

213

First, one must distinguish between the form in which an idea is expressed and the process of communication. Although the form of edifying discourse is direct, the process is always rather indirect where subjectivity is concerned, because its reception involves the "double reflection" of personal appropriation--grasping the ideal requirement abstractly and intellectually and then applying it to oneself concretely and existentially. [26]

Kierkegaard's basic technique for attaining indirection and the consequent lingering upon an idea is ambiguity; thus, if the recipient is to learn anything, he must discover it for himself. As compared to lucid discourse, this ambiguity serves two purposes: (a) It arouses attention to a high degree by confronting the recipient with a puzzle; (b) it evokes a response at a deep level of the personality by requiring a decision. The goal of indirect communication, then, is not to clarify an idea, secure acceptance of a proposal, or arouse emotion, but to stimulate the recipient into independent activity. [27]

The means by which indirectness produces this stimulation is the "sign of contradiction," a concept which includes all forms of ambiguity used for purposes of communication. [28] As Kierkegaard illustrates by the following situation, such a sign may involve more than the use of unclear language:

> If a man were to stand on one leg, or pose in a queer dancing attitude swinging his hat, and in this attitude propound something true, his few auditors would provide themselves into two groups; and many listeners he would not have, since most men would give him up at once. The one class would say: "How can what he says be true, when he gesticulates in that fashion?" The other class would say: "Well, whether he cuts capers or stands on his head, even if he were to throw handsprings, what he says is true and I propose to appropriate it, letting him go." [29]

Here the indirection arises out of an ambiguity regarding the communicator himself, and the auditor is forced to make a judgment. If the speaker were then to abandon this queer posture, he might still continue to communicate indirectly by giving his discourse an indirect form. For example, he might combine jest and earnestness so deftly that one could scarcely tell whether he was serious, or he might combine attack and defense so cleverly that one would not know whether it was the one or the other. Whether the ambiguity arises from the communicator or from the form of the discourse, the recipient is faced with a puzzle which he must unlock for himself.

Kierkegaard observed that the most striking instance of indirect communication in the religious sphere is Christianity. When God assumes the form of a man and walks among men incognito, he reasons, men reveal themselves by how they respond. In this case, Jesus is the "sign of contradiction."

> And this only the sign of contradiction can do:
> it draws attention to itself, and then it presents
> a contradiction. There is something which makes
> it impossible to desist from looking--and lo!
> while one looks, one sees as in a mirror, one
> gets to see oneself . . . . A contradiction placed
> directly in front of a man--if only one can get
> him to look upon it--is a mirror; while he is
> judging, what dwells within him must be revealed.
> . . . The contradiction puts before him a choice,
> and while he is choosing, he himself is revealed. 30

In conclusion of this section, two further points may be raised: whether Kierkegaard as an author took his own advice and whether indirection is ethical. The answer to the first of these points is that Kierkegaard in his own writings makes extensive use of various forms of indirect communication. One of the most novel of these is the use of pseudonyms. To give alternative views of life both concreteness and dramatic power, he employs the technique of the playwright and invents imaginary characters who speak for themselves. They not only express their own views, but also, like participants in a dialogue, interact with one another. 31 Realizing that many readers would be impatient with this method and would ask why he did not come right out and say what he meant, Kierkegaard prepared a reply:

> I will be quite frank about it; my conception of
> communication by means of books is very dif-
> ferent from what I generally see put forward
> respecting it, and what seems silently to be taken
> for granted. The indirect mode of communication
> makes communication an art in quite a different
> sense than when it is conceived in the usual man-
> ner: that the maker of the communication has to

present something to the attention of one who
knows, that he may judge it, or to the attention
of one who does not know, that he may learn
something. But no one bothers himself about the
next consideration, that which makes communication dialectically so difficult, that the recipient is
an existing individual, and that this is essential. [32]

Elsewhere Kierkegaard goes beyond explaining his
method to giving an argument for it:

If anyone were to say that this is mere declama-
tion, that all I have at my disposal is a little
irony, a little pathos, a little dialectics, my reply
would be "What else should anyone have who proposes to set forth the ethical?" Should he perhaps
set it objectively in a framework of paragraphs
and get it smoothly by rote, so as to contradict
himself by his form? [33, 34]

As a final note for this section, is indirect communication ethical? Is it not a form of deception to keep the
reader or the listener in the dark regarding one's position
or one's intentions? Kierkegaard admits the accuracy of
the criticism, but then he adds: "One must not let oneself
be deceived by the word 'deception'." As Socrates pointed
out, deception may be used in the service of truth, or at
least may be a means of eliminating illusion:

Indeed, it is only by this means, i. e., by de-
ceiving him, that it is possible to bring into the
truth one who is in an illusion. Whoever rejects
this opinion betrays the fact that he is not over-
well versed in dialectics, and that is precisely
what is especially needed when operating in this
field. For there is an immense difference, a
dialectical difference, between these two cases:
the case of a man who is ignorant and is to have
a piece of knowledge imparted to him, so that he
is like an empty vessel which is to be filled or a
blank sheet of paper on which something is to be
written; and the case of a man who is under an
illusion and must be first delivered from that. [35]

Temporarily to suppress the truth "in order that
truth may become truer," therefore, is both right and
essential. The device should be understood as a "teleological suspension" of the ethical principle that one ought

216

always to tell the truth.

Edifying Discourse

In addition to his observations on the limitations of traditional forms of discourse and his theory of indirect communication, Kierkegaard has a great deal to say regarding edifying discourse. This branch of communication is a broad category which includes all forms of speaking or writing designed to cultivate subjectivity by addressing the recipient directly and intimately rather than indirectly through literary media. [36], [37] The edifying speaker may employ techniques of indirection, but his form is direct in that the meaning is not hidden ambiguity. Obscurity is considered unnecessary because the discourse addresses itself to the individual who already has some interest in the ethical or the religious quality of his life. [38]

What are the practical implications of using existentialism as a viewpoint for examining edifying discourse as an attempt to cultivate subjectivity? The following are a few of Kierkegaard's many suggestions to the speaker employing this form of public address:

1. Edifying discourse should address itself to the individual. [39] In a peculiar way, edifying discourse speaks to each listener individually, for edification, like love, has to do only with individuals. This type of communication, in other words, deals with a kind of truth "whose chief feature is that one must be alone about it . . . since it is just this solitariness which is the way."[40]

Each listener should be helped to see himself as individually and solely responsible for the quality of his own life. An edifying address is not a call to a united endeavor but a "summons to a separate accounting."[41]

2. Edifying discourse should be personal and subjective. The proper mood is that of earnest admonition and exhortation: "Do not check your soul's flight, do not grieve the better promptings within you, do not dull your spirit with half wishes and half thoughts . . ."[42] Kierkegaard notes that during such an address the usual relation of subject and object is reversed. Whereas at an ordinary lecture the speaker and the listener examine the subject matter, at an edifying address they are the objects of the examination, so to speak, by the content. [43]

217

In contrast, if the speaker deals with his topic in a straightforward manner, he cultivates objectivity in the listener rather than subjectivity and thus gives a simple lecture. His presentation lacks a distinguishing feature of edifying discourse--namely, the emphasis upon the listener's relation to what is understood--that is, upon the obligation to act with all one's might in pursuance of what one does understand. Objectivity should be viewed, therefore, as a temptation for both speaker and audience, for in ethical and religious matters, personal detachment is a convenient means of escape from the pain of self-examination and personal responsibility. [44]

3. Edifying discourse should be concrete rather than abstract so as to communicate ideality effectively through the medium of the imagination. Since edification is an effort to communicate subjective thought, it is an attempt to talk about that which cannot be verbalized. Words, being categories, are unavoidably abstract and are thus inherently limited in dealing with the existential. [45]

In view of this difficulty, the preacher makes a serious error if he tries to deliver "eternal truths in abstracto" instead of setting forth "what the ordinary man fills out the day with in the living room."[46] To be effective, the edifying speaker must be something of a poet, and his discourse must have a strong imaginative element. This imaginative material should penetrate beneath the surface and bring to light the hidden thoughts, wishes, and fantasies which characterize the subjective valuative life. The goal in such probing is not merely to "hold the mirror up to nature" so that the listener can see his own inner life; the aim also is to help him to see himself in the light of an ideal conception of what it is to be a man.

4. Edifying discourse should stress process rather that result. Since this type of communication is concerned with subjectivity--with inwardness and with the "existential dialectic" of striving with oneself in relation to the ideal-- the emphasis is always upon the process of valuation (of "existing") rather than upon external conduct. The basic technique is to bring inwardness to the light by making the listener "contemporary with an existing individual in his existence."[47]

Although the edifying speaker may use artistic means to bring inwardness to the level of self-realization, the essential nature of edification makes it possible for the speaker to achieve the same result simply and directly. The reason for this, as Kierkegaard observes, is that the edifying address is essentially an earnest man talking aloud to himself. 48 His discourse, in other words, is such that, although he is the speaker, he also is a hearer who feels himself examined by his own presentation. If in earnestness he permeates his own daily existence with an awareness of the ideality contained in his address, he has the true power of eloquence at hand every moment. He has only to think aloud about the particulars of life to make the hearer contemporary with an existing individual.

5. The edifying speaker should respect the independence of the listener. One of the many things Kierkegaard admired about Socrates was his way of holding the pupil at a little distance so as to preserve the learner's freedom. He remarks that "Socrates was an ethical teacher, but he took cognizance of the absence of any direct relationship between teacher and pupil, because the truth is inwardness, and because this inwardness is precisely the road which leads them away from one another. "49

The respondent's right of ethical self-determination does not come to light when discourse is analyzed from the standpoint of psychology, but from the ethico-religious point of view this right becomes a matter of importance. The edifying speaker, as one practical implication, should refrain from the use of techniques designed to put psychological pressure on the listener: ". . . gesticulation and wiping the sweat from the brow, strength of voice and vigor of fist, along with deliberate employment of the same in order to accomplish something, are aesthetic reminiscences . . . "50 Thus, with a relatively modest approach, the edifying speaker ". . . lets God keep the thunder and the might and the glory. "51

6. Edifying discourse should stress possibility more than reality. Although listeners are more impressed by heroic deeds performed in real life than by similar exploits recounted in tales of the imagination, the edifying speaker should see a certain danger in the use of "real life" illustrations. The listener should not admire what he ought to imitate, for, as Kierkegaard explains, ". . . there is a certain ingenuousness of spirit which seeks to protect itself against the ethical impression precisely by means of admiration. "52

When religious heroes appear in the edifying address,

219

therefore, the emphasis is not on the fact that they actually performed their reputed deeds but on the thought that such achievements are possible for all and indeed are required. The ideal should sting the listener and thus play a more active role than evoking admiration.   "A communication in terms of the possible operates in terms of the ideal man (not the differential ideal but the universal ideal), whose relationship to every man is that of a requirement."53

In addition to developing these general principles of edification, Kierkegaard has a great deal to say about the uniqueness of the Christian sermon.   The following are among the more unusual features of his analysis: the "Absolute Paradox" as an instrument of communication; the "offense" of Christianity as a factor in eliciting an existential response; "sin" as a uniquely Christian concept which is important to the sermon; and "contemporaneousness" as a basic technique of Christian preaching.   In addition, Kierkegaard criticizes Christian preachers by showing how they lecture, argue, and persuade rather than preach, how they falsify Christianity by transforming it from a "paradoxical existence-communication" into a doctrine, how they reduce Christianity to a sentimental paganism, and how they misconstrue and misuse the dialectic of authority and revelation. 54, 55, 56, 57

Kierkegaard sometimes talks of edifying discourse as "a healing art" and refers to the edifying speaker as a "physician of souls. "   The illness with which this physician is concerned is the "sickness of the self" which is essentially a lack of subjectivity.   This malady takes many forms which are characterized variously by "spiritlessness," disillusionment, hopelessness, remorse, negativism, or defiance.   Fleeing from freedom and moral responsibility, the individual prefers "unfreedom" and clings tenaciously to protective views, such as scientific "explanations" of his condition. 58

Kierkegaard considers it important for the edifying speaker to understand the sickness of the self from the existential point of view, since from this position one gets a clear picture of the dynamics of sickness and health; one sees what the individual is doing to perpetuate his illness and what he must do to move toward health.   It is important also for the edifying speaker to realize that a person who clings to "unfreedom" has a "dread of the good"--anxiety at the thought of freedom and responsibility.   As a consequence, he is resistant to influences which tend in this direction.[59]

The Kierkegaardian literature thus leads us to an understanding of edifying discourse in several ways. His analysis of the traditional forms helps us to see what edifying discourse is not; his theory of indirect communication and his use of imaginative literature show how one may present alternative views of life concretely and imaginatively. His own edifying discourses (some eighty in all) serve as models for study and analysis.[60] His conception of health and sickness in the self, his analysis of the forms of this sickness, and his theory of anxiety have many implications for the edifying speaker. Finally, his interpretation of Christianity, his criticism of the preachers, and his description of the Christian sermon are of special interest to students of Christian communication.

Kierkegaard's Significance for Rhetoric

Kierkegaard's insights regarding religious communication and the new dimensions which he provided for individual aspects of rhetoric are important, but what are his more general contributions? First, he gives us new vantage points for viewing Socrates and Aristotle. Second, he illuminates the thesis that a philosophy of rhetoric has practical importance. Third, he strengthens rhetoric as a humane study and broadens its base.

Kierkegaard's Relation to Socrates and Aristotle

The views of Socrates on communication were greatly admired by the Danish philosopher. In the words of David F. Swenson: "It is because Kierkegaard reveals an inner sympathy with him, an understanding of the Greek thinker which is unexampled for its intimacy, and because he seems to have fulfilled, in relation to his own time and age, an ethical task analogous to that which Socrates fulfilled in Greece, that we are justified in calling him a modern Socrates."[61] If Kierkegaard's interpretation of Socrates is valid, his analysis of the significance of the Socratic dialectic and of Socratic irony helps us to appreciate the Greek master's method of teaching as well as his frequent attacks on the rhetoricians.

The ethical passion of Socrates and the objectivity and the theoretical interest of Aristotle are combined in Kierkegaard. Like the former, he goes beyond the role of the pedagogue to that of a rhetorician who seeks to perfect a method of communication which will be consistent with an ethical teacher's respect for his pupil's right of self-determination. With Aristotle he shares an interest in formulating a practical system for the management of discourse--a system grounded in a psychologically correct analysis of the relevant motivational processes.

How is the existential analysis of communication related to Aristotle's Rhetoric? Although the two differ in purpose, in the standpoint from which discourse is analyzed, and in the categories employed, Kierkegaard apparently has no objection to the Rhetoric as a general study of the means of persuasion. He is convinced, however, that Aristotelian logic and psychology do not provide the most appropriate categories for analyzing and evaluating ethical and religious discourse. The two theories of communication, thus, are not in conflict; rather, they are parallel efforts within different domains of inquiry. Both are within the scope of rhetoric as that term is used today.

Practical Importance of a Philosophy of Rhetoric

From time to time rhetoricians have been reminded that they should take "a broad philosophical view of the principles of the Art,"[62] should "attend to the philosophical problems which are at the root of the discipline,"[63] and should not concern themselves merely with the formulation and the arrangement of rules. Kierkegaard's theory of communication demonstrates the importance of this advice by pointing up what has not always been obvious to students of rhetoric--the intimate relation which exists between a theory of discourse and the philosophic outlook which underlies and nourishes it.

This relationship may be clarified by recalling the different aspects of rhetoric. Rhetoric involves (1) discourse to be composed or analyzed, (2) rules, principles, and evaluative criteria to guide these activities, (3) rationale or basic theory derived from the relevant subject matter of various fields, and (4) metatheory and philosophy of rhetoric.[64] These levels are richly illustrated and interrelated in Kierkegaard. For example, his distinction between subjective and objective thought leads to a corresponding differentiation between ethico-religious language and language about ethics and religion; and this distinction, in turn, is the basis for both a discussion of the differences between a lecture and an edifying address and for an explication of the principles of edifying discourse. Nor is this example unique. On the contrary, one can point to any aspect of Kierkegaard's theory of communication and rather easily relate it to the basic categories and presuppositions of his philosophy. Thus, by illustrating the dependence of a theory of discourse upon its presuppositions, Kierkegaard demonstrates the practical importance of the philosophy of rhetoric.

Rhetoric as a Humane Study

Finally, what is Kierkegaard's most significant contribution to rhetoric? Although a fresh point of view and a new set of categories for the analysis and the evaluation of communication are significant existentialist offerings, the truly important consideration is that Kierkegaard's philosophy is a protest against the dehumanization of modern man. A human approach to the study of human beings, it broadens the base of rhetorical theory and thus strengthens rhetoric as a humane study.

Some years ago, Everett Hunt defended a humanistic view of rhetoric in these words: "Rhetoric is the study of men persuading men to make free choices. "[65] As profound as it is simple, this definition expresses in a few words a whole philosophy of rhetoric. Kierkegaard, too, feels that the highest power and the noblest use of discourse is not in the area of compulsion. "Socrates, " he remarks, "knew better: the art of using power to make men free. "[66]

The emphasis upon humaneness is obtained in two major ways. First, existentialism puts science as a philosophic influence into its proper place. The temptation to overemphasize science, so well known today, was great even in the early part of the nineteenth century, and it was important then, as it is now, to make it clear that knowledge only clarifies the possibilities for action, that choice is a distinctive human act, and that the capability of analyzing life scientifically does not mean that it can be lived scientifically. Man's capacity to consider the possibilities and to choose constitutes his freedom, and his freedom, together with his ability to use it responsibly, is his uniqueness and his dignity.

This stress upon humaneness, however, does not become an antiscience. The existentialist realizes that science is one valid approach to the study and the interpretation of human experience. However, although not a revolt against the systematic study of human beings, exis-

223

tentialism is a protest against the imperialism of the scientific outlook and against the uncritical acceptance of the scientific account as the interpretation of man. Science is not the explanation of the world; it is only a very special sort of elucidation which uses abstract entities and which states mathematical relations between measurable aspects of selected bits of experience. The limitations of science as a picture of reality are inherent in its method and in its presuppositions. The quantitative and the real are not identical. [67]

Second, existentialism emphasizes humaneness through its affirmation of the reality of the inner experience of man --a recognition that these inner "events" can be located, precisely indicated, clarified and confirmed, and tested and attested. The human mind may be seen both from within and from without, so to speak, and observations from both viewpoints yield clues to its nature. Even if it were demonstrated that every thought and every act is finally determined, each individual would still have to face all of the decisions and crises of a personal existence, and the existential point of view would remain as important and as legitimate as ever. Nietzsche's affirmation would still stand--that man is the only being who makes promises and thus determines his future and who renders changes insignificant by subjecting them to a sovereign principle. [68]

In other words, Kierkegaard's theory of communication is founded upon an affirmation of the inner man and upon a sensible view of science--both of which remain valid. This approach to the study of personality, as the Danish philosopher saw clearly, was necessary and could be defended against the charge that it was unscientific. [69] Kierkegaard's theory of communication, thus, is a distinguished contribution to our understanding of rhetoric as a humane study.

Conclusion

The theory of communication implicit in the writings of Søren Kierkegaard is provocative, practical, informative, and even inspiring. His existential philosophy leads him to the concept of subjectivity as a general end of discourse, to an analysis of the limitations of the traditional forms of communication, and to an explication of indirect communication and edifying discourse. Although his immediate objective was to assist speakers and writers who dealt with ethico-religious topics, his ideas are seminal for rhetoric generally.

1. Søren Kierkegaard, Training in Christianity, trans. Walter Lowrie (Princeton, N. J. : Princeton University Press, 1947), p. 188.

2. Søren Kierkegaard, Concluding Unscientific Postscript to the "Philosophical Fragments," trans. David F. Swenson and Walter Lowrie; ed. Walter Lowrie (Princeton, N. J. : Princeton University Press, 1944), p. 182.

3. Postscript, pp. 79 note, 84-85, 171, 227, 273, 313.

4. Søren Kierkegaard, Either/Or, trans. Walter Lowrie (Princeton, N. J. : Princeton University Press, 1949), II, 192.

5. Søren Kierkegaard, Philosophical Fragments, trans. David F. Swenson (Princeton, N. J. : Princeton University Press, 1936), pp. 5-8.

6. Postscript, p. 243.

7. Postscript, pp. 169-170.

8. Ibid., pp. 67-86.

9. Training, pp. 227-228.

10. Postscript, pp. 15-16, 49-55, 86-113.

11. Ibid., pp. 25-48.

12. Training, pp. 31, 98-99.

13. Fragments, pp. 67-69.

14. Postscript, pp. 380-381.

15. Training, p. 144.

16. Postscript, pp. 16, 22-23, 47, 65, 73-74, 92-94, 117, 215, 221, 232-233, 247, 347-353, 362, 379, 399 note, 430-431, 436-437.

17. Søren Kierkegaard, The Point of View, trans. Walter Lowrie (London: Oxford University Press, 1939),

pp. 21, 61, 112-113, 129, 136-138.

18. _Training_, pp. 222-223, 361.

19. _Postscript_, p. 217.

20. _Point of View_, pp. 22-27.

21. _Kierkegaard's Attack Upon "Christendom_," trans.
    Walter Lowrie (Princeton, N. J.: Princeton Univer-
    sity Press, 1946), pp. 283-285.

22. Søren Kierkegaard, _Stages on Life's Way_, trans.
    Walter Lowrie (Princeton, N. J.: Princeton Univer-
    sity Press, 1945), pp. 437-438.

23. _Point of View_, p. 38.

24. _Ibid._, p. 24.

25. _Postscript_, pp. 71-73.

26. _Ibid._, pp. 67-74.

27. _Postscript_, pp. 216-217.

28. _Training_, pp. 124-125.

29. _Postscript_, pp. 235-236.

30. _Training_, p. 126.

31. This device creates problems for the scholar who
    wants to know what Kierkegaard himself believed,
    since to be strictly correct, one ought never to
    attribute to Kierkegaard any statement that appears
    under a pseudonym.

32. _Postscript_, pp. 246-247.

33. _Ibid._, p. 137.

34. No mention is made here of Kierkegaard's theory of
    the comic. It should be noted, however, that he
    wrote a dissertation on Socratic irony and that his
    writings contain many interesting observations on the
    use of the comic in ethico-religious communication.

35. Point of View, pp. 39-40.

36. Postscript, pp. 229, 241, 243, 244.

37. On the basis of Kierkegaard's thought edifying discourse may be classified into three forms: ethical, immanental religious, and transcendental religious. To define these categories would require an exposition of the "existence spheres," a task beyond the scope of this article.

38. Postscript, p. 217.

39. Point of View, pp. 111- 138.

40. Postscript, p. 65.

41. Søren Kierkegaard, Purity of Heart, trans. Douglas V. Steere, Torchbook ed. (New York: Harper & Brothers, 1956), pp. 184-197.

42. Either/Or, II, 294.

43. Training, pp. 228-229.

44. Postscript, pp. 173ff.

45. Ibid., pp. 276, 312-322, 414.

46. Ibid., p. 415.

47. Postscript, p. 257.

48. Stages, pp. 419-420.

49. Postscript, p. 221.

50. Stages, p. 419.

51. Ibid., p. 419.

52. Postscript, p. 321.

53. Ibid., p. 321.

54. Postscript, pp. 229-230, 493, 518.

55. Training, Parts I-II.

56. Fragments, Chapters I-III.

57. Søren Kierkegaard, On Authority and Revelation, trans.
     Walter Lowrie (Princeton, N. J. : Princeton Univer-
     sity Press, 1955), pp. 105-120.

58. Søren Kierkegaard, Fear and Trembling and The Sick-
     ness Unto Death, trans. Walter Lowrie (New York:
     Doubleday and Company, 1954), pp. 142-262.

59. Søren Kierkegaard, The Concept of Dread, trans.
     Walter Lowrie (Princeton, N. J. : Princeton Univer-
     sity Press, 1946), pp. 105-137.

60. Søren Kierkegaard, Edifying Discourses, 4 vols. ,
     trans. David F. Swenson and Lillian Marvin Swenson
     (New York: Harper & Brothers, 1943-1946).   Ad-
     ditional discourses appear in the following works:
     Christian Discourses (London: Oxford, 1952); For
     Self-Examination (Minneapolis, Minn. : Augsburg
     Publishing House, 1940); The Gospel of Suffering and
     Lilies of the Field (Minneapolis, Minn. : Augsburg
     Publishing House, 1948); Purity of Heart (New York:
     Harper & Row, 1938, 1956); Thoughts on Crucial
     Situations in Human Life (Minneapolis, Minn. : Augs-
     burg Publishing House, 1941); Training in Christianity
     (Princeton, N. J. : Princeton University Press, 1947);
     Works of Love (Princeton, N. J. : Princeton Univer-
     sity Press, 1946).

61. David F. Swenson, Something about Kierkegaard
     (Minneapolis, Minn. : Augsburg Publishing House,
     1945), p. 37.

62. I. A. Richards, The Philosophy of Rhetoric (New York
     and London: Oxford University Press, 1936), p. 7.

63. Maurice Natanson, "The Limits of Rhetoric," QIS,
     XLI (April, 1955), 135.

64. Natanson, p. 139.

65. "Rhetoric as a Humane Study," QIS, XLI (April, 1955),
     p. 114.

66. The Journals of Søren Kierkegaard, A Selection, ed.
     and trans. Alexander Dru (London: Oxford Univer-
     sity Press, 1938), No. 616, p. 180.

67. J. W. N. Sullivan, The Limitations of Science, Mentor ed. (New York: The Viking Press, 1949), p. 135.

68. H. J. Blackham, Six Existentialist Thinkers, Torchbook ed. (New York: Harper & Row, 1959), p. 74.

69. Among the modern psychological works which recognize the importance of Kierkegaard's interpretation of personality are these: Gordon Allport, Becoming (New Haven: Yale University Press, 1955), pp. 79-84; Rollo May, The Meaning of Anxiety (New York: The Ronald Press Company, 1950), passim.

Kierkegaard and Counseling
for Individuality

Ben Strickland

First published in the Personnel and Guidance Journal,
XLIV (January 1966), 470-474, and is here reprinted with
the kind permission of the American Personnel and Guidance
Association and of the author, who is at present Director
of Counselor Education, Texas Christian University.

Not too long ago existentialism was considered
largely an atheistic philosophy. Today many
disciplines are considering the philosophy for its
positive attributes. One of the more recent
areas to be influenced by existentialism seems
to be that of individual counseling as indicated by
the appearance of numerous journal articles within the last few years. One of the more prominent writers in the school of existentialism,
Søren Kierkegaard, sometimes called the "father
of existentialism," seems to have been speaking
to the modern day counselor as he attempted to
describe the process and climate wherein such
characteristics as individuality are fostered.

An attempt to identify or define a philosophical approach to counseling that is widely respected by guidance
personnel today would encounter some difficulty. This is
not to suggest that any one philosophy of counseling would
be adequate in terms of the varied concepts and personalities represented by guidance programs across the country.
This does point up the absence of philosophical contributions
to current literature related to guidance and/or counseling.
Such literature contains large quantities of research employing experimental, descriptive, and historical approaches
with only an occasional reference to philosophical aspects of
counseling. This disproportionate lack of concern for counseling philosophy seems to have been characteristic of the

230

guidance movement.

Some authorities suggest that the basis for the lack of emphasis on counseling philosophy can be found in the origin and development of guidance. Williamson (1961), for example, has suggested that guidance services have arisen out of problems rather than from a system of philosophy. Wrenn (1963) has indicated that another reason for the lack of attention to counseling philosophy can be found in the rapidity with which guidance programs have developed, leaving little time for the evolvement of a philosophy.

Allport (1962) and Maslow (1962) have also pointed up the lack of philosophical emphases in psychological literature, wherein no commonly accepted comprehensive theory of man can be found. Such a lack of philosophical emphasis in psychology could partially explain some of the lack of philosophical bases in counseling theory that has drawn heavily from psychological theory. The neglect of philosophical application in psychology or counseling cannot be attributed to any lack of interest in philosophy in general; that is, if quantity of publications available is an indicator of interest. A reader can find an ample supply of publications in many areas of philosophical thought. At least some of this interest seems to have been stimulated by the advent of the contemporary philosophy of existentialism. The problem of adapting various philosophical emphases--including existentialism--for practical utilization is indeed difficult, however, and supposedly could account for some of the lack of philosophical emphases in the various areas.

The difficulty of philosophical adaptation would not seem so great as to justify the omission of such emphasis in the development of a theory of human behavior, particularly in view of the current interest expressed by various writers. In a recent publication (May, 1961), for example, Allport, Maslow, Rogers, May, and others suggested the importance of a revaluation of current psychological emphases in terms of philosophical association or content. The particular philosophical emphasis to which these writers were referring was that of existentialism, which they felt could contribute significantly to the development of philosophical bases for psychology and related fields.

What is existentialism? Although somewhat difficult to define in operational terms, existentialism is a school of thought that is concerned with the individual and his attempt to retain his identity, make his own choices, and provide his own self-direction. The reason for this very general definition is that there is no single philosophy of existentialism. Instead, the existential school of thought has developed around the works of many different individuals whose concept of man has varied greatly. Who, then, is an existentialist? According to the general definition suggested above, anyone who chooses to evaluate and determine his own destiny could be considered an existentialist. One of the first existentialists, according to many contemporary scholars, was Søren Kierkegaard, a Danish religious writer of the 19th century. Although there is some disagreement as to who provided the first emphasis for the existentialist school of thought, some scholars insist that this emphasis dates back to Plato and possibly even before his time, many contemporary writers consider Kierkegaard to be the "father of existentialism." In keeping with this recognition, it would seem appropriate to consider Kierkegaard's emphases in any attempt to relate the philosophy of existentialism to counseling theory.

Kierkegaardian Individuality

Individuality was a prime concern of Kierkegaard, as indicated by the fact that he attempted to describe the various aspects of individuality in all his 43 works. He has devoted much effort to the development of this concept as can be found in such works as The Point of View for My Work as an Author (1962). To Kierkegaard, individuality was an accomplishment rather than an endowment; an active rather than passive endeavor. Physical characteristics, for example, would not be criteria for individuality because these are natural endowments. A person is born with a certain physical structure, body chemistry, and chromosomal arrangement that make him unlike any other person. Yet these possessions were acquired through no effort on the part of each person; and, although these may be desirable or undesirable, they did not result from active pursuits. Briefly then, individuality is the extent to which a person is realizing his potential. According to Kierkegaard, this potential is not necessarily the potential to become a great orator or athlete "for the greatest thing is not to be this or that but to be oneself, and this everyone can be" (1944a). It is the potential to become himself. Since the phrase, "to become himself," is subject to a variety of contemporary meanings, it will be necessary to describe briefly the process as suggested by Kierkegaard.

To Become Himself

As has been previously suggested, to become oneself requires an active engagement on the part of each person. This is a process that begins early in life as a person begins to establish some sort of identity. He recognizes that he is something different from his environment and that he has control, to some extent, over this something. As he begins to exercise control, he develops a frame of reference, or self, that represents a synthesis of his past experiences and his aspirations, his potentials and limitations. As he experiences life, his frame of reference enlarges; he understands more of himself and begins to develop a more realistic frame of reference wherein he realizes that although he may have certain limitations, he will have a busy existence realizing the potential that he does have. Furthermore, he begins to realize that to attempt to achieve the potentials of others may prevent the development of his own potentials. This does not mean (according to Kierkegaard) that a person should not identify with a great artist, for example, and attempt to develop his potential in that direction. It does mean, however, that as the person tests reality, he begins to identify the direction of his potential and realizes that coping in a direction wherein he has limitations might be obstructive to the development of his own potential.

To become oneself, then, refers to the recognition of one's own potentials and the acceptance of the challenge of realizing them. To become oneself is to develop individuality, according to Kierkegaard, and it is "in everyman's power to become what he is, an individual" (1962).

Thus, individuality is itself a potential. Yet it is a potential that every man possesses. Victor Frankl's (1963) vivid description of the behavior of prisoners of war suggests that once this individuality is initiated it persists even under extreme conditions of discouragement.

Individuality may be considered an emergence. One does not just acquire individuality just as the apple tree does not acquire apples. It is an intrinsic potential which manifests itself as a result of a continual life process. It is continual because man can never completely understand himself.

Individuality as Social, Not Antisocial

A person does not develop individuality in a vacuum,

233

according to Kierkegaard. He belongs to his environment although separate from it. Although groups may influence the development of individuality, it must evolve from within the individual. In John Steinbeck's words, this is a process wherein the person would "merge successfully with his habitat." He must find himself within his environment, and must identify that which is truly himself. During this, according to Rogers (1963b), the individual seeks empathy, rather than rebellion, with the values of his culture.

From this frame of reference it would seem that individuality would be a desirable accomplishment, and one which might be encouraged in a counseling relationship. If the client can more completely realize his potential, his worth to himself and to society might be enhanced.

Counseling for Individuality

The most important result of an interpersonal relationship, from a Kierkegaardian frame of reference, would be that of choice. Furthermore, choice-making is encouraged in an atmosphere that encourages introspection, self-revaluation, and self-direction. Such an environment could be established through the following counselor approaches.

1. Adopt the role of learner rather than teacher. Allow the client to do the teaching since his understanding of his own feelings is superior to that of the counselor. Such an approach requires humility since the counselor must step down from his role as expert. "Instruction begins when you, the teacher, learn from the learner," according to Kierkegaard (1962). Then the client, or individual, will have greater reason to evaluate his existence in his role as teacher.

2. Try to understand what the client understands. Don't make assumptions. Attempt to find the client where he now is and begin there. "This is the secret to the art of helping others" (1962). Until the individual's frame of reference is understook, another person can be of little value to him, according to Kierkegaard.

3. Utilize any technique available which seems appropriate, always remembering that the truth that the client seeks or the choice that he must make must come from within his own frame of reference if individuality is to be fostered. To encourage the individual to seek else-

234

where for his answers is to detract from the significance of these answers.

Caution should be used with techniques such as advice or condemnation, since Kierkegaard felt that these approaches presuppose two possible fallacies: (1) certainty, when the only thing for certain is the existence of the client--or individual; and (2) the ability of the client to evaluate in the same manner as the counselor, when in reality he may be deluded. Both of these suppositions could easily be obstructive to the counseling process.

4. Use objective information discreetly. Increased self-knowledge might be useless or even obstructive. "To exist and to know are two very different things," says Kierkegaard, and "to understand everything except one's own self is very comical" (1941). A vocational choice made by a person who has only matched test scores with the Dictionary of Occupational Titles, for example, might require revaluation at some future date and this might be difficult.

5. Help the client find truth for himself. This is not a universal truth, however. This is truth that has meaning to the client. "The underlying principle of all questions is that the one who is asked must have the Truth in himself and be able to acquire it by himself" (1939). Kierkegaard felt that each individual has the freedom to decide what is appropriate for himself, and that only when he exercises this freedom can he find truth for himself. This truth must be actively acquired and must come from within. It cannot be merely known. It must be experienced in order to produce changes in behavior. Unless the individual produces truth within himself, he will not live by it. "Truth exists for the particular individual only as he himself produces it in action," says Kierkegaard (1944b). The counselor can only provide an occasion for the client to develop his own truths.

6. Assist the client in developing an inward frame of reference. Encourage him to look to his inner self for direction. "Only when the individual turns to his inner self," states Kierkegaard, "does he have his attention aroused" (1941). He may arrive at the same answers that others have held for centuries, but this must be accomplished through introspection rather than injection. Although he may seek evidence from without, he must make decisions from within.

7.   Encourage him in articulating all areas of his existence. The existence of every person, according to Kierkegaard, represents some form of articulation between the objective and subjective, between facts and feelings, between the external and the inward. Of equal importance is the synthesis of past and future into present reality, for man "lives at once in hope and recollection" (1944a). Neither alone is sufficient. Existence is not determined solely by reason, pure thought, imagination, history, or any combination of these. It is a recurring, temporary, becoming phenomena that represents the articulation of everything the individual is, has been, or strives to be with his own contemporary reality.

The foregoing would seem to represent the major suggestions for the counselor in his attempt to encourage individuality from a Kierkegaardian frame of reference. Kierkegaard would, in general, seem to have visualized the purposes of the counselor as being that of assisting the client in self-exploration in an effort to gain greater self-understanding, and ultimately greater self-fulfillment. Yet the counselor can only provide an environment conducive to this process, since to attempt to impart truths to another individual is to indicate a lack of respect for his individuality.

Indications of Development in Behavior

The development of individuality would seem to follow similar patterns in most people. These would be general patterns, however, for each person might react in a unique manner to specific environmental settings. The following changes would seem appropriate to most people.

1.   From choices based on pleasure-pain to choices that encourage the realization of potentials. Instead of making decisions that allow temporary satisfactions, the individual would begin to make decisions that would lead ultimately to more permanent gratifications. His decisions would become associated with intrinsic rather than extrinsic gratifications.

2.   From an existence containing isolated sequences to an existence representing a directional synthesis of past and future into the present. The individual with little concern for his own individuality would seem to possess little concern for his own direction. His existence would consist of meaningless, nonrelated moments. With the development of individuality would occur direction and more im-

236

portant--self-direction.

3. From an existence chained to the present to an existence that can transcend the present and give some consideration for the future. Instead of a day-to-day existence, the individual would become able to make choices that would contribute toward the development of his potential. He would be as much a process as a product. He would be forever realizing his potentials--to become himself.

4. From values based on external consensus to values based on an inner frame of reference. Instead of arbitrarily adopting the values of others, the individual would come to respect his own valuing system.

5. From direction-from-without to direction-from-within. Instead of asking others to make his decisions for him, the individual would begin to make his own and to have confidence in his ability to make his own decisions. He would begin to recognize that he alone is responsible for his direction, and he alone must accept the consequences of his behavior.

6. From concern for certainty to acceptance of uncertainty. Decisions require change, and change is accompanied by some uncertainty. Since the realization of potentials requires many decisions, the individual would have to begin to accept the uncertainty that will be present frequently. He would begin to tolerate ambiguity and uncertainty.

7. From knowledge to self-knowledge. Instead of merely seeking knowledge, the client would begin to use knowledge to discover self-knowledge. Instead of seeking only objective knowledge, the client would also seek subjective wisdom. Instead of only objective understanding, the client would seek self-understanding.

8. From unrealistic coping to acceptance of limitations. Instead of seeking to achieve in areas wherein the individual has considerable limitation, he would begin to accept his limitations and strive in areas wherein his potentials could be utilized.

9. From selfish to more altruistic concerns. Instead of being concerned only with himself, the individual would begin to recognize his responsibilities to others as well as to himself. Without interaction with others there

would be no realization of potential--no individuality.

Some of the evolving contemporary emphases concerning human behavior seem to offer the field of counseling a refreshing approach to some of the traditionally exploited concepts such as individuality. According to these emphases, individuality is viewed as a positive, actively attained attribute. Although some of these emphases might seem too abstract to be meaningful, it must be remembered that many of the objective personality inventories in use today were developed on premises equally intangible. Furthermore, although these contemporary emphases may not provide for a revolutionary new philosophy of counseling, at least these will only add a few more ambiguities to our present philosophies of counseling.

References

Allport, Gordon. Becoming. New Haven: Yale Univ. Press, 1963.

Allport, Gordon. "Psychological Models for Guidance," Harvard Educational Review, 1962, 23, 373-382.

Frankl, Victor E. Man's Search for Meaning. New York: Washington Square Press, 1963.

Kierkegaard, Søren. Philosophical Fragments, translated by David Swenson. London: Oxford Univ. Press, 1939.

Kierkegaard, Søren. Concluding Unscientific Postscript, translated by David F. Swenson and Walter Lowrie. Princeton, N. J.: Princeton Univ. Press, 1941.

Kierkegaard, Søren. Either/Or. Vol. 2, translated by Walter Lowrie: Princeton, N. J.: Princeton Univ. Press, 1944. (a)

Kierkegaard, Søren. The Concept of Dread, translated by Walter Lowrie. Princeton, N. J.: Princeton Univ. Press, 1944. (b)

Kierkegaard, Søren. The Point of View for My Work as an Author, translated by Walter Lowrie. New York: Harper, 1962.

Maslow, Abraham H.   Toward a Psychology of Being.   New
    York: D. Van Nostrand, 1962.

May, Rollo.   Existential Psychology.   New York: Random
    House, 1961.

Rogers, Carl R.   "The Concept of the Fully Functioning
    Person, " Psychotherapy, 1963, 1, 17-26.   (a)

Rogers, Carl R.   "Toward a Modern Approach to Values, "
    Paper read at a symposium at The University of
    Houston, 1963.   (b)

Williamson, E. G.   Student Personnel Services in Colleges
    and Universities.   New York: McGraw-Hill, 1961.

Wrenn, C. Gilbert.   "School Counseling. "   In Van Cleve
    Morris (Ed.), Becoming an Educator.   Boston:
    Houghton Mifflin, 1963.

Kierkegaard and the Responsible
Enjoyment of Children

John R. Scudder, Jr.

First published in the Educational Forum, XXX (May 1966), 497-503, the article is here reprinted with the kind permission of its editor and of Kappa Delta Pi, owners of the copyright, and of the author, who is at present Professor of Philosophy and Education, Lynchburg College.

What possible contribution could Kierkegaard make to one's relationship to children? He lacks all the qualifications for pedagogical insight. He lacked the experience of a parent or a teacher, the knowledge of an expert in child development, and the special understanding of children given to a few geniuses.

Certainly, if one wanted help from a nineteenth century Dane in understanding his relationships to children, he would turn to Hans Christian Andersen. Both authorities and experienced amateurs agree that he possessed a rare genius for understanding children. Child psychologists get that "I-told-you-so" look when they read how the ugly duckling achieved the status and self-acceptance that every child needs. Parents and teachers, weary of being told by experts of stages, needs, and inner direction which they cannot find in their daily relationship with children, laugh when the naive child exposes the nakedness of the king. Irate at being lectured at about their duties to the child, they eagerly heed the warning not to be an inch worm who measures rather than enjoys children. Yet, they cannot completely follow Andersen's one-sided advice because as parents and teachers they face concretely the primary problem of adult relationships with children: How can one spontaneously enjoy children and at the same time be responsible for them?

Seeking a solution to this problem is confused by current tensions between practitioners, with their claims to methodological insight which springs automatically from "actual experience," and experts with their authoritative prescriptions dictated by what the evidence "indicates." In my first encounter with this conflict, my knowledge of family life garnered from books in graduate school was summarily rejected by parents because I was not one of their number. Ironically, the same knowledge is now accepted as sage wisdom because I sprinkle it liberally with anecdotes from my relationships with my own children. These parents actually listen to me now because I speak as an involved parent and not, as they mistakenly believe, because experience has taught me correct methodology. Believing that method springs automatically from experience is not only naive but it misdirects both parents and teachers. They look to experience for methods with which to manipulate children rather than for insight into developing individual relationships with particular children.

Parents and teachers are justly suspicious of experts as outsiders. Could it be that concern with children because of "expertness" rather than involvement has produced that abstract monster of modern pedagogy, the child? If so, the experts are responsible for substituting adult guidance of the child through stages of development for normal and enjoyable relationships between adults and particular children.

I was attempting to re-establish such relationships when by serendipity I "discovered" Kierkegaard. His insight that·life passes through three stages helped me combine spontaneous enjoyment with duty in my relationship with children. According to Kierkegaard, in the first stage, the aesthetic stage, man is basically concerned with his own enjoyment. It is a stage characterized by spontaneity and play. The second stage is the ethical stage in which man by making either/or decisions assumes responsibility for determining the kind of person he becomes. This stage is characterized by a sense of duty and a desire to reform. The third stage is the religious stage in which man surrenders his life to God and receives forgiveness. It is characterized by spontaneity, concern, and acceptance. In applying Kierkegaard's "three stages on life's way" to adult relationships with children, I shall designate the three stages as enjoyment, duty, and acceptance.[1]

The stage of enjoyment can be easily understood by anyone who has been an older brother, a favorite uncle, or a bachelor friend of the family. He enters a home with great gusto, armed with goodies, and proceeds to enchant

241

the children. He tells them stories, gives them horseback rides, and scuffles with them on the floor. He simply cannot understand why parents are so "long-faced" and stuffy with their children. Why can't they merely enjoy them?

When this same debonair Prince Charming has his own children, he is unable simply to enjoy them. He usually attributes this to his age. No longer can he get down on the floor without great effort and the disturbance of creaking joints. He blames his impatience with the children on his tiring day at the office. While there is some truth to his rationalizations, his difficulty lies not in himself, but in his change of status. He now feels responsible for what his children will become. He is no longer free merely to enjoy them. He must teach them right and wrong, help them to make A's, and show them the way to personal popularity. He has discovered what every conscientious teacher and parent knows, namely, the awesome duty of being responsible for the welfare of children.

Even the student teacher never feels the full weight of duty because, although she teaches and sometimes controls the class, the final responsibility rests with her supervising teacher. Having been spared the awesome experience of being completely responsible for the children in the class, she finds them "cute" and merely enjoys them. Once the yoke of duty is placed on the neck of the teacher, as with the favorite uncle, the enjoyment that comes from playing with children vanishes.

Faced with the demands of duty to use what Kierkegaard calls "the terrible freedom" to mold in part the life of a child by our decisions and actions, we are tempted to flee from our responsibilities into legalistic control and then into rosy rationalization. Our efforts at legalistic control usually take the form of seeking "scientifically proved" principles to apply to our children. Often teachers who complain that their courses in pedagogy are impractical want to be furnished with maxims which they can apply to their students and get proved results. Their anxious desire for crutches in the form of principles results not so much from pedagogical insensitivity as from the desire to escape the pressures of responsibility.

When "proved" principles and magic methods fail to yield the utopian classroom situations which education texts predict, these teachers are totally unprepared for this normal state of affairs. Having been well schooled in the art of rationalization by the glowing descriptions of the ideal classes which their professors taught many years ago, they waste effort and ingenuity white-washing rather than improving themselves. By remaining in this arrested state of development, they evade their duty to children and their profession.

Kierkegaard believed that the normal progression[2] in life was from the aesthetic stage of play and art to the stage of duty and responsibility. In one's relations with children, this would mean moving from merely enjoying them to accepting one's responsibility for them as a duty.

A responsible parent and teacher must give his children both the best of the cultural heritage and help them develop their natural potential. He must share with them his values and on the basis of these teach them to make right rather than wrong decisions. This heavy yoke of duty is an awesome responsibility at best.

Unfortunately, the attitude of a stoic subverts his relationship with children. His tendency to regiment and drive is foreign to their natural capriciousness. Moreover, they unconsciously resent his teaching them because it is his duty rather than from his concern for them. Their revulsion at this type of personality is increased by his treatment of his students. He tends either to do his duty as a teacher and then "wash his hands" of them or to accept them to the degree that they achieve, or try to meet, his high standards. The point here is certainly not that authoritarian teaching fails and permissive acceptance succeeds, for as Harry S. Broudy cleverly points out through his story about an authoritarian teacher:

> The point of all this is that Katie and her methods could not be reduced to a formula which could then be judged pedagogically good or bad, any more than a particular painting can be judged good or bad simply because it was done in the Romantic style. [3]

Indeed, Miss Dove, who through a popular novel[4] and movie became for many the exemplar of the old-fashioned authoritarian teacher, illustrates my point perfectly. Miss Dove's rapport with children came not from demands on them, as many of her admirers mistakenly believe, but rather from her concern for them. Her disciplining of them was her natural way of expressing this concern. Certainly, we need more discipline and a greater sense of duty in both home and school. My point is simply that duty is an inadequate foundation for one's relationship with children.

Kierkegaard rejected duty as foundation for life in a time when there was a solid foundation for it. Most people in his day were idealists. Today, as Martin Buber points out, we live in an "age of confusion" in which the young "no longer receive direction from eternal values." Even the loyalty to the state or the party which, according to Buber, filled the vacuum left by the decline of idealism, no longer evokes duty. [5] Appeals to duty beg the question; duty to what or whom? To espouse the doctrine of duty for duty's sake seems like whistling in the dark to frighten off the emptiness left by the loss of value which formerly demanded duty. Lest one be tempted to join Sisyphus in rolling the marble block up the hill, he should recall that this unfortunate Greek was condemned to this fate as punishment.

Kierkegaard believed many persons would recoil from the fearful responsibility imposed by duty into aesthetic retreat. Certainly, this is tempting to the parent and teacher, especially when failure is added to the heavy burden of responsibility. The novice teacher or parent is buttressed against the pressures imposed by duty because he believes that he is actually molding the personalities of future generations. Therefore, he is a savior of the world. When he discovers that his students are mainly interested in getting to the next grade, that his "special" student has forsaken his teachings for those of another mentor, and that magic methods which he learned in college do not produce the predicted results, he is likely to seek refuge in aesthetic retreat. He soon learns, however, that simply enjoying children is no longer as spontaneous and natural as it once was. His playful attitude lacks contagious effect. The children rapidly become bored with mere play. Some become indignant because, as Broudy has pointed out, "when children are immersed in this world of make-believe they are probably not playful at all; the odds are in favor of their being serious."[6] In addition, while he may not want to teach them, many of his students, although they would never admit it, will want to learn. Moreover, they will reject him because unconsciously they will know that he is using them for his own enjoyment. Eventually, our would-be Epicurean will join many of his colleagues in counting the days until Friday.

244

With children, we clearly need a playful, aesthetic tone, and at the same time, a stoic determination to help them develop their potential; but our relationship with them must be based upon a concern for the welfare of each child rather than a desire to play or do our duty. Inability to achieve this ourselves leads us to despair. This kind of despair, according to Kierkegaard, creates the climate in which one is willing to make the leap of faith. The leap of faith places our relationship with others, including children, in a different dimension. Our main concern shifts from our relationship with man to our relationship to God. In the leap of faith we surrender our lives to God, confident of His forgiveness. To the degree that we are willing to accept God's love and forgiveness, we are able to accept ourselves--we need not reform our children to prove our worthiness. In turn, we are able to accept them as they are, for they, being children of God as we are, do not need to prove themselves worthy of our love and concern. When we no longer have to reform children, we are able to give ourselves freely to them in the spirit of Anne Morrow Lindbergh's poem.

> Like birds in winter
> You fed me;
> Knowing the ground was frozen,
> Knowing
> I should never come to your hand,
> Knowing
> You did not need my gratitude.
> Softly,
> Like snow falling on snow,
> Softly, so not to frighten me,
> Softly,
> You threw your crumbs upon the
> ground--
> And walked away. [7]

Now we seek to help our children grow merely because they need our help rather than because it is our duty. We are free to enjoy them and they to enjoy us, but enjoyment is not the end of our relationship. Indeed, it is not even a means, but rather the product of our acceptance of self and of our children. In short, it is a gift of God.

This gift certainly is no panacea. Kierkegaard's approach to life cannot be regarded as the solution to the problem of adult relationships with children. Even formulating it in the "sacred" five steps of problem solving would not make it a solution. The problem-solving method rests on the assumption that life is a series of problems which can be formulated and solved by human ingenuity. Therefore, educators who claim that education is problem-solving are forced to regard educators who view their vocation from the perspective of their relationship with God as "poachers" to be tolerated in the name of democracy. If, however, they really apply the implications of pluralism to education, they would welcome Charles S. McCoy's position:

> Aware that other standpoints of faith are not only possible but present around us, we center our lives as scholars upon Christian faith in God and the view which this position provides of man and the world. As participants in the exhilarating enterprise of scholarly reflection, we can be aware of the theological dimensions of our own thought and illumine the concealed theological elements in the thought of our colleagues. This process will not "convert" others, but it will enrich the intellectual quest of the university and clarify the situation of real choice with reference to ultimate alternatives of faith. [8]

Most educators would consider it ridiculous, indeed, to urge a teacher who was an agnostic to become a Christian in order to save a pedagogical problem. Is it not equally ludicrous to call on Christians, who once faced lions rather than bow to Rome, to become Pragmatists in order to improve their pedagogical methods? How can one who believes with Paul "that when I want to do right, evil lies close at hand"[9] claim to have solved the problem of his relationship with children even with the help of Kierkegaard's valuable insight?

In illumining "the concealed theological elements" in pedagogical thought, many theologians deliver a scathing attack on those who naively call for building the kingdom in a local classroom through guiding the whole child, providing for individual differences, teaching children rather than subjexts, and pupil-teacher planning. Such an assault could well be made in the name of Kierkegaard, who over a hundred years before Dachau, the bomb, and the Iron Curtain, warned western man of the dire consequences of trying to build man-made utopias. Certainly, we educators need to be wary of the exaggerated claims made for education in our day, but we surely do not need another attack on Progressivism. By now, even its critics must be bored

246

with their own polemics. As an educator, I am weary of
clergymen, who, however sophisticated in theology, show
their pedagogical illiteracy, by tilting with windmills. Furthermore, as a clergyman, I am cautious about hurling
epithets at what Broudy calls "those godless" schools because of his judicious warning that I live in a glass house
where the inhabitants are prone to criticize and instruct the
public schools while neglecting basic concerns within the
church which potentially could make contributions to public
education. [10]

Certainly, one such area is the relationship of the
Christian faith to the life of public school teachers. In
dealing with this relationship we need more than sermons
on the general topic of Christian vocation. As Thomas F.
Green points out, "instead of asking what must be the educational implications of the Christian faith, we would ask
what particular problems are raised by one's involvement
in education which demand religious or theological illumi-
nation. "[11] There are two dimensions to this type of dialogue.

> Theology points in one sense to the presuppositions
> on which all academic discipline and intellectual
> system rest, and in another sense, beyond these
> presuppositions to the commitments of personal
> existence, to the final place of the heart's trust. [12]

The academic dialogue attempting to relate the discipline of
education (pedagogy) to that of theology has received more
attention than the existential one. One reason for this is
that many modern educators like Dewey are more "at home"
with that aspect of experience which is subject to "test"
rather than "testimony. "[13] Moreover, the existential dialogue is academically uncomfortable because although a
Christian teacher may couch it in terms of the relevance
of theological insight to his life and work as teacher, ultimately he must confront his actual relationship with God.

Kierkegaard's view of the three stages of life speaks
at once to both dimensions of the problem of a relationship
of responsible enjoyment between adults and children. To
the degree that one enters the third stage of life by accepting children and himself as children of God and receiv-
ing God's love and forgiveness, he can combine the spontaneous enjoyment of children of the first stage with the sense
of duty to them of the second stage. It is my testimony
that this insight has helped me let God transform my re-

lationship with children as a teacher and parent.

Notes

1. One desiring to pursue the stages further could, of course, read Kierkegaard's Stages on Life's Way, translated by Walter Lowrie (Princeton: Princeton University Press, 1945) and his interpretation of the stages in the Concluding Unscientific Postscript (Princeton: Princeton University Press, 1941), pp. 252-266. For a concise treatment through selections and interpretation see Carl Michalson, The Witness of Kierkegaard (New York: Association Press, 1960), pp. 27-74, 118-127.

2. In pursuing this line of reasoning one should heed Walter Lowrie: "We need in fact to be warned not to regard the three stages as a prescribed curriculum which one must pass through in advancing from youth to age." Stages on Life's Way, p. 6.

3. Paradox and Promise, Essays on American Life and Education (Englewood Cliffs, N. J.: Prentice-Hall, Inc., 1961), p. 80.

4. Frances Gray Patton, Good Morning, Miss Dove (New York: Mead and Company, 1954).

5. Between Man and Man, trans. by Ronald Gregor Smith (New York: The Macmillan Company, 1948), p. 115.

6. Op. cit., p. 28.

7. The Unicorn and Other Poems, 1935-1955 (New York: Pantheon Books, Inc., 1956), p. 10. Used with permission of the publisher.

8. Charles S. McCoy, "The Meaning of Theological Reflection," Faith-Learning Studies, I, (New York: Faculty Christian Fellowship, 1964), p. 24.

9. Romans 7:21

10. Broudy, "Those Godless Schools," Paradox and Promise, pp. 138-148.

11. Thomas F. Green, "Education and Epistemology,"

Faith-Learning Studies, p. 14.

12. McCoy, op. cit., pp. 23-24.

13. Isaac B. Berkson, "Science, Ethics, and Education in the Deweyan Experimentalist Philosophy," School and Society, 87 (October 10, 1959), p. 389.

A Bibliography of Periodical Articles

in the English Language about Sören Kierkegaard

Compiled by

Lewis A. Lawson

Preface to the Bibliography

There have been bibliographies of articles about
Sören Kierkegaard compiled before. But they are now both
dated (as this one will be soon) and incomplete (also as
this one undoubtedly is), both in the number of citations
offered and in the amount of information given within each
citation. I have tried to provide as many citations as possible. I have therefore spent a good deal of time in various
libraries in the vicinity of Washington: McKeldin Library,
University of Maryland; the Library of Congress; Enoch
Pratt Free Library, Baltimore; Johns Hopkins University
Library; and the Library of the Catholic University of
America.

My principles of limitation are: (1) I have not
included any books or self-contained essays within books;
(2) I have included only articles or review-articles; thus
I have omitted all single book reviews; (3) I have included
only articles in the English language, either in English-
language or foreign periodicals; readers interested in articles in languages other than English will still need to consult Jens Himmelstrup's Søren Kierkegaard International
Bibliografi for articles before 1962 or such annual bibliographies as Bibliographie der fremdsprachigen Zeitschriftenliteratur or Répertoire bibliographique de la philosophie
since that date.

Beyond these limitations, I have attempted to cover
every discipline, including literary history, music history,
education, even sociology or economics, where the thought
of Sören Kierkegaard may have been discussed or applied.

253

Bibliographical Sources

Any bibliographical treatment of Sören Kierkegaard would be, in one sense, merely a continuation of Jens Himmelstrup's extremely useful Søren Kierkegaard International Bibliografi (Copenhagen, 1962). But, quite understandably, Professor Himmelstrup did not have access to many English-language periodicals, especially American, so that his coverage in this area is somewhat incomplete. And, too, there has been a remarkable spate of articles published in the few years since the Bibliografi was published. For these reasons several sources other than the Bibliografi must be consulted in order to compile a reasonably full listing:

Abstracts of English Studies

American Literary Scholarship

Annual Subject Index to Periodicals

Bibliographie der fremdsprachigen Zeitschriftenliteratur

Bibliography of Comparative Literature, edited by Fernand Baldensperger and Werner P. Friederich (New York: Russell and Russell, 1960).

British Humanities Index

Bulletin Signaletique

Canadian Index to Periodicals

Catholic Periodicals Index

Denmark: Country, People, Culture (Copenhagen: The Royal Library, 1966), pp. 96-112.

Education Index

Guide to Religious Periodicals

Index to Little Magazines

Index to Religious Periodical Literature

Indian Periodicals Index

International Index to Periodical Literature

International Institute of Philosophy Bibliography

Methodist Periodical Index

Philosopher's Index

Poole's Index

Psychological Abstracts

Publications of the Modern Language Association Annual
    Bibliography

Reader's Guide to Periodical Literature

Répertoire bibliographique de la philosophie

Scandinavian Studies Annual Bibliography

Year's Work in English Studies

Year's Work in Modern Language Studies

Bibliography

Abbagano, Nicola. "Kierkegaard in Italy," Meddelelser fra
    Søren Kierkegaard Selskabet, II (1950), 49-53.

Adorno, T. W. "On Kierkegaard's Doctrine of Love,"
    Studies in Philosophy and Social Science, VIII (1940)
    413-429.

Ahlstrom, Sidney E. "The Continental Influence on Ameri-
    can Christian Thought Since World War I," Church
    History, XXVIII (September 1958), 256-272.

Allen, E. L. "Grundtvig and Kierkegaard," Congregational
    Quarterly, XXIV (July 1946), 205-212.

_____. "Introduction to Kierkegaard," Durham Univer-
    sity Journal, XXXVI (December 1943), 9-14.

_____. "Kierkegaard and Karl Marx," Theology, XL
    (February 1940), 117-121.

_____. "Pascal and Kierkegaard," London Quarterly
    and Holborn Review, CLXII (April 1937), 150-164.

Allison, Henry E. "Christianity and Nonsense," Review of
    Metaphysics, XX (March 1967), 432-460.

_____. "Kierkegaard's Dialectic of the Religious Con-
    sciousness," Union Seminary Quarterly Review, XX
    (March 1965), 225-233.

Anderson, James Maitland. "Søren Kierkegaard and the
    English-Speaking World," Hovedstaden, IV (April 5,
    1913), 7-8.

Anderson, Raymond E. "Kierkegaard's Theory of Com-
    munication," Speech Monographs, XXX (March 1963),
    1-14.

Angoff, Charles. "Letters and the Arts," Living Age,

256

CCCLVIII (March 1940), 89.

Ansbro, John J. "Kierkegaard's Gospel of Suffering,"
Philosophical Studies, XVI (1967), 182-192.

Arendt, Hannah. "Tradition and the Modern Age," Partisan
Review, XXI (January 1954), 53-75.

Auden, W. H. "Knight of Doleful Countenance," New Yorker,
XLIV (May 25, 1968), 141-142, 146-148, 151-154,
157-158.

_____. "Preface to Kierkegaard," New Republic, CX
(May 15, 1944), 683-684.

Babbage, S. Barton. "Soren Kierkegaard," Evangelical
Quarterly, (January 1943), 56-72.

Barrett, Cyril. "Soren Kierkegaard: An Exception, 1813-
1855," Studies, XLV (Spring 1956), 77-83.

Barrett, E. E. "Beyond Absurdity," Asbury Seminarian,
XI (Summer 1957), 33-45.

Barth, Karl. "Kierkegaard and the Theologians," tr. by
H. M. Rumscheidt, Canadian Journal of Theology,
XIII (January 1967), 64-65.

_____. "Thank You and a Bow: Kierkegaard's Reveille,"
tr. by H. M. Rumscheidt, Canadian Journal of Theology, XI (January 1965), 3-7.

Beck, Maximillan. "Existentialism, Rationalism, and
Christian Faith," Journal of Religion, XXVI (October
1946), 283-295.

_____. "Existentialism versus Naturalism and Idealism,"
South Atlantic Quarterly, XLVII (April 1948), 157-
163.

Belitt, Ben. "A Reading in Kierkegaard," Quarterly Review of Literature, IV (Number 7, 1947), 67-76.

Bethurum, Dorothy. "The Retreat of the Intellectuals,"
Vanderbilt Alumnus, XXXVI (December 1950), 6-7.

Bixler, Julius Seelye. "The Contribution of Existenz-
Philosophie," Harvard Theological Review, XXXIII

(January 1940), 35-63.

Blackham, H. J. "The Comparison of Herzen with Kierkegaard: A Comment," Slavic Review, XXV (June 1966), 215-217.

Blanshard, Brand. "Kierkegaard on Faith," Personalist, XLIX (Winter 1968), 5-23.

Bogen, James. "Kierkegaard and the 'Teleological Suspension of the Ethical'," Inquiry, V (Winter 1962), 305-317.

_____. "Remarks on the Kierkegaard-Hegel Controversy," Synthese, XIII (December 1961), 372-389.

Bolman, Frederick de W., Jr. "Kierkegaard in Limbo," Journal of Philosophy, XLI (December 21, 1944), 711-721.

_____. "Reply to Mrs. Hess," Journal of Philosophy, XLII (April 13, 1945), 219-220.

Brackett, Richard M., S. J. "Kierkegaard: A Christian Protest," America, XC (January 8, 1955), 380-382.

_____. "Soren Kierkegaard: Back to Christianity," Downside Review, LXXIII (July 1955), 241-255.

Brandt, Frithiof. "The Great Earthquake in Soren Kierkegaard's Life," Theoria, XV (1949), 38-53.

Bretall, Robert W. "Soren Kierkegaard: A Critical Survey," Examiner, II (Autumn 1939), 327-345.

Brookfield, Christopher M. "What was Kierkegaard's Task? A Frontier to be Explored," Union Seminary Quarterly Review, XVIII (November 1962), 23-35.

Brophy, Liam. "Soren Kierkegaard: the Hamlet in Search of Holiness," Social Justice Review, XLVII (January 1955), 291-292.

Broudy, Harry S. "Kierkegaard on Indirect Communication" Journal of Philosophy, LVIII (April 27, 1961), 225-233.

_____. "Kierkegaard's Levels of Existence," Philosophy

and Phenomenological Research, I (March 1941), 294-312.

Buch, Jørgen. "Kierkegaard Anniversary," Hibbert Journal, LXII (October 1963), 24-26.

———. "A Kierkegaard Museum," American Book Collector, XII (December 1961), 5-7.

Butler, Christopher. "Impressions of Kierkegaard," Downside Review, LV (July 1937), 363-369.

Callan, Edward. "Auden and Kierkegaard: The Artistic Framework of For the Time Being," Christian Scholar, XLVIII (Fall 1965), 211-223.

———. "Auden's New Year Letter: A New Style of Architecture," Renascence, XVI (Fall 1963), 13-19.

Campbell, R. "Lessing's Problem and Kierkegaard's Answer," Scottish Journal of Theology, XIX (March 1966), 35-54.

Cant, Reginald. "Søren Kierkegaard," Church Quarterly Review, CXXVII (January 1939), 268-294.

Cattaui, Georges. "Bergson, Kierkegaard, and Mysticism," tr. by Alexander Dru, Dublin Review, CXCII (January 1933), 70-78.

Celestin, George. "Kierkegaard and Christian Renewal," Dominicana, XLIX (Summer 1964), 149-157.

Chaning-Pearce, Melville. "Kierkegaard's Message to our Age," Journal of the Transactions of the Victoria Institute, LXXIV (1945), 27-52.

———. "Repetition: A Kierkegaardian Study," Hibbert Journal, XLI (July 1943), 361-364.

Chari, C. T. K. "On the Dialectic of Swami Vivekenanda and Sören Kierkegaard," Revue internationale de philosophie, X (Fascicule 3, 1956), 315-331.

———. "Soren Kierkegaard and Swami Vivekenanda: A Study in Religious Dialectics," Vedanda Kesari, XXXIX (May 1952), 67-71.

_____. "Søren Kierkegaard and Swami Vivekenanda: A Study in Religious Dialectics," Vedanda Kesari, XXXIX (June 1952), 107-110.

Charlesworth, Max. "The Meaning of Existentialism," Thomist, XVI (October 1953), 472-496.

"Choose, Leap and Be Free," Times Literary Supplement, XLV (March 9, 1946), 109-111.

Christensen, Arild. "Kierkegaard's Secret Affliction: An Explanation of His Term 'The Thorn in the Flesh'," Harvard Theological Review, XLII (October 1949), 255-271.

Christensen, M. G. "Grundtvig and Kierkegaard," Lutheran Quarterly, II (November 1950), 441-446.

Clive, Geoffrey. "The Demonic in Mozart," Music and Letters, XXXVII (January 1956), 1-13.

_____. "Seven Types of Offense," Lutheran Quarterly, X (Fall 1958), 11-25.

_____. "The Sickness unto Death in the Underworld: A Study of Nihilism," Harvard Theological Review, LI (July 1958), 135-167.

_____. "Teleological Suspension of the Ethical in Nineteenth-Century Literature," Journal of Religion, XXXIV (April 1954), 75-87.

Closs, August. "Goethe and Kierkegaard," Modern Language Quarterly, X (September 1949), 264-280.

Coates, J. B. "Soren Kierkegaard," Fortnightly Review, CLXVII (April 1950), 243-250.

Cochrane, A. C. "On the Anniversaries of Mozart, Kierkegaard, and Barth," Scottish Journal of Theology, IX (September 1956), 251-263.

Cole, J. Preston. "The Existential Reality of God: A Kierkegaardian Study," Christian Scholar, XLVIII (Fall 1965), 224-235.

_____. "The Function of Choice in Human Existence," Journal of Religion, XLV (July 1965), 196-210.

. "Kierkegaard's Doctrine of the Atonement,"
Religion in Life, XXXIII (Autumn 1964), 592-601.

Collins, James Daniel. "Faith and Reflection in Kierkegaard," Journal of Religion, XXXVII (January 1957),
10-19.

. "The Fashionableness of Kierkegaard," Thought,
XXII (June 1947), 211-215.

. "Kierkegaard and Christian Philosophy," Thomist,
XIV (October 1951), 441-465.

. "Kierkegaard's Critique of Hegel," Thought,
XVIII (March 1943), 74-100.

. "The Mind of Kierkegaard: The Problem and
the Personal Outlook," Modern Schoolman, XXVI
(November 1948), 1-22.

. "The Mind of Kierkegaard: The Spheres of
Existence and the Romantic Outlook," Modern Schoolman, XXVI (January 1949), 121-147.

. "The Mind of Kierkegaard: The Attack upon
Hegelianism," Modern Schoolman, XXVI (March
1949), 219-251.

. "The Mind of Kierkegaard: Becoming a Christian in Christendom," Modern Schoolman, XXVI
(May 1949), 293-322.

. "The Relevance of Kierkegaard," Commonweal,
LXII (August 5, 1955), 439-442.

. "Three Kierkegaardian Problems: The Meaning
of Existence," New Scholasticism, XXII (October
1948), 371-416.

. "Three Kierkegaardian Problems: The Ethical
View and Its Limits," New Scholasticism, XXIII
(January 1949), 3-37.

. "Three Kierkegaardian Problems: The Nature
of the Human Individual," New Scholasticism, XXIII
(April 1949), 147-185.

Comstock, W. Richard. "Aspects of Aesthetic Existence:

Kierkegaard and Santayana," International Philosophical Quarterly, VI (June 1966), 189-213.

Cook, E. J. Raymond. "Kierkegaard's Literary Art," Listener, LXXII (November 5, 1964), 713-714.

Copleston, Frederick C. "Existence and Religion," Dublin Review, CCXX (Spring 1947), 50-63.

Croxall, Thomas Henry. "The Christian Doctrine of Hope and the Kierkegaardian Doctrine of 'the Moment'," Expository Times, LVI (August 1945), 292-295.

_____. "The Death of Kierkegaard," Church Quarterly Review, CLVII (July-September 1956), 271-286.

_____. "Facets of Kierkegaard's Christology," Theology Today, VIII (October 1951), 327-339.

_____. "The Importance of Kierkegaard," Danish Foreign Office Journal, Number 2 (April-June 1948), 30-33.

_____. "Kierkegaard and Mozart," Music and Letters, XXVI (July 1945), 151-158.

_____. "Kierkegaard as Seen by an Englishman," Danish Foreign Office Journal, Number 17 (October 1955), 11-14.

_____. "Kierkegaard on 'Authority'," Hibbert Journal, XLVII (January 1950), 145-152.

_____. "Kierkegaard on the Choice," Meddelelser fra Søren Kierkegaard Selskabet, II (1950), 37-38.

_____. "Kierkegaard on Music," Publications of the Royal Music Association, LXXIII (1946-1947), 1-11.

_____. "Man's Inner Condition: A Study in Kierkegaard," Philosophy, XXII (November 1947), 252-255.

_____. "A Strange but Stimulating Essay on Music," Musical Times, XC (February 1949), 46-48.

_____. "Was Kierkegaard a Cripple?" Meddelelser fra Søren Kierkegaard Selskabet, II (1950), 58-60.

Cumming, Robert. "Existence and Communication," Ethics,

LXV (January 1955), 79-101.

Dallen, James. "Existentialism and the Catholic Thinker," Catholic World, CC (February 1965), 294-299.

Davison, R. M. "Herzen and Kierkegaard," Slavic Review, XXV (June 1966), 191-209.

_____. "Reply," Slavic Review, XXV (June 1966), 218-221.

Demant, V. A. "Sören Kierkegaard: Knight of Faith," Nineteenth Century, CXXVII (January 1940), 70-77.

Demson, David. "Kierkegaard's Sociology, with Notes on Its Relevance to the Church," Religion in Life, XXVII (Spring 1958), 257-265.

DeRosa, Peter. "Some Reflexions on Kierkegaard and Christian Love," Clergy Review, XLIV (October 1959), 616-622.

DeRougement, Denis. "Kierkegaard Revealed in His Irony," Arizona Quarterly, I (Summer 1945), 4-6.

Dewey, Bradley Rau. "Kierkegaard and the Blue Testament," Harvard Theological Review, LX (October 1967), 391-409.

Diamond, Malcolm L. "Faith and Its Tensions: A Criticism of Religious Existentialism," Judaism, XIII (Summer 1964), 317-327.

_____. "Kierkegaard and Apologetics," Journal of Religion, IV (April 1964), 122-132.

Dietrichson, Paul. "Kierkegaard's Concept of Self," Inquiry, VIII (Spring 1965), 1-32.

Dodd, E. M. "Kierkegaard and Schweitzer: An Essay in Comparison and Contrast," London Quarterly and Holborn Review, CLXX (April 1945), 148-153.

Driscoll, Giles. "Heidegger's Ethical Monism," New Scholasticism, XLII (Fall 1968), 497-510.

Dru, Alexander. "Kierkegaard: A Great Christian Thinker," Listener, LIV (November 17, 1955), 841-842.

_____. "Reply with Rejoinder," <u>Dublin Review,</u> CCXXI (Spring 1948), 183-188.

Drucker, Peter F. "Unfashionable Kierkegaard," <u>Sewanee Review,</u> LVII (October 1949), 587-602.

Duncan, Elmer H. "Kierkegaard's Teleological Suspension of the Ethical: A Study of Exception-Cases," <u>Southern Journal of Philosophy,</u> I (Winter 1963), 9-18.

_____. "Kierkegaard's Uses of Paradox--Yet Once More," <u>Journal of Existentialism,</u> VII (Spring 1967), 319-328.

Dunstan, J. Leslie. "The Bible in <u>Either/Or,</u>" <u>Interpretation,</u> VI (July 1952), 310-320.

_____. "Kierkegaard and Jeremiah," <u>Andover Newton Bulletin,</u> XLVII (February 1955), 17-24.

Dupré, Louis K. "The Constitution of the Self in Kierkegaard's Philosophy," <u>International Philosophical Quarterly,</u> III (December 1963), 506-526.

_____. "Kierkegaard: Melancholy Dane," <u>America,</u> XCIV (March 24, 1956), 689-690.

Durfee, Harold A. "The Second Stage of Kierkegaardian Scholarship in America," <u>International Philosophical Quarterly,</u> III (February 1963), 121-139.

Durkan, John. "Kierkegaard and Aristotle," <u>Dublin Review,</u> CCXIII (October 1943), 136-148.

Earle, William. "Hegel and Some Contemporary Philosophies," <u>Philosophy and Phenomenological Research,</u> XX (March 1960), 352-364.

_____. "Phenomenology and Existentialism," <u>Journal of Philosophy,</u> LVII (January 21, 1960), 75-84.

Edwards, Brian F. M. "Kafka and Kierkegaard: A Reassessment," <u>German Life and Letters,</u> XX (April 1967), 218-225.

Edwards, C. N. "Guilt in the Thought of Soren Kierkegaard," <u>Encounter,</u> XXVII (Spring 1966), 141-157.

Eller, Vernard. "Existentialism and the Brethren,"
Brethren Life and Thought, V (Summer 1960), 31-38.

_____. "Fact, Faith, and Foolishness: Kierkegaard and
the New Quest," Journal of Religion, XLVIII (January
1968), 54-68.

_____. "Kierkegaard Knew the Brethren! Sort of,"
Brethren Life and Thought, VIII (Winter 1963), 57-60.

Emmet, Dorothy M. "Kierkegaard and the 'Existential'
Philosophy," Philosophy, XVI (July 1941), 257-271.

Evans, Oliver. "The Rise of Existentialism," South Atlantic
Quarterly, XLVII (April 1948), 152-156.

Evans, Robert O. "Existentialism in Greene's 'The Quite
American'," Modern Fiction Studies, III (Autumn
1957), 241-248.

Fabro, Cornelio. "The Problem of Desperation and Christian Spirituality in Kierkegaard," Kierkegaardiana,
IV (1962), 63-69.

_____. "Why Did Kierkegaard Break Up with Regina?"
Orbis Litterarum, XXII (1967), 387-392.

Fairhurst, Stanley J. "Sören Kierkegaard [a Bibliography],"
Modern Schoolman, XXI (November 1953), 19-22.

Farber, Marjorie. "Subjectivity in Modern Fiction,"
Kenyon Review, VII (Autumn 1945), 645-652.

Fasel, Oscar A. "Observations on Unamuno and Kierkegaard," Hispania, XXXVIII (December 1955), 443-450.

Faussit, Hugh I'Anson. "Kierkegaard and the Present Age,"
Aryan Path, XIII (June 1942), 259-263.

Fenger, Henning. "Kierkegaard--A Literary Approach,"
Scandinavica, III (May 1964), 1-16.

Ferm, Deane W. "Two Conflicting Trends in Protestant
Theological Thinking," Religion in Life, XXV (Autumn
1956), 582-594.

Ferrie, W. S. "Soren Kierkegaard: Hamlet or Jeremiah?"
Evangelical Quarterly, VIII (April 1936), 142-147.

Fitzpatrick, Mallory. "Kierkegaard and the Church,"
Journal of Religion, XXVII (October 1947), 255-262.

Fleissner, E. M. "Legacy of Kierkegaard," New Republic,
CXXXIII (December 26, 1955), 16-18.

Ford, Richard S. "Existentialism: Philosophy or Theology?" Religion in Life, XXVIII (Summer 1959),
433-442.

Forgey, Wallace. "A Pastor Looks at Kierkegaard,"
Andover Newton Bulletin, XLVII (February 1955),
32-39.

Forshey, Gerald. "Pharaoh, Kierkegaard, and Black
Power," Christian Advocate, XII (May 30, 1968),
7-8.

Fowler, Albert. "Waters from His Own Well," University
of Kansas City Review, XXII (December 1955), 89-92.

Fox, Marvin. "Kierkegaard and Rabinic Judaism," Judaism,
II (April 1953), 160-169.

Freehof, Solomon B. "Aspects of Existentialism," Carnegie
Magazine, XXII (April 1949), 292-294.

Friedman, Rudolph. "Kierkegaard: The Analysis of the
Psychological Personality," Horizon, VIII (October
1943), 252-273.

Friedrich, Gerhard. "Reply to Llewellyn Jones," Christian
Century, LXIX (June 4, 1952), 674-675.

Fromm, Harold. "Emerson and Kierkegaard: The Problem
of Historical Christianity," Massachusetts Review,
IX (Autumn 1968), 741-752.

Gallagher, Michael P. "Wittgenstein's Admiration for
Kierkegaard," Month, XXXIX (January 1968), 43-49.

Garelick, Herbert. "The Irrationality and Supra-rationality
of Kierkegaard's Paradox," Southern Journal of
Philosophy, II (Summer 1964), 75-86.

Geismar, Eduard. "Soren Kierkegaard," American-Scandinavian Review, XVII (October 1929), 591-599.

Genêt. "Letter from Paris," New Yorker, XL (May 16, 1964), 170.

Gerber, Rudolph J. "Kierkegaard, Reason, and Faith," Thought, XLIV (Spring 1969), 29-52.

Gill, Jerry H. "Kant, Kierkegaard, and Religious Knowledge," Philosophy and Phenomenological Research, XXVIII (December 1967), 188-204.

Gimblett, Charles. "S. K. : A Strange Saint," London Quarterly and Holborn Review, CLXXX (October 1955), 280-282.

Glicksberg, Charles I. "The Aesthetics of Nihilism," University of Kansas City Review, XXVII (December 1960), 127-130.

"Gloomy Dane: The Sesquicentennial of Kierkegaard's Birth," Tablet, CCXVII (May 4, 1963), 482.

Golding, Henry J. "Kierkegaard: A Neglected Thinker," Standard, XII (January 1926), 142-148.

Goulet, Denis A. "Kierkegaard, Aquinas, and the Dilemma of Abraham," Thought, XXXII (Summer 1957), 165-188.

Graef, H. C. "Prophets of Doom," Catholic World, CLXXXII (June 1956), 202-206.

Graham, D. Aelred. "Introducing Christianity into Christendom: An Impression of Soren Kierkegaard," Clergy Review, XXIV (December 1944), 535-541.

Gregory, T. S. "Kierkegaard: The Only Philosopher?" Listener, XXXVI (1946), 798.

_____. "Kierkegaard: The Prophet of Now," Listener, XXXVI (1942), 717-719.

_____. "Kierkegaard: The Prophet of Now," Current Religious Thought, X (November 1950), 7-11.

Grene, Marjorie. "Kierkegaard: The Philosophy," Kenyon Review, IX (Winter 1947), 48-69.

Grieve, Alexander. "Soren Kierkegaard," Expository Times,

XIX (February 1908), 206-209.

Griffin, J. T. "Fathers of Existentialism," Philippine Studies, VI (June 1958), 155-164.

Griffith, Gwilym O. "Kierkegaard on Faith: A Study of Fear and Trembling," Hibbert Journal, XLII (October 1943), 58-63.

Griffith, Richard M. "Repetition: Constantine (S.) Constantius," Journal of Existential Psychiatry, II (Summer 1962), 437-448.

Grimsley, Ronald. "The Don Juan Theme in Molière and Kierkegaard," Comparative Literature, VI (Fall 1954), 316-334.

_____. "Hugo, Kierkegaard and the Character of Nero," Revue de littérature comparée, XXXII (April-June 1958), 230-236.

_____. "Kierkegaard and Descartes," Journal of the History of Philosophy, IV (January 1966), 31-41.

_____. "Kierkegaard and Leibniz," Journal of the History of Ideas, XXVI (July-September 1965), 383-396.

_____. "Kierkegaard and Scribe," Revue de littérature comparée, XXXVIII (October-December 1964), 512-530.

_____. "Kierkegaard, Vigny, and 'The Poet'," Revue de littérature comparée, XXXIV (January-March 1960), 52-80.

_____. "Modern Conceptions of the Demonic," Church Quarterly Review, CLXXXV (April-June 1957), 185-194.

_____. "Romantic Melancholy in Chateaubriand and Kierkegaard," Comparative Literature, VIII (Summer 1956), 227-244.

_____. "Rousseau and Kierkegaard," Cambridge Journal, VII (July 1954), 615-626.

Gumbiner, Joseph Henry. "Existentialism and Father Abraham," Commentary, V (February 1948), 143-148.

268

Guterman, Norbert. "Kierkegaard and His Faith," Partisan Review, X (March-April 1943), 134-142.

Halevi, Jacob L. "Kierkegaard and the Midrash," Judaism, IV (Winter 1955), 13-28.

———. "Kierkegaard's Teleological Suspension of the Ethical: Is It Jewish?" Judaism, VIII (Fall 1959), 291-302.

Halvorsen, Wendell Q. "Ibsen and Kierkegaard," Union Seminary Quarterly Review, II (November 1946), 13-17.

Hamilton, Kenneth M. "Created Soul - Eternal Spirit: A Continuing Theological Thorn," Scottish Journal of Theology, XIX (March 1966), 23-34.

———. "Kierkegaard on Sin," Scottish Journal of Theology, XVII (September 1964), 289-302.

———. "Man: Anxious or Guilty? A Second Look at Kierkegaard's The Concept of Dread," Christian Scholar, XLVI (Winter 1963), 293-299.

Hamilton, William. "Daring to be the Enemy of God: Some Reflections on the Life and Death of Mozart's Don Giovanni," Christian Scholar, XLVI (Spring 1963), 40-54.

Handa, Ichiro. "Japan and Kierkegaard," Meddelelser fra Søren Kierkegaard Selskabet, II (1950), 38-41.

Hanzo, Thomas. "Eliot and Kierkegaard: 'The Meaning of Happening' in The Cocktail Party," Modern Drama, III (May 1960), 52-59.

Hare, Peter H. "Is There an Existential Theory of Truth?" Journal of Existentialism, VII (Summer 1967), 417-424.

Haroutunian, Joseph. "Protest to the Lord," Theology Today, XII (October 1955), 295-296.

Harper, Ralph. "Two Existential Interpretations," Philosophy and Phenomenological Research, V (March 1945) 392-400.

Harrelson, Walter J. "Kierkegaard and Abraham," Andover Newton Bulletin, XLVII (February 1955), 12-16.

Hartman, Robert S. "The Self in Kierkegaard," Journal of Existential Psychiatry, II (Spring 1962), 409-436.

Hartt, Julian N. "Christian Freedom Reconsidered: The Case of Kierkegaard," Harvard Theological Review, LX (April 1967), 133-144.

Heinecken, Martin J. "Kierkegaard as Christian," Journal of Religion, XXXVII (January 1957), 20-30.

Heinemann, F. H. "Origin and Repetition," Review of Metaphysics, IV (December 1950), 201-214.

Held, Matthew. "The Historical Kierkegaard: Faith or Gnosis," Journal of Religion, XXXVII (October 1957), 260-266.

Hems, John M. "Abraham and Brand," Philosophy, XXXIX (April 1964), 137-144.

Hendel, Charles W. "The Subjective as a Problem," Philosophical Review, LXII (July 1953), 327-354.

Hendry, George S. "The Gospel in an Age of Anxiety," Theology Today, XII (October 1955), 283-289.

Henriksen, Aage. "Kierkegaard's Reviews of Literature," Orbis Litterarum, X (1955), 1-2, 75-83.

Herbert, Robert. "Two of Kierkegaard's Uses of 'Paradox'," Philosophical Review, LXX (January 1961), 41-55.

Hess, Mary Whitcomb. "Browning: An English Kierkegaard," Christian Century, LXXIX (May 2, 1962), 569-571.

_____. "Browning and Kierkegaard as Heirs of Luther," Christian Century, LXXX (June 19, 1963), 799-801.

_____. "The Death of Sören Kierkegaard," Catholic World, CLXXXII (November 1955), 92-98.

_____. "The Dilemma in Kierkegaard's 'Either/Or'," Journal of Philosophy, XLII (April 13, 1945), 216-219.

270

_____. "Kierkegaard and Isaac Pennington," Catholic World, CLXII (February 1946), 434-437.

_____. "Kierkegaard and Socrates," Christian Century, LXXXII (June 9, 1965), 736-738.

_____. "A Last Century Liberal: Heinrich Heine," Catholic World, CLXXXIII (July 1956), 281-285.

_____. "Three Christians in Literature: Browning, Kierkegaard, Heine," Christianity Today, VIII (April 24, 1964), 13-15.

_____. "What Luther Meant by Faith Alone," Catholic World, CXCIX (May 1964), 96-101.

Hill, Brian V. "Soren Kierkegaard and Educational Theory," Educational Theory, XVI (October 1966), 344-353.

Hill, E. F. F. "Kierkegaard: The Man and His Thought," World Review, (December 1948), 58-62.

Høirup, Henning. "Grundtvig and Kierkegaard: Their Views of the Church," tr. by Johannes Knudsen, Theology Today, XII (October 1955), 328-342.

Holmer, Paul Leroy. "James Collins and Kierkegaard," Middelelser fra Søren Kierkegaard Selskabet, V (1954), 1-8.

_____. "Kierkegaard, a Religious Author," American-Scandinavian Review, XXXIII (June 1945), 147-152.

_____. "Kierkegaard and Ethical Theory," Ethics, LXIII (April 1953), 157-170.

_____. "Kierkegaard and Kinds of Discourse," Middelelser fra Søren Kierkegaard Selskabet, IV (1954), 1-5.

_____. "Kierkegaard and Logic," Kierkegaardiana, II (1957), 25-42.

_____. "Kierkegaard and Religious Propositions," Journal of Religion, XXXV (July 1955), 135-146.

_____. "Kierkegaard and the Sermon," Journal of Religion, XXXVIII (January 1957), 1-9.

_____. "Kierkegaard and Theology," Union Seminary Quarterly Review, XII (March 1957), 23-31.

_____. "On Understanding Kierkegaard," Orbis Litterarum, X (1955), 93-106.

_____. "Søren Kierkegaard and the University of Minnesota," Meddelelser fra Søren Kierkegaard Selskabet, III (1951), 73-76.

Holmes, Roger W. "The Problems of Philosophy in the Twentieth Century," Antioch Review, XXII (Fall 1962), 287-296.

Hong, Howard. "The Kierkegaard Papers," TriQuarterly, Number 16 (Fall 1969), 100-123.

Hook, Sidney. "Two Types of Existential Religion and Ethics," Partisan Review, XXVI (Winter 1959), 58-63.

Horgby, Ingvar. "Immediacy--Subjectivity--Revelation," Inquiry, VIII (Spring 1965), 84-117.

Horn, Robert L. "On Understanding Kierkegaard Understanding . . .," Union Seminary Quarterly Review, XXI (March 1966), 341-345.

Horton, William. "British Theological Leadership," Christendom, I (Spring 1936), 515-524.

Hubben, William. "Kierkegaard and the Friends," Friends Intelligencer, (October 1953), 230-234.

Huszar, George de. "Preface to Kierkegaard," South Atlantic Quarterly, XLVIII (January 1949), 100-106.

Hyman, Frieda Clark. "Kierkegaard and the Hebraic Mind," Journal of Ecumenical Studies, IV (Summer 1967), 554-556.

Irving, John A. "Thoughts on Existentialism," Queen's Quarterly, LVII (Autumn 1950), 298-303.

Ishag, Saada. "Herman Melville as Existentialist: An Analysis of Typee, Mardi, Moby Dick, and The Confidence Man," Emporia State Research Studies, XIV (December 1965), 5-41, 60-62.

Jacobson, Nolon Pliny. "The Predicament of Man in Zen Buddhism and Kierkegaard," Philosophy East and West, II (October 1952), 238-253.

Jagal, Ernest. "Malicious Philosophers of Science," Partisan Review, X (January-February 1943), 40-57.

James, Ingli. "The Autonomy of the Work of Art: Modern Criticism and the Christian Tradition," Sewanee Review, LXX (Spring 1962), 296-318.

Jansen, F. J. Billeskov. "The Universality of Kierkegaard," American-Scandinavian Review, L (June 1963), 145-149.

Jaspers, Karl. "The Importance of Kierkegaard," Cross Currents, II (Spring 1952), 5-16.

_____. "The Importance of Nietzsche, Marx, and Kierkegaard in the History of Philosophy," Hibbert Journal, XLIX (April 1951), 226-234.

Johannesson, Eric O. "Isak Dinesen, Soren Kierkegaard, and the Present Age," Books Abroad, XXXVI (Winter 1962), 20-24.

Johnson, Howard. "The Diety in Time: An Introduction to Kierkegaard," Theology Today, I (January 1945), 517-536.

_____. "Kierkegaard and Politics," American-Scandinavian Review, XLIII (September 1955), 246-254. [Reprinted in Anglican Theological Review, XXXVIII (January 1956), 32-41.]

_____. "Kierkegaard and Sartre," American-Scandinavian Review, XXXV (September 1947), 220-225.

Johnson, William A. "The Anthropology of Soren Kierkegaard," Hartford Quarterly, IV (Summer 1964), 43-52.

_____. "Guilt According to Freud and Kierkegaard," Hartford Quarterly, 14-54.

Jones, Llewellyn. "Kierkegaard or Grundtvig?" Christian Century, LXIX (May 14, 1952), 588-589.

_____. "The Transmigration of Kierkegaard," Humanist, II (Spring 1942), 21-27.

Jones, W. Glyn. "Søren Kierkegaard and Poul Martin Møller," Modern Language Review, LX (January 1965), 73-82.

Jorgensen, K. E. J. "Karl Barth in the Light of Danish Theology," Lutheran Church Quarterly, IV (April 1931), 175-181.

Kaufmann, R. J. "A Poetry for Sisyphus," Prairie Schooner, XL (Spring 1966), 23-43.

Kaufmann, Walter. "A Hundred Years After Kierkegaard. II: Kierkegaard," Kenyon Review, XVIII (Spring 1956), 182-211.

Kerr, Hugh T. "A Kierkegaard Centenary," Theology Today, XII (October 1955), 291.

"Kierkegaard," Sign, XXV (July 1946), 28.

"Kierkegaard and the Bible," Theology Today, X (July 1953), 247-248.

"Kierkegaard in France," Times Literary Supplement, XXXIV (May 23, 1935), 324.

Killinger, John. "Existentialism and Human Freedom," English Journal, L (May 1961), 303-313.

King, Joe M. "Kierkegaard as an Existentialist," Furman Studies, XV, 35-44.

King, Winston L. "Negation as a Religious Category," Journal of Religion, XXXVII (April 1957), 105-118.

Klemke, E. D. "Logicality versus Alogicality in the Christian Faith," Journal of Religion, XXXVIII (April 1958), 107-115.

_____. "Some Insights for Ethical Theory from Kierkegaard," Philosophical Quarterly, X (October 1960), 322-330.

_____. "Some Misinterpretations of Kierkegaard," Hibbert Journal, LVII (April 1959), 259-270.

Kraft, Julius. "The Philosophy of Existence," Philosophy
and Phenomenological Research, I (March 1941),
339-358.

Kraushaar, Otto Frederick. "Kierkegaard in English,"
Journal of Philosophy, XXXIX (October 8, 1942),
561-583.

_____. "Kierkegaard in English," Journal of Philosophy,
XXXIX (October 22, 1942), 589-607.

Kreyche, G. "A Glance at Existentialism," Ave, CII
(October 9, 1965), 10-13.

Kritzeck, James. "Philosophers of Anxiety," Commonweal,
LXIII (March 2, 1956), 572-574.

Kroner, Richard J. "Existentialism and Christianity,"
Encounter, XVII (Summer 1956), 219-244.

_____. "Kierkegaard or Hegel?" Revue internationale
de philosophie, VI (1952), 79-96.

_____. "Kierkegaard's Either/Or Today," Union Review,
VI (December 1944), 23-26.

_____. "Kierkegaard's Understanding of Hegel," Union
Seminary Quarterly Review, XXI (January 1966),
233-244.

Kuhn, Helmut. "Existentialism and Metaphysics," Review
of Metaphysics, I (December 1947), 37-60.

_____. "Existentialism, Christian and anti-Christian,"
Theology Today, VI (October 1949), 311-323.

Kurtz, Paul W. "Kierkegaard, Existentialism, and the
Contemporary Scene," Antioch Review, XXI (Winter
1961-1962), 471-487.

Lal, Basant Kumar. "Kierkegaard's Approach to Ethics,"
Philosophic Quarterly, XXXVIII (October 1965), 181-
190.

Lampert, E. "Herzen or Kierkegaard," Slavic Review,
XXV (June 1966), 210-214.

Larsen, Robert E. "Kierkegaard's Absolute Paradox,"

Journal of Religion, LXII (January 1962), 34-43.

Larson, Curtis W. R. "Kierkegaard and Sartre," Personalist, XXXV (Spring 1954), 128-136.

Lawson, Lewis A. "Cass Kinsolving: Kierkegaardian Man
of Despair," Wisconsin Studies in Contemporary
Literature, III (Fall 1962), 54-66.

_____ . "Walker Percy's Indirect Communications,"
Texas Studies in Literature and Language, XI (Spring
1969), 867-900.

Lee, Roland F. "Emerson Through Kierkegaard: Toward
a Definition of Emerson's Theory of Communication,"
English Literary History, XXIV (September 1957),
229-248.

Leendertz, W. "Søren Kierkegaard: An Interpretation,"
Mennonite Quarterly Review, XXIII (October 1949),
203-231.

LeFevre, P. D. "Snare of Truth," Pastoral Psychology,
XIX (October 1968), 33-44.

Lessing, Arthur. "Hegel and Existentialism: On Unhappi-
ness," Personalist, XLIX (Winter 1968), 67-77.

Levertoff, P. "On Some Reflections on Kierkegaard,"
Quest, XVI.

Levi, Albert William. "A Hundred Years after Kierkegaard.
I: The Three Masks," Kenyon Review, XVIII (Spring
1956), 169-182.

_____ . "The Idea of Socrates: The Philosophic Hero
in the Nineteenth Century," Journal of the History
of Ideas, XVII (January 1956), 89-108.

Levy, G. E. "Kierkegaard's Significance as a 'Corrective',"
Colgate-Rochester Divinity School Bulletin, XIX
(1942).

Lindström, Valter. "A Contribution to the Interpretation of
Kierkegaard's book: The Works of Love," Studia
Theologica, VI (1952), 1-29.

Livingston, G. H. "Kierkegaard and Jeremiah," Asbury

Seminarian, XI (Summer 1957), 46-61.

Lønning, Per. "The Dilemma of 'Grace Alone'," Dialog,
VI (Spring 1967), 108-114.

_____. "Kierkegaard's 'Paradox'," Orbis Litterarum,
X (1955), 156-165.

Löwith, Karl. "Nature, History, and Existentialism,"
Social Research, XIX (March 1952), 79-94.

_____. "On the Historical Understanding of Kierkegaard,"
Journal of Philosophy, XXXVIII (December 4, 1941),
677-678.

_____. "On the Historical Understanding of Kierkegaard,"
Review of Religion, VII (March 1943), 227-241.

Lowrie, Walter. "Existence as Understood by Kierkegaard
and/or Sartre," Sewanee Review, LVIII (July 1950),
379-401.

_____. "Kierkegaard," Church Review, II (April-June
1941), 8-10.

_____. "Qualified Retraction and Unqualified Apology,"
Theology Today, XVI (July 1959), 267.

_____. "Translators and Interpretators of Soren Kierke-
gaard," Theology Today, XII (October 1955), 312-327.

Lucas, Ernest. "Soren Kierkegaard," Holborn Review,
CLVII (January 1932), 7-17.

Lund, Margaret. "The Single Ones," Personalist, XLI
(Winter 1960), 15-24.

Lund, Mary Graham. "The Existentialism of Ibsen,"
Personalist, XLI (Summer 1960), 310-317.

MacCallum, Henry Reid. "Kierkegaard and the Levels of
Existence," University of Toronto Quarterly, XIII
(April 1944), 258-275.

McEachran, F. "The Significance of Soren Kierkegaard,"
Hibbert Journal, XLIV (January 1946), 135-141.

McFadden, R. "Nuclear Dilemma, with a Nod to Kierkegaard," Theology Today, XVII (January 1961), 505-518.

MacGillivray, Arthur, S. J. "Melancholy Dane: Soren Kierkegaard," Catholic World, CLXIII (July 1946), 338-342.

McInerny, Ralph. "The Ambiguity of Existential Metaphysics," Laval théologique et philosophique, XII (Number 1, 1956), 120-124.

_____. "Connection Seen in Ethics of Kierkegaard and Aquinas," Christian Messenger, LXXXII (March 5, 1964), 4.

_____. "Ethics and Persuasion: Kierkegaard's Existential Dialectic," Modern Schoolman, XXXIII (May 1956), 219-239.

_____. "Kierkegaard and Speculative Thought," New Scholasticism, XL (January 1966), 23-25.

_____. "A Note on the Kierkegaardian Either/Or," Laval théologique et philosophique, VIII (Number 2, 1952), 230-242.

_____. "The Teleological Suspension of the Ethical," Thomist, XX (July 1957), 295-310.

Mackey, Louis H. "Kierkegaard and the Problem of Existential Philosophy," Review of Metaphysics, IX (March 1956), 404-419.

_____. "Kierkegaard and the Problem of Existential Philosophy," Review of Metaphysics, IX (June 1956), 569-588.

_____. "Kierkegaard's Lyric of Faith: A Look at Fear and Trembling," Rice Institute Pamphlet, XLVII (July 1960), 30-47.

_____. "Loss of the world in Kierkegaard," Review of Metaphysics, XV (June 1962), 602-620.

_____. "Loss of the World in Kierkegaard's Ethics," Journal of Philosophy, LVIII (October 26, 1961), 701.

_____. "Some Versions of the Aesthetic: Kierkegaard's

Either/Or," Rice University Studies, L (Winter 1964), 39-54.

McKinnon, Alastair. "Barth's Relation to Kierkegaard: Some Further Light," Canadian Journal of Theology, XIII (January 1967), 31-41.

_____. "Believing the Paradoks: A Contradiction in Kierkegaard?" Harvard Theological Review, LXI (November 1968), 633-636.

_____. "Kierkegaard: 'Paradox' and Irrationalism," Journal of Philosophy, LXII (November 4, 1965), 651-652.

_____. "Kierkegaard: 'Paradox' and Irrationalism," Journal of Existentialism, VII (Spring 1967), 401-416.

Mackintosh, Hugh Ross. "A Great Danish Thinker," Expository Times, XIII (June 1902), 404.

_____. "The Theology of Kierkegaard," Congregational Quarterly, VII (July 1929), 282-296.

McMinn, J. B. "Value and Subjectivity in Kierkegaard," Review and Expositor, LIII (October 1956), 477-488.

McPherson, Thomas. "Second Great Commandment: Religion and Morality," Congregational Quarterly, XXXV (July 1957), 212-222.

MacRae, D. G. "The Danish Malady," Life & Letters Today, XLVII (November 1945), 85-90.

Madden, M. C. "Kierkegaard on Self-Acceptance," Review and Expositor, XLVIII (July 1951), 302-309.

Magel, Charles R. "Kierkegaard's Logically Contradictory Christianity," Graduate Review of Philosophy, III (Winter 1960).

Malantschuk, Gregory. "Kierkegaard and the Totalitarians," American-Scandinavian Review, XXXI (September 1946), 246-248.

Malmquist, C. P. "A Comparison of Orthodox and Existential Psychoanalytic Concepts of Anxiety," Journal of the Nervous and Mental Diseases, CXXXI (1960), 371-382.

Manasee, E. M. "Conversion and Liberation: A Comparison of Augustine and Kierkegaard," Review of Religion, XVII (May 1943), 361-383.

Manger, Philip. "Kierkegaard in Max Frisch's Novel Stiller," German Life and Letters, XX (January 1967), 119-131.

Mantripp, J. C. "Sören Kierkegaard," London Quarterly and Holborn Review, CLXIV (April 1939), 237-243.

Marcel, Gabriel. "Some Reflections on Existentialism," Philosophy Today, VIII (Winter 1964), 248-257.

Maritain, Jacques. "From Existential Existentialism to Academic Existentialism," Sewanee Review, LVI (Spring 1948), 210-229.

Martin, H. V. "Kierkegaard's Attack upon Christendom," Congregational Quarterly, XXIV (April 1946), 139-144.

_____. "Kierkegaard's Category of Repetition," Expository Times, XLIV (July 1943), 265-268.

Maude, Mother Mary. "A Kierkegaard Bibliography," Theology, XLI (May 1941), 297-300.

Maxwell, Robert. "Walker Percy's Fancy," Minnesota Review, VII (1967), 3-4, 231-237.

"Meant for Mankind: Kierkegaard and Christianity as the Regulating Weight," Times Literary Supplement, LXVIII (March 20, 1969), 281-283.

Merlan, Philip. "Toward the Understanding of Kierkegaard," Journal of Religion, XXIII (April 1943), 77-90.

Mesnard, Pierre. "The Character of Kierkegaard's Philosophy," Philosophy Today, I (June 1957), 84-89.

Michalson, Carl. "Kierkegaard's Theology of Faith," Religion in Life, XXXII (Spring 1963), 225-237.

Michalson, Gordon Elliott. "A Dramatic Approach to Christianity," Christendom, IX (Autumn 1944), 462-475.

Miller, Samuel H. "Kierkegaard: Then and Now," Andover

Newton Bulletin, XLVII (February 1955), 5-11.

Minear, Paul S. "The Church: Militant or Triumphant?" Andover Newton Bulletin, XLVII (February 1955), 25-31.

_____. "Kierkegaard Centennial," Theology Today, XII (July 1955), 244-246.

_____. "Thanksgiving as a Synthesis of the Temporal and the Eternal," Anglican Theological Review, XXXVIII (January 1956), 4-14.

Mitchell, Charles. "The Lord of the Flies and the Escape from Freedom," Arizona Quarterly, XXII (Spring 1966), 27-40.

Mondoca, A. de. "The Origin of Existentialism," Journal of the University of Bombay, XXI (1952), 107-119.

Moore, S. "Religion as the True Humanism--Reflections on Kierkegaard's Social Philosophy," Journal of the American Academy of Religion, (March 1969), 15.

Moore, W. G. "Kierkegaard and His Century," Hibbert Journal, XXXVI (July 1938), 568-582.

_____. "Recent Studies of Kierkegaard," Journal of Theological Studies, XL (July 1939), 225-231.

Mourant, John A. "The Ethics of Kierkegaard," Giornale Metafisica, VII (1952), 202-226.

_____. "The Limitations of Religious Existentialism: The Problem of Communication," International Philosophical Quarterly, I (Spring 1961), 437-452.

_____. "The Place of God in the Philosophy of Kierkegaard," Giornale Metafisica, VIII (1953), 207-221.

Muggeridge, Malcolm. "Books," Esquire, LXX (September 1968), 30.

Munz, Peter. "Sum qui sum," Hibbert Journal, L (January 1952), 143-152.

Murphy, John L. "Faith and Reason in the Teaching of Kierkegaard," American Ecclesiastical Review, CXLV

(October 1961), 233-265.

Mustard, Helen M. "Sören Kierkegaard in German Literary Periodicals, 1860-1930," Germanic Review, XXVI (April 1951), 83-101.

Naess, Arne. "Kierkegaard and the Values of Education," Journal of Value Inquiry, II (Fall 1968), 196-200.

Nageley, Winfield E. "Kierkegaard on Liberation," Ethics, LXX (October 1959), 47-58.

_____. "Kierkegaard's Irony in the 'Diapsalmata'," Kierkegaardiana, VI (1966), 51-75.

Nelson, Clifford A. "The Dimension of Inwardness in Christianity," Augustana Quarterly, XXI (1941), 125-144.

Neumann, Harry. "Kierkegaard and Socrates on the Dignity of Man," Personalist, XLVIII (Autumn 1967), 453-460.

Nicholson, G. E. "A Dramatic Approach to Christianity," Christendom, IX (Autumn 1944), 462-475.

Niebuhr, Reinhold. "Coherence, Incoherence, and Christian Faith," Journal of Religion, XXXI (July 1951), 155-168.

Noxon, James. "Kierkegaard's Stages and A Burnt-Out Case," Review of English Literature, III (January 1962), 90-101.

Noyce, Gaylord B. "Wounded by Christ's Sword," Interpretation, VIII (October 1954), 433-443.

O'Donnell, William G. "Kierkegaard: The Literary Manner," Kenyon Review, IX (Winter 1947), 35-47.

"The 'Offence' of the God-Man: Kierkegaard's Way of Faith," Times Literary Supplement, XXXVI (March 27, 1937), 229-230.

Ofstad, Harald. "Morality, Choice, and Inwardness," Inquiry, VIII (Spring 1965), 33-72.

Oke, C. Clare. "Kierkegaard as a Major Prophet," Expository Times, LXII (November 1950), 61-62.

Øksenhalt, Svein. "Kierkegaard's Lichtenberg: A Reconsideration," Proceedings of the Pacific Northwest Conference on Foreign Languages, XVI (1965), 50-56.

Oliver, W. Donald. "The Concept and the Thing," Journal of Philosophy, XXXIII (January 30, 1936), 69-80.

O'Malley, Frank. "The Passion of Leon Bloy," Review of Politics, X (January 1948), 100-115.

O'Mara, Joseph. "Kierkegaard Revealed," Studies, XXXVIII (December 1949), 447-456.

Otani, Hidehito. "The Concept of a Christian in Kierkegaard," Inquiry, VIII (Spring 1965), 74-83.

Otani, Masaru. "Introduction to Kierkegaard," Meddelelser fra Søren Kierkegaard Selskabet, V (1955), 3-5.

_____. "The Past and Present State of Kierkegaard Studies in Japan," Orbis Litterarum, XVIII (1963), 54-59.

_____. "Self-Manifestation of 'Freedom in Anxiety' by Kierkegaard," Orbis Litterarum, XXII (1967), 393-398.

_____: "Something about Kierkegaard's Inner History," Orbis Litterarum, X (1955), 191-195.

Owen, H. P. "Existentialism and Ascetical Theology," Church Quarterly Review, CLX (April-June 1959), 226-231.

Pait, James A. "Kierkegaard and the Problem of Choice," Emory University Quarterly, II (December 1946), 237-245.

Paul, William W. "Faith and Reason in Kierkegaard and Modern Existentialism," Review of Religion, XX (March 1956), 149-163.

Percy, Walker. "The Message in the Bottle," Thought, XXXIV (Fall 1959), 405-433.

Perkins, Robert L. "Soren Kierkegaard's Library," American Book Collector, XII (December 1961), 8-16.

Perry, Edmund. "Was Kierkegaard a Biblical Existentialist?" Journal of Religion, XXXVI (January 1956), 17-23.

Petras, John W. "God, Man and Society, the Perspectives of Buber and Kierkegaard," Journal of Religious Thought, XXIII (1966-1967), 119-128.

Pittenger, W. Norman. "Soren Kierkegaard," Anglican Theological Review, XXXVIII (January 1956), 1-3.

Poole, Roger C. "Hegel, Kierkegaard and Sartre," New Blackfriars, XLVII (July 1966), 532-541.

_____. "Kierkegaard on Irony," New Blackfriars, XLVIII (February 1967), 245-249.

Pope, R. Martin. "Impressions of Kierkegaard," London Quarterly Review, CLXVI (January 1941), 17-24.

Popkin, Richard H. "Hume and Kierkegaard," Journal of Religion, XXXI (October 1951), 274-281.

_____. "Kierkegaard and Scepticism," Algemene Nederlands Tijdschrift voor Wijsbegeerte en Psychologie, LI (February 1958-1959), 123-141.

_____. "Theological and Religious Scepticism," Christian Scholar, XXXIX (June 1956), 150-158.

Prenter, R. "The Concept of Freedom in Sartre against a Kierkegaardian Background," tr. by H. Kaasa, Dialog, VII (Spring 1968), 132-137.

"Queues for Kierkegaard," Times Educational Supplement, 2554 (May 1, 1964), 1149.

Rahv, Philip. "Kafka's Hero," Kenyon Review, I (Winter 1939), 60-74.

Ramsey, Robert Paul. "Existenz and the Existence of God: A Study of Kierkegaard and Hegel," Journal of Religion, XXVIII (July 1948), 157-176.

_____. "Natural Law and the Nature of Man," Christendom, IX (Summer 1944), 369-381.

Rappoport, Angelo S. "Ibsen, Nietzsche, and Kierkegaard,"
New Age, III (1908), 21-22, 408-409, 428-429.

Ratcliffe, S. K. "Kierkegaard, the Only Philosopher?"
Listener, XXXVI (November 28, 1946), 755.

Reichmann, Ernani. "Kierkegaard in Brazil," Kierkegaardiana, V (1964), 78-79.

Reinhardt, Kurt F. "The Cleavage of Minds: Kierkegaard
and Hegel," Commonweal, XXIV (October 2, 1936),
523-524.

Reinhold, Hans A. "Soren Kierkegaard: Great Christian
of the Nineteenth Century," Commonweal, XXXV
(April 10, 1942), 608-611.

Replogle, Justin. "Auden's Religious Leap," Wisconsin
Studies in Contemporary Literature, VII (Winter
1966), 47-75.

Rhodes, Donald W. "The Christianity of Sören Kierkegaard," Canadian Journal of Theology, XII (April
1966), 85-97.

Riding, Laura. "Soren Kierkegaard," Times Literary
Supplement, XXXVI (April 10. 1937), 275.

Riviere, William T. "Introducing Kierkegaard," Christian
Century, LVI (September 27, 1939), 1164-1166.

Robb, Kenneth A. "William Styron's Don Juan," Critique,
VIII (Winter 1965-1966), 34-46.

Roberts, David Everett. "The Concept of Dread," Review
of Religion, XI (March 1947), 272-284.

_____. "Faith and Freedom in Existentialism: A Study
of Kierkegaard and Sartre," Theology Today, VIII
(January 1952), 469-482.

_____. "A Review of Kierkegaard's Writings," Review
of Religion, VII (March 1943), 300-317.

Roberts, James Deotis. "Kierkegaard on Truth and Subjectivity," Journal of Religious Thought, XVIII (Win-
ter-Spring 1961), 41-56.

Robertson, John George. "Soren Kierkegaard," Modern Language Review, IX (October 1914), 500-513.

Robinson, William. "Objectivity of the Subjective in Kierkegaard," Shane Quarterly, XVI (July 1955), 144-150.

Rohde, Peter P. "Kierkegaard and our Time," Arena, 1949, No. 2, 84-94.

Rougemont, Denis de. "Kierkegaard and Hamlet: Two Danish Princes," Anchor Review, I (1955), 109-127.

Rowell, Ethel M. "The Interplay of the Past and Present," Hibbert Journal, XLI (July 1943), 355-360.

Ruoff, James E. "Kierkegaard and Shakespeare," Comparative Literature, XX (Fall 1968), 343-354.

Ruotolo, L. "Keats and Kierkegaard: The Tragedy of Two Worlds," Renascence, XVI (Summer 1964), 175-190.

Savage, Donald S. "Genius or Apostle," Changing World, No. 6, 20-31.

Schmitt, Richard. "Kierkegaard's Ethics and Its Teleological Suspension," Journal of Philosophy, LVIII (October 26, 1961), 701-702.

_____. "The Paradox in Kierkegaard's Religiousness A," Inquiry, VIII (Spring 1965), 118-135.

Schrader, George A. "Kant and Kierkegaard on Duty and Inclination," Journal of Philosophy, LXV (November 7, 1968), 688-701.

_____. "Norman Mailer and the Despair of Defiance," Yale Review, LI (December 1961), 267-280.

Schrag, Calvin O. "Existence and History," Review of Metaphysics, XIII (September 1959), 28-44.

_____. "Kierkegaard's Existential Reflections on Time," Personalist, XLII (Spring 1961), 149-164.

_____. "A Note on Kierkegaard's Teleological Suspension of the Ethical," Ethics, LXX (October 1959), 66-68.

Schrag, Oswald O. "Existential Ethics and Axiology,"

Southern Journal of Philosophy, I (Summer 1963), 39-47.

_____. "The Main Types of Existentialism," Religion in Life, XXIII (Winter 1953-1954), 103-113.

Schutz, Alfred. "Mozart and the Philosophers," Social Research, XXIII (Summer 1956), 219-242.

Scudder, J. R., Jr. "Kierkegaard and the Responsible Enjoyment of Children," Educational Forum, XXX (May 1966), 497-503.

Searles, Herbert L. "Kierkegaard's Philosophy as a Source of Existentialism," Personalist, XXIX (April 1948), 173-186.

Seaver, George. "Denmark's Dead Man," Nineteenth Century, CXXXIX (June 1946), 287-291.

Sechi, Vanina. "Perspectives in Contemporary Kierkegaard Research," Meddelelser fra Søren Kierkegaard Selskabet, IV (1953), 10-12.

Seidlin, Oskar. "Georg Brandes," Journal of the History of Ideas, III (October 1942), 415-442.

Sen, Krishna. "A Comparative Study of the Concept of Faith of Stace, Dewey, Kierkegaard, and St. Thomas Aquinas," Philosophical Quarterly, XXIX (1956-1957), 69-74.

Short, John. "The Journals of Soren Kierkegaard," Theology, XLI (July 1940), 36-43.

Skinhøj, Erik, and Kirsten Skinhøj. "Soren Kierkegaard in American Psychology," Acta Psychiatrica et Neurologica Scandinavica, XXX (1955), 315-325.

Skinner, J. E. "Philosophical Megalomania," Theology and Life, IX (Summer 1966), 146-159.

Slaatte, Howard A. "Kierkegaard's Introduction to American Methodists," Drew Gateway, XXX (Spring 1960), 161-167.

Smith, Constance J. "The Single One and the Other," Hibbert Journal, XLVI (July 1948), 315-321.

Smith, Elwyn A. "Kierkegaard and Dogmatic Theology: An Epistemological Impasse," Evangelical Quarterly, (April 1945), 106-123.

————. "Psychological Aspects of Kierkegaard," Character and Personality, XII (March 1944), 195-206.

Smith, J. Weldon. "Religion A/Religion B," Scottish Journal of Theology, XV (September 1962), 245-265.

Smith, John E. "The Revolt of Existence," Yale Review, XLIII (Spring 1964), 364-371.

Smith, Joyce Carol Oates. "The Existential Comedy of Conrad's Youth," Renascence, XVI (Fall 1963), 22-28.

————. "Ritual and Violence in Flannery O'Connor," Thought, XLI (Winter 1966), 545-560.

Smith, Ronald Gregor. "Hamann and Kierkegaard," Kierkegaardiana, V (1964), 52-67.

————. "Hamann Renaissance," Christian Century, LXXVII (June 29, 1960), 768-769.

————. "Kierkegaard's Library," Hibbert Journal, L (October 1951), 18-21.

Smith, Vincent E. "Existentialism and Existence," Thomist, XI (April 1948), 141-196.

————. "Existentialism and Existence," Thomist, XI (July 1948), 297-329.

Sokel, Walter H. "Kleist's Marquise of O, Kierkegaard's Abraham, and Musil's Tonka: Three Stages of the Absurd as the Touchstone of Faith," Wisconsin Studies in Contemporary Literature, VIII (Autumn 1967), 505-516.

Sontag, Frederick. "Kierkegaard and the Search for a Self," Journal of Existentialism, VII (Summer 1967), 443-457.

Soper, David Wesley. "Kierkegaard: The Danish Jeremiah," Religion in Life, XIII (Autumn 1944), 522-535.

"Soren Kierkegaard: The Attack upon Christendom," Together, (January 1967), 58.

"Soren Kierkegaard: Danish Moralist and Author," Review of Reviews, IX (February 1894), 236.

"Soren Kierkegaard: Prophet with Honor," Christian Century, LXXX (July 24, 1963), 943.

Spiegelberg, Herbert. "Husserl's Phenomenology and Existentialism," Journal of Philosophy, LVII (January 21, 1960), 62-74.

Sponheim, Paul R. "Kierkegaard and the Suffering of the Christian Man," Dialog, III (Summer 1964), 199-206.

Stack, George J. "Aristotle and Kierkegaard's Concept of Choice," Modern Schoolman, XLVI (November 1948), 11-23.

_____. "Kierkegaard and the Phenomenology of Repetition," Journal of Existentialism, VII (Winter 1966-1967), 111-128.

Stanford, Derek. "The Aesthetics of Kierkegaard," Twentieth Century, CLI (October 1952), 348-354.

Stanley, Rupert. "Soren Kierkegaard," New-Church Magazine, (April-June 1947), 23-27.

Stark, Werner. "Kierkegaard and Capitalism," Sociological Review, XLII (Section 5, 1950), 87-114.

Starkoff, C. "The Election: Choice of Faith," Review of Religion, XXIV (May 1965), 444-454.

Steere, Douglas V. "Discovering Kierkegaard," Christendom, III (Winter 1938), 146-151.

_____. "Kierkegaard in English," Journal of Religion, XXIV (October 1944), 271-278.

Steinberg, Milton. "Kierkegaard and Judaism," Menorah Journal, XXXVII (Spring 1949), 163-180.

Stern, Guenther. "On the Pseudo-Concreteness of Heidegger's Philosophy," Philosophy and Phenomenological Research, VIII (March 1948), 337-370.

Stewart, H. L. "Soren Kierkegaard as a Major Prophet of the Nineteenth Century," Expository Times, LXI (June 1950), 271-273.

_____. "Soren Kierkegaard as a Major Prophet of the Nineteenth Century," Expository Times, LXII (June 1951), 284-285.

Stewart, R. W. "Existential Christianity," Expository Times, LXIII (January 1952), 118-120.

_____. "Is Church Like a Theatre?" Expository Times, LXII (October 1950), 27-28.

_____. "A Neglected Prophet," Expository Times, XXXVIII (August 1927), 520-521.

Stobart, Mabel Annie. "The 'Either/Or' of Søren Kirkegaard [sic]," Fortnightly Review, n. s. LXXI (January 1902), 53-60.

_____. "New Light on Ibsen's 'Brand'," Fortnightly Review, n. s. LXVI (August 1, 1899), 227-239.

Strickland, Ben. "Kierkegaard and Counseling for Individuality," Personnel and Guidance Journal, XLIV (January 1966), 470-474.

Sulzbach, Marian Fuerth. "Time, Eschatology, and the Human Problem," Theology Today, VII (October 1950), 321-330.

Swenson, David F. "The Anti-Intellectualism of Sören Kierkegaard," Philosophical Review, XXV (July 1916), 567-586.

_____. "A Danish Thinker's Estimate of Journalism," International Journal of Ethics, XXXVIII (October 1927), 70-87.

_____. "The 'Existential Dialectic' of Kierkegaard," Journal of Philosophy, XXXV (December 8, 1938), 684-685.

_____. "The Existential Dialectic of Sören Kierkegaard," Ethics, XLIX (April 1939), 309-328.

_____. "Soren Kierkegaard," Scandinavian Studies and

Notes, VI (1920-1921), 1-41.

Tavard, George H. "Christianity and the Philosophy of Existence," Theological Studies, XVIII (March 1957), 1-16.

"That Blessed Word, Existential," Christian Century, LXXII (November 30, 1955), 1390-1392.

Thomas, John Heywood. "The Christology of Søren Kierkegaard and Karl Barth," Hibbert Journal, LIII (April 1955), 280-288.

_____. "Kierkegaard and Existentialism," Scottish Journal of Theology, VI (December 1953), 379-395.

_____. "Kierkegaard on the Existence of God," Review of Religion, XVIII (November 1953), 18-30.

_____. "The Relevance of Kierkegaard to the Demythologizing Controversy," Scottish Journal of Theology, X (September 1957), 239-252.

Thomas, J. M. Lloyd. "The Modernness of Kierkegaard," Hibbert Journal, XLV (July 1947), 309-320.

_____. "Pascal and Kierkegaard," Hibbert Journal, XLVII (October 1948), 36-40.

Thompson, Josiah. "Søren Kierkegaard and His Sister-in-Law Henrietta Kierkegaard," Fund og Forskning, XII (1965), 101-120.

Thomsen, Eric H. "That Tremendous Dane," Religion in Life, II (Spring 1933), 247-260.

Thomte, Reidar. "Kierkegaard in American Religious Thought," Lutheran World, II (Summer 1955), 137-146.

_____. "New Reflections on the Great Dane," Discourse, VI (Spring 1963), 144-155.

Thulstrup, Niels. "America Discovers a New 'Classic'," Danish Foreign Office Journal [Special Number for the United States], (1955), 19-20.

_____. "Theological and Philosophical Kierkegaardian

Studies in Scandinavia, 1945-1953," tr. by Paul
Holmer, <u>Theology Today</u>, XII (October 1955), 297-
312.

Tillich, Paul. "Existential Philosophy," <u>Journal of the</u>
<u>History of Ideas</u>, V (January 1944), 44-70.

_____. "Kierkegaard as an Existential Thinker," <u>Union</u>
<u>Review</u>, IV (December 1942), 5-7.

_____. "Kierkegaard in English," <u>American-Scandinavian</u>
<u>Review</u>, XXX (September 1942), 254-257.

Tracy, David. "Kierkegaard's Concept of the Act of Faith:
Its Structure and Significance," <u>Dunwoodie Review</u>,
(1963), 194-215.

_____. "Kierkegaard's Concept of the Act of Faith:
Its Structure and Significance," <u>Dunwoodie Review</u>,
IV (1964), 133-176.

Updike, John. "The Fork," <u>New Yorker</u>, XLII (February
26, 1966), 115-118, 121-124, 128-130, 133-134.

Wadia, A. R. "Soren Kierkegaard," <u>Aryan Path</u>, XXXV
(October 1964), 446-450.

Wahl, Jean. "Existentialism: A Preface," <u>New Republic</u>,
CXIII (October 1, 1945), 442-444.

_____. "Freedom and Existence in Some Recent Philos-
ophies," <u>Philosophy and Phenomenological Research</u>,
VIII (June 1948), 538-556.

Walen, Georg J. M. "Kierkegaard's Existential System,"
<u>Journal of Liberal Religion</u>, II (Spring 1941), 187-
196.

Walker, Jeremy. "Kierkegaard's Concept of Truthfulness,"
<u>Inquiry</u>, XII (Summer 1969), 209-224.

Webb, Clement C. J. "Apropos de Kierkegaard," <u>Philosophy</u>,
XVIII (April 1943), 68-74.

Webber, Ruth House. "Kierkegaard and the Elaboration of
Unamuno's Niebla," <u>Hispanic Review</u>, XXXII (April
1964), 118-134.

Weiss, Robert O. "The Leveling Process as a Function of the Masses in the View of Kierkegaard and Ortega y Gasset," Kentucky Foreign Language Quarterly, VII (First Quarter, 1960), 27-36.

Whitehead, Lee M. "Art as Communion: Auden's The Sea and the Mirror," Perspective, XIV (Spring 1966), 171-178.

Whittemore, Robert C. "Of History, Time, and Kierkegaard's Problem," Journal of Religious Thought, XI (Spring-Summer 1954), 134-155.

_____. "Pro Hegel, Contra Kierkegaard," Journal of Religious Thought, XIII (Spring-Summer 1956), 131-144.

Wiegand, William. "Salinger and Kierkegaard," Minnesota Review, V (May-July 1965), 137-156.

Wieman, Henry Nelson. "The Interpretation of Christianity," Christian Century, LVI (April 5, 1939), 444-446.

Wilburn, Ralph G. "The Philosophy of Existence and the Faith-Relation," Religion in Life, XXX (Autumn 1961), 497-517.

Wild, John. "Existentialism: A New View of Man," University of Toronto Quarterly, XXVII (October 1957), 79-95.

_____. "Kierkegaard and Classical Philosophy," Journal of Philosophy, XXXV (December 8, 1938), 685-686.

_____. "Kierkegaard and Classical Philosophy," Philosophical Review, XLIX (September 1940), 536-551.

_____. "Kierkegaard and Contemporary Existential Philosophy," Anglican Theological Review, XXXVIII (January 1956), 15-32.

Will, Frederick. "A Confrontation of Kierkegaard and Keats," Personalist, XLIII (Summer 1962), 338-351.

Williams, Forest. "A Problem in Values: The Faustian Motivation in Kierkegaard and Goethe," Ethics, LXIII (July 1953), 251-261.

Wilshire, Bruce W. "Kierkegaard's Theory of Knowledge and New Directions in Psychology and Psychoanalysis," Review of Existential Psychology and Psychiatry, III (1963), 249-261.

Winkler, R. O. C. "The Significance of Kafka," Scrutiny, VII (December 1938), 354-360.

Wolf, H. C. "Kierkegaard and the Quest of the Historical Jesus," Lutheran Quarterly, XVI (February 1964), 3-40.

Woodbridge, Hensley Charles. "A Bibliography of Dissertations Concerning Kierkegaard Written in the United States, Canada, and Great Britain," American Book Collector, XII (December 1961), 21-22.

_____. "Søren Kierkegaard: A Bibliography of His Works in English Translation," American Book Collector, XII (December 1961), 17-20.

Wrighton, B. "Thoughts on Kierkegaard," Arena, I (1933), 317.

Yanitelli, Victor. "A Bibliographical Introduction to Kierkegaard," Modern Schoolman, XXVI (May 1949), 345-363.

_____. "Types of Existentialism," Thought, XXIV (September 1954), 495-508.

Zeigler, Leslie. "Personal Existence: A Study of Buber and Kierkegaard," Journal of Religion, XL (April 1960), 80-94.

Zweig, P. "A Genius for Unsavoriness," Nation, CCVII (September 23, 1968), 283-284.

INDEX